TWO, FOUR, SIX, EIGHT,
WHEN YOU GONNA INTEGRATE?*

*Plains High School cheer

TWO, FOUR, SIX, EIGHT,
WHEN YOU GONNA INTEGRATE?

LIVERIGHT / NEW YORK

ISBN 978-0-87140-241-7

Library of Congress Catalog Card Number 77-130912

LIVERIGHT PAPERBOUND EDITION 1971

Published by arrangement with Behavioral Publications,
2852 Broadway-Morningside Heights, New York, New York

Printed in the United States of America

To the students at Plains High School who made it possible

Contents

Acknowledgments

We would like to express our gratitude to the various people who helped to make this book possible. Above all, we are indebted to the students at what we have called Plains High School who consented to be interviewed. They made this book possible, and it is to them that we owe our greatest debt. We hope that this book will in part diminish the debt and make life at Plains High more pleasant, more productive and generally more rewarding.

We wish to extend special gratitude to our colleague, Dr. James B. Taylor, Director of the Department of Research, The Menninger Foundation, for his encouragement to undertake the research, and for his moral and professional support when it was most needed. We are also grateful to Mrs. Martha Carithers from the Division of Social Science Research, who, in the planning stages of the research, contributed immensely to our thinking. Miss Carol Griffin and Miss Marianne Ptacek provided us with the benefit of their interest and good will.

To Mrs. Sherry Schiller goes our deepest appreciation for undertaking the task of typing the original interviews. And for typing more drafts of this book than we care to remember, we are indebted to Mrs. Barbara Crites, Mrs. Winnie Anderson, and Mrs. Jean Hahn.

We are grateful to Drs. Gardner Murphy and Howard Shevrin of the Menninger Foundation Research Department for their constructive suggestions for improving earlier versions of the manuscript.

Finally, we are indebted to The Menninger Foundation for providing the opportunity to explore our own interests.

Frank A. Petroni
Ernest A. Hirsch
C. Lillian Petroni
Topeka, Kansas 1970

CHAPTER 1

Introduction: What This Book is About

To talk about the relationship between the white and black races as though all whites, on the one hand, and all blacks, on the other, were the same—homogeneous, uniform, and unvarying—is to oversimplify matters greatly. In every race and ethnic constellation one finds that individual and subgroup differences, competitions, antagonisms and variations exist within, just as much as between, groups. The way the adolescent views various members of his own race, the way he perceives individual representatives of other races, the way he understands the abstractions of being black or white, the racial attitudes he develops, the actions he undertakes with regard to matters related to race, these are determined in part by such seemingly inharmonious factors as family background, status needs, athletic ability, recreational preferences, darkness of skin, ability in and attitudes toward school, age-peer relations and pressures, dating patterns, individually developed attitudes and so on. We want to illustrate this sort of variability, to show with a fairly small (and not a particularly representative or balanced) group of young people how variable they are in their attitudes and actions regarding the race question—both as far as relations between races, and within the same race are concerned.

This book is not written in the style of a textbook. Its purpose is not to add to the number of scholarly books in the area, but to be a work which can profitably be read by professionals and nonprofessionals, by educators and factory workers, by students and housewives, and which can be appreciated by them all.

The writing of the book is partly the result of the urgings of a number of students who gave us the mandate to "Tell it like it is." We thought we could best respond to the students' mandate by sharing our interviews *directly* with the reader, instead of talking only *about* the dynamics of intergroup relations as they occurred in an integrated high school. By writing about what went on, we felt we would be once or twice removed from the actors, from the action, and from the stage on which it all took place. Hence, we reproduced the interviews directly as they were given to us; of course, we disguised names, situations, relationships and so on. We hoped, in this way, to prevent, or at least to baffle, recognition.

1

Two things ought to be said in connection with our interviewing sample. First, we were amazed how well these young people agreed on major facts. Even though we chose adolescents from a variety of social, economic and scholastic areas, they often gave very similar factual information on major topics. They agreed, for example that, while young black men dated white young women, white young men never dated black young women. This "fact" always remained the same, even though its interpretation might differ from one person, or one sub-group, to another. Thus, black young men might evaluate the dating situation somewhat differently from white young men, and both might again interpret it differently from white or black young women. Still, all agreed on the major factual outlines of the dating patterns.

A second characteristic which we felt to be noteworthy was the degree to which the interview permitted us to participate in the concrete way the students saw and reacted both to their own and to the more general racial situation. In other words, while there was agreement on the outlines of various life areas, the young people saw each actual situation in their own way, through their own eyes, with their own thoughts and emotions. They evaluated, interpreted, and commented upon circumstances on the basis of unique perceptions, needs, wishes, and companionships and according to other unique background and future-oriented factors. The more we had the opportunity to listen to the spontaneous reactions of small groups of individuals, the more we realized that these reactions were fresh and three-dimensional. True, occasionally we felt we were being told the "expected" thing, but usually we felt that what we were told was genuine.

Originally, we had planned to talk about problems of integration in general—problems related to housing, jobs, schools, recreation, and the like. Then we felt that we were being too ambitious, that to do what we originally had in mind would take a book of enormous proportions and for that reason we decided to focus on the problems of integration in education. But even this, after a while, seemed too ambitious an undertaking, and so we decided to focus on student feelings about race relations in one border state high school.

We limited our interviews to high school students because we considered a great deal of the "action" to take place in high schools. School, we feel, tends to represent a central life interest to many students, much of whose social life with one another takes place there. This is less apt to be true of teachers, counselors, administrators and parents, whose time at the school occupies considerably less of a central place in their lives.

So this is what this book is—a concrete, vivid, first-hand account of how various black, Mexican-American, and white students see the problem of being black or being white, both with respect to others of their own group and vis-à-vis each others' race or ethnic group. We interviewed a number of students, and their thoughts about racial matters follow in the various chapters to come. While many of the books we have read in this area have tended to describe integration abstractly, to record events related to integration historically and theoretically, we wish to emphasize the liveliness of everyday interactions. In a sense, we are trying to present a composite *case study* which will illustrate how the integration effort is both succeeding and coming up against obstacles among these young people who attend school in a border state. Although each chapter presents the views of several adolescents, the reader may find that the chapters read as though each contained a *single* case study. While the students who participate in each interview may differ somewhat from each other, they were interviewed as a group of friends or acquaintances, and so they are usually of rather similar minds. As a result, differences in points of view tend to be apparent between, rather than within, the various chapters.

Our sampling procedure was unorthodox. We knew that the kind of rather unstructured interview we planned would run from two to three hours in length. (None, in fact, lasted less than two and one-half hours.) Further, we knew from past experience, that small groups of from three to four made for good interview situations. While the danger always existed, particularly among adolescents, that the presence of others would inhibit spontaneity and the expression of an unpopular position, we found that mutual stimulation by and large outweighed any mutual inhibiting influence. Thus, we informally made contact with one white student whom we asked to bring along two friends. From these three initial students, we obtained further names. Contact was then made with one of these additional young persons, and he (or she) was also asked to bring two friends. Then the whole process was repeated. Non-white students were obtained the same way. The first non-white contact was made through a friend in a civil rights organization. In the course of an interview, we carefully recorded all names that came up, and the context in which they were used, such as, "R_____ is a hippie," or "I_____ is a militant," and the like. Additional subjects were obtained in this way.

We conducted our interviews in the evenings, at the home of one of the authors (F.P.) whose wife (L.P.) recorded what was said in speedwriting, and who helped to keep the interviews conversational. We met with only two refusals to be interviewed—a Negro girl canceled her appointment after Dr. Martin Luther King's death, and a black "militant" would not "talk to white people."

Plains High School, which most of the adolescents in our sample attend, or did attend, has actually been "integrated" for many years. Even before the Supreme Court Brown decision of 1954, Plains High was at least formally integrated. Both blacks and whites had been going to the high school for a long time. Only rather recently, however, and largely as a result of the major emphasis placed on it nationally, has integration begun to mean more than merely the side by side placement of white and black in one location. Only lately has the process become one in which integration is a conscious issue and aim. At this time, approximately one student in six at Plains High School is Negro. In addition, there is a much smaller group of Mexican-American students, most of whom live in a Mexican-American section of town. Finally, there is a very small scattering of American-Indian students.

Throughout the book we present our ideas about why we think certain things are happening as far as racial feelings among adolescents are concerned. We feel that something more than simply an unadorned presentation of events is needed, and that a look at reasons, motivations, group processes and social trends is therefore desirable. Our ideas can obviously be right or wrong, and it will be up to the reader to decide which ideas he wants to accept and which he wants to reject.

What we try to emphasize in this small study (and what may emerge in a much more violent form on the national scene), is how the various participants that are involved in race relations interact. We wanted to find out if and how prejudiced white persons helped to create an atmosphere of hypersensitivity and, ultimately, of *reactive prejudice*. We felt that prejudice, particularly these days, did not consist simply of one group's wanting to subjugate, or isolate, or condescend to, or treat with cruelty and anger, another group, with the overt situation ending there. Nowadays, the minority group that is treated in a prejudicial way tends to react, less internally as it has done in the past, and more overtly, often with reactive hatred, disparagement, bravado and ridicule. We wanted to see if this type of situation also held for the kind of adolescent groups we were trying to study. Would we find a black *reaction* toward prejudice which could easily become a prejudice (in the sense of a blind, illogical, all-or-none reaction) of its own?

It occurred to us that prejudicial behavior would have particularly serious effects when it occurred during a major period of personality growth, a period when the person was developing and discovering who and what he was and who he could become. We felt that the atmosphere in which prejudice existed had an effect of making inflexible, not only the self organization of the person against whom prejudice was directed, but also the self organization of the person who was doing the directing. We wanted to see whether the adolescent victim of aggression would also enhance the very self characteristics to which prejudices were attached in the first place. Would these young people, as do their elders, develop a pride in the superficiality of being black, for example? We feel that, while it surely enriches a person to take pride and active interest in his cultural and historical heritage and background, it is as unrealistic to take pride in skin color (or in any other purely physical self characteristics), as it is irrational to be ashamed or to feel degraded because of it. While one might assume responsibility for what one does, thinks, or feels, one can hardly do so with regard to characteristics with which one has entered the world.

Another destructive and unfortunate impact on the self-concept, we felt, could be seen in the tendency of some black persons to deny their blackness—to say in one way or another, "I'm as white as you are." While such allegations may be presented in fun, they are sometimes meant quite seriously. (Such a statement may, of course, also mean, "I'm as good as you.") The young black person who makes such a statement volunteers to give up his right to be who he is. Such a youth does not develop a complete identity of his own. Instead, he borrows portions of an "approved" identity from his prejudice-steeped surroundings. While he does this, he rejects important parts of the identity which are genuinely and rightly his.

The prejudiced white person's self is also hampered. His restricted views narrow his growth and do not permit him to develop as widely, flexibly and, above all, maturely as he otherwise could. His biased, unrealistic convictions direct the flow of his life outlook into narrowed and emotionally distorted channels which hinder an accurate view of reality and prevent a broad, inclusive sweep of activities, thoughts, attitudes, and interests.

Some whites and blacks use denial to maintain the position that the relations between the races could hardly be better (at least right here, right now, in their own community.) This is a further identity-stunting maneuver— another way of distorting reality, of being less true in relation to others and, more important, in relation to oneself.

The pervasive helplessness the Negro feels to act in line with his human inclinations has further damaging effects on his conception of himself. He tends to think of himself either as a person who cannot, as a matter of course, obtain what should rightly be his, or as someone who must fight or beg for his share. One can imagine what effects such alternatives must have on a person's conception of himself.

As will be fully apparent in later chapters, the young black student, although he may not be aware of the precise ways in which self-fulfilling prophecies operate, often deeply and rightly resents their results, preventing as they do his ability to step out from his present inferior social and economic position in order to achieve a more satisfactory one. The prophecy becomes self-fulfilling when it says, for example, "You can't get ahead, so there's no use in your taking college preparatory courses. We don't expect you to accomplish much later on, because you're not going to be able to achieve it.

People won't let you, and you don't demonstrate that you have the ability." As a result of such a "prediction," the black adolescent is generally not prepared—or only poorly—socially, educationally, and vocationally. As a result, he has difficulty even approximating a status resembling that of his white peers.

But we expected to find little of such theoretical reasoning in our respondents. Instead, we expected to find rage, resentment, and indignation about the *immorality* of prejudice. We expected to find deep anger, both among the many black young people who were being prejudiced against, and among some of their white fellow students who thought about racial matters, and who considered prejudice as evil.

As will become evident in later sections of the book, most black, Mexican-American and many white students do indeed react with anger at the unfairness of prejudice, while a few black, Mexican-American and some white students feel there to exist only a minor racial problem or no such problem at all. These latter students think that integration is going ahead just as it should, but once one goes below the initial public-directed veneer, one finds that these students often tend to demonstrate, if they are black, resentment about the role in which the black student is being placed, and, if they are white, they often slowly give vent to more or less successfully disguised, increasingly prejudicial attitudes.

We see no purpose in placing blame on individuals or groups, because we feel that placing blame results more in defensive emotionality than in rational understanding. We make an effort to show how segregation, either legal or de facto, explicit or implicit, is the result of *pressures*—pressures resulting from familial and from other social, historical, religious, and economic factors; pressures which exert their effects on the growing child and adolescent; pressures which peers and important adults exert from an early age on; pressures which create attitudes that seem "right" and "reasonable"; pressures of cultural preference, i.e., of arbitrarily defined "rights" and "wrongs"; pressures exerted by persons of status in the community and so on. Often, as a result of the multitude of such pressures, while persons may sincerely feel that they have no prejudice, prejudicial evidences may nevertheless be apparent in some of their reactions. It is hardly much of a triumph, however, to discover that someone is "really" prejudiced, since most people, of all races, are. Until a time when the physical characteristics of race cease to offer a basis for superficial discrimination, the person who seeks to find a total lack of prejudice will probably be unsuccessful. He will have to satisfy himself with good intentions, which will necessarily fall short of any "unprejudiced" ideal.

It has been the tendency to think of persons against whom prejudice is directed as "victims." While the objects of prejudice undoubtedly are victims, it is our feeling that persons who hold prejudice are victims as well, even if in a different way. While the lives of prejudiced persons are not affected in the same economic, psychological, physical, or political sense, prejudiced persons, as already has been suggested, suffer damage because of the mentally narrowing effects of their prejudice. Not only does prejudice narrow, it also makes shallower a person's capacity to experience the fullness and depth of his life. Because prejudice is illogical and unrealistic, it cuts out areas of life that require an openness and a nondefensiveness to all sorts of experience, all sorts of perception, all sorts of thought. "Victors," in this sense, are those who live without fear of objectively looking at areas which might go counter to preconceived points of view, points of view that support prejudice, whether the prejudice is that of the white, the reactive anger of the black, or the isolation of the Mexican-American.

Although it is easy to be seduced into thinking of persons as types, as one reads the interviews that follow, one becomes aware of the three-dimensionality of the young people that are telling us their views. They are certainly not "types" in the sense of always reacting the way one expects. They are, instead, natural and human. The young people who speak in this book react to their human situations in altogether human ways—rarely in terms of stereotypes or formulas. It is easy to put oneself in the shoes of whoever is talking. These young people speak as Fred, or Mildred, or Joe, or Betsy; not as slogan-ridden abstractions. They have human needs and talk about human activities. We have set the stage for them to talk about race relations. At other times they have other things that they talk and think about and do. They sleep, eat, work, date, study, play, plan their futures, and spend time with friends and relatives.

Nevertheless, while there are things other than racial matters in the lives of these young people, it has been our experience that the lives of the black adolescents are more filled with concerns relating to racial matters than are the lives of whites. For the whites, when they are concerned about race, such questions occupy a relatively peripheral aspect of their lives (although fear and mistrust of black persons by many white persons has become an increasingly prominent feature.) For the black person, racial questions are much more central; they occupy consciousness more vividly, more frequently, and more strongly.

While we consider this book to be a modest contribution to any effort to present racial inequities, we feel that what is said needs to be said, particularly by the young persons who are saying it. And we feel that what is said needs to be heard. We hope that, after reading the points of view of these young people, the reader will be able to have a fuller appreciation of the magnitude and complexity of the problems of racial relations and will be able to deal with them with increased wisdom.

CHAPTER 2

The Black "Elite"

Part 1

This group of young people is considered to be at the top of the black social ladder by both blacks and whites. Elites mix easily with whites, go to white parties, achieve good grades, take school seriously, are often in better financial circumstances than other blacks, and in general identify themselves with what they consider to be the values of the "white community." For those reasons, they are frequently resented by other blacks, particularly since they often disown, or at least seem to disown, their black heritage. Often they are considered "Uncle Toms" or "White Negroes" and resented because they are not "average." Other blacks think that the elites are trying to be just like the whites and are irritated with them because of this. Whites tend to like them more than they do other blacks because they consider elite blacks to be more like themselves. Most whites do not believe there is a great chasm between themselves and elite blacks. The elites are considered "Uncle Toms" by other blacks, even when there are no whites around with whom elites can associate. Perhaps the feeling of the elites' detractors is that eventually the elites will go into the white community, live in suburbia and participate in other trappings of "whiteness."

Even among elites, there is a hierarchy of "eliteness." The elite Negro tends to feel that the lighter his skin, the better. Thus, certain parents want their children to associate only with blacks whose skin is of as light or lighter color than their own. One can understand this type of injunction as an effort to be "white"—the lighter the skin, the nearer the approximation to the white ideal, and the higher the social status—at least in the eyes of the people to whom lightness of skin is important.

The first interview, which follows below, involves two elite black young women, named Carol and Debbie, and a black elite young man, named Al.

[QUESTION: What pressures do you feel from the fact that you attend a desegregated school?
AL: Well, I participate in speech; I'm the only Negro in the whole group. I find it kind of interesting that I'm the only Negro. I'm always contrasted in

pictures of the group. However, the Negroes accuse me of thinking I'm white. In the bathroom one day, they'd written across the wall in big letters, "Al Carter is an Uncle Tom." I think it's this kind of pressure from the other Negro kids which causes me the greatest concern.]

Segregation does not have to be imposed only by outsiders; it can also be imposed from within, by the members of the segregated group itself. It is difficult to separate the effects of segregation in the prejudicial sense from segregation which is a secondary effect of staying with one's own group because it is socially more comfortable to do so.

[CAROL: You should come to school in the morning before school starts. It's really segregated in the morning. The second floor is traditionally Negro. The white kids are traditionally on the third floor by the music room. But, the Negro kids are on the main floor, right there in front. They're on the main floor because nobody will put them down. It's the best place. It's like riding in front of a bus. All the Negro kids always make it a point to go out the front door, never the back door, and that's why they're in the main hall, I guess.]

[AL: I went to a segregated grade and junior high school. It was quite different there, because if you wanted to say something, you went ahead and said it, because everybody was black and it didn't make any difference. The discipline was very strict there, and the teaching was really good, too. The kids were afraid of the teachers. There weren't any fights in that school. Here the teachers aren't strict at all; the kids are able to get away with an awful lot.

QUESTION: Were the teachers in this elementary and junior high school black or white?

AL: They were all Negro, and they made no bones about letting you know where you stood. They were strictly interested in teaching, and they maintained firm control over the class at all times.

DEBBIE: There are four Negro teachers at Plains High School right now, and they're all excellent. I guess they had to be excellent, though, in order to get the job. They're really better than most of the white teachers there.

CAROL: Well, our Spanish teacher is white, and she's very brilliant.]

The prejudiced teacher is a particularly destructive influence, since the teacher should ideally offer a model for identification, a model for fairness and wisdom—dispassionate and not influenced by attitudes which grow out of immature and nonobjective impressions.

[AL: Well, one of the music teachers—he really gives me the creeps. He loses his temper a great deal, and his tongue goes wild. He actually discriminates. He called me a cross-eyed pygmy once. All the other Negro kids said, "You gonna let him call you that?" I just laughed about it. I thought it was kind of funny. Only two of the kids in my class are Negro. He always apologizes after one of his temper attacks, but the Negro kids are afraid of him, and he seems to discriminate openly. But that's the only real case of open discrimination that I can think of.]

[QUESTION: Carol, was there much change from elementary, to junior high school, to high school in your relationship to white kids? [Carol is the only one in the room who had attended integrated schools throughout her school career].

CAROL: Kids change in general as they get older. I still have some friends that I had in grammar and junior high school. About half of my friends are white and about half of them are Negro. In school we eat together, we sit together in assembly hall, we walk home together and so on. So I really haven't noticed that much change in my own relationship with white kids. But, I think there's a change for most people.]

Almost all the students, black and white, agree that the most integration takes place in sports. By "integration" they mean that Negro athletes play side by side with white athletes. The "side-by-sideness," however, lasts only so long as the athletic event. Usually, once the event is over, so is the integration. The "integration" of activities also varies with individual students; that is, some black and white students attend certain activities, and some do not. Students tend to agree that some sports, such as swimming, are primarily white activities.

Carol's comment about having to be careful about what one says is of interest because, usually, it is the *white* students who say they have to be careful about what they say to *black* students. Carol, a black student, feels she, too, has to be careful about what she says to other black students. One of the major pressures which the students at Plains High School speak of again and again involves their need to be careful about what they say to each other.

[QUESTION: In what areas and activities at school do you find the most integration?

AL: Sports. [Debbie and Carol agree.]

CAROL: Well, the Business Club is also mostly integrated, and Negro kids very often win awards in that.

DEBBIE: The Home Economics Club is also integrated now, since last year when I became Vice-President. I was the only Negro in the club for a while. Once the Negro kids saw that I made it, they were more willing to go ahead and apply for membership themselves. Now we have more Negroes in this club as well. It's fun to be the only Negro. You don't have to watch what you say.

You have to be very careful, you know, about what the Negro kids will react to. You have to be very careful about what you say in front of other Negro kids, because they become very angry.

QUESTION: Could you give me some examples?

DEBBIE: Well, you don't mention swimming and anything about hair. You don't talk about Martin Luther King, either. I didn't really care for Martin Luther King so much. He was just the leader of the Southern Christian Leadership Conference.

QUESTION: Why don't you mention swimming?

DEBBIE: Well, you haven't been around Negroes much, have you?

AL: Well, look at my hair. You know, it's cut pretty close, but look at how kinky it is. See these girls? Their hair is nice and straight. They spend a lot of time at it, and a lot of money. If they went swimming and got it wet, it would be just as wirey as mine. [The girls agree and tell about how long it takes to straighten out their hair. They explain that they straighten it with an iron placed in fire—not an electric iron, because they once had an experience with an electric iron catching on fire.]

Almost all these students, both white and black, note a change in racial attitudes over the generations, in the direction of less prejudice. Not only do they describe less prejudice, but they also describe a greater freedom regarding the interracial sharing of activities. The question is, of course, whether these changes will continue—whether there is enough momentum to keep change moving in the direction in which it has begun. It is certainly possible that segregation will continue in a more "pleasant" context, i.e. in what, superficially, seems simply a more amicable relation between two separate races.

[QUESTION: Do you notice any changes between generations, regarding attitudes about race?

AL: My parents put a lot of pressure on me and don't really want to have our race mix with the white race. They're far more racist than I am, and it's very difficult for me to get along in that house.

DEBBIE: Well, I think the family is getting better in each generation. For example, my grandmother is very much for the Negro and thinks of herself as a Negro. And my parents do a little less. But I think of myself as a person, and not a Negro.

AL: My grandfather has money. But he wants to live like a Negro and wants to look like a Negro. He doesn't want to change our ways; he doesn't want to integrate with the whites. Both of my grandparents' parents were slaves. And most of my family doesn't like to have whites in their home. My aunt just flat refuses to have any white people at her house. She even went ahead and painted her children's dolls brown, because in those days they didn't have Negro dolls. My parents don't like my best friend, who's white. They put a lot of pressure on me not to go with whites, but I don't want to stay in the ghetto; I hate the ghetto. I want to get out and better myself. I want to go to college and move as far away from them as I can. They're all racists. They don't want to change. They want me to be just like them. Even my sister is racist. I'm trying very hard to get away from black people. When I was in that all Negro school, of course, my friends were all Negroes. But I don't have any more Negro friends right now. I live in a Negro area, but I don't even talk to anybody who lives near me. I wanted to find out what white people were all about. So when I went to high school, I tried to make new friends and get away from the black people as much as possible. My parents said, for example, if Adam Clayton Powell was white, he wouldn't have been publicized the way he was and censured the way he was. When a Negro is on TV, everybody watches in my family. They all crowd around. We go to Negro stores to shop; we used to go to a Negro school; we go to Negro churches; we live in a Negro neighborhood. Our grandfather thought we were better than other Negroes, but he still wanted to remain where the other Negroes live.]

[DEBBIE: My grandmother seemed to like to feel that she is lower than other people, lower than white people. She likes the people she worked for, but she seemed to also like to be obsequious in front of white people. When we moved into a white neighborhood, the next door neighbor was a colonel in the Air Force and was transferred to another city. My grandmother came over and said, "You should go over there and apologize and tell them that you didn't mean to have them move out." We tried to tell her that it wasn't our fault that he was moving. It was because he was transferred by the military and had to move to Omaha.]

But even when pride in race does occur, one still finds criteria for "acceptability," and the elite criteria are very similar to those applied by whites. The present generation of young people seem to resent their parents' stress on lightness of skin color as a criterion for social acceptability, and seem to look for more significant measures of worth. The adult elite's concern with the "lower class" is also very similar to the white middle class's concern with it. Thus, in some respects black elites share a number of racial and social attitudes with many whites. It is no wonder that the elite young people are confused—it often seems to them that whatever they do, they do wrong, either as far as adults or peers are concerned. They frequently hear one of two accusations: "You think you're better than we are," or, "Don't forget, you're better than they are."

[DEBBIE: My parents want me to just bring home Negroes, but not lower class Negroes.

CAROL: Well, my parents feel the same way about lower class Negroes. We're not permitted to hang around with any lower class Negroes. In fact, my mother gets very upset if I'm dated by a Negro boy who is darker than I am.

DEBBIE: My parents feel the same way. It seems kind of odd. The kids at school act that way, too. They seem to prefer lighter-skinned Negroes. But, then, if you're always seen with light-skinned Negroes, they come up to you and say, "What do you think, that you're better than we are? Why don't you hang around with real Negroes?" So it's very confusing sometimes.]

Willingness and desire to integrate is seen as a positive act by the younger elite Negro. He feels that he is more willing to integrate, while the "lower class" Negro takes greater pride in his blackness (and his separateness). The implication is that integration is good and that the elite Negro leads the way towards it, while others drag their feet, or go in another direction.

[QUESTION: Who is more clannish—Negro girls or Negro boys?

CAROL: Well, Negro boys hang around with each other more than Negro girls. I think the boys are less willing to integrate. In general, I'd say that the elite Negro kids, like ourselves, are more willing to integrate. The other Negro kids, the lower class kids, the hoodlums, the tough kids, the kids who're flunking out and don't pay any attention to their school work, they don't like others to integrate. They don't try to keep themselves up. They don't try to better themselves. These are the kids in the vast majority. These trashy kids don't influence us. We just don't listen to them.

AL: Well, there're about 300 Negro kids in the high school, and over 200 of them are the real trashy ones. There're only about 50 of us who're more or less in the elite group, and we hang around with each other, and with white kids. These trashy kids even go to different churches. They speak a different language. Their language is very much Negro. Their diction is poor. They're hypocrites, as well. They're very nice to white kids in front of them, but behind their backs they always pick on the white kids. They always have something negative to say. They also pick on Mexicans.

CAROL: Those of us in the elite group more or less know each other very well. But we're not necessarily in the same social groups. We all go our own separate ways and pursue our separate interests.

AL: I don't even like to go on the second floor where all the Negro kids hang out. The boys will get your name, and they bug you. [The girls agree. They say they rarely go up to the second floor.]

DEBBIE: I'm a monitor and sometimes I have to take notes to classes. It's really difficult going into some classes, because you walk in and there're all these Negro kids, and they make obscene remarks. They whistle and ask you for dates right out loud. It's very embarrassing. I try to avoid the bad kids. I try to avoid coming into contact with them to avoid being embarrassed.]

The elites sometimes speak derogatively of the "lower class" Negroes in ways that many white persons would not. Al mentions the "trashy Nigger." Few white persons carrying on a serious interracial discussion, as Al is doing, would permit themselves to speak like this. In a sense, some elite Negroes seem to manifest as much, if not more, racial discrimination as do whites.

[QUESTION: Are you ever threatened because of your attitudes, which are so different from the majority of the other Negro students?

AL: Well, I was threatened a few times, but I learned to avoid these trashy niggers. But most of the time there aren't too many fights. The girls seem to fight a lot more than the boys. Of course, everyone likes to see the girls fight. They pull each other's hair, and they'd just as soon rip off each other's clothing, right in front of everyone. So as soon as anybody hears of a couple of girls fighting, everyone gathers around.]

[QUESTION: Are there different classes of white kids?

AL: Oh, yes, there's white trash just like there's Negro trash, and the white trash and Negro trash sometimes hang around together. The white trash looks up to the Negro for that soul stuff, and things like that. Then there're also some whites who're so elite they look down on all of us Negroes. These are the real rich kids. In fact, they look down upon everyone in that school except themselves, and there're only a handful of them. Then there's the middle class whites. Now these are the ones that we usually get along with. These are the ones that the elite Negroes are friendly with. They accept us pretty much. The white trash looks down on us, though. The white trash, just like Negro trash, comprise the majority group among the whites.]

We will continue to hear about the kind of classroom segregation which Al talks about in what follows. For example, only one or two black students are present in each of the college preparatory classes; most other black students seem to be in courses such as shop or others which involve manual work. This is the kind of de facto segregation which keeps the races separate and which requires thoughtful creativity to solve.

[AL: Fortunately, the classes are divided in school according to college preparatory, business preparation, and things like this. So we don't come into contact with them very much, because most of these kids are in shop or the business courses, but not in the college preparatory courses. You find them in study halls, but anyone with any brains avoids taking study hall. First of all, it has the connotation that you need help and that you need study. And second of all, if you've ever seen a study hall, it's perfectly ridiculous; it really just wastes time. Kids in there really cut up. They can't study there at all. I have a study hall this semester. I had to have some time filled in, and I couldn't get into this other course, so I got stuck in this study hall. You should see the things that go on there. There's one Negro boy in this study hall who just gets away with murder. He argues with the teacher all the time. The other day he was arguing with her, and then he pretended he was crying. He's a fantastic actor. And then he went up to her, sat on her lap, and kissed her. The kids clown around a lot all the time. This big fat girl came in the other day, and all the boys started whistling and yelling, "Man, oh man, isn't she pretty! How about a date honey?" and all kinds of things. These are the kinds of things that go on in the study halls.]

[QUESTION: How often do you interact with white kids in school?

DEBBIE: Well, after King died, things were pretty bad. You didn't see whites and Negroes hanging around together too much for a while. People were pretty mad. Negro kids were pretty angry. I was mad at the white kids, too, but for a different reason—not because Dr. King was killed. I was angry with them because all of a sudden they thought we were experts on race relations. They asked us if we were going to riot and other stupid questions. They'd ask us why we were going to riot.

AL: I saw the ghettos in Detroit, and when I was there I was sick to my stomach. I knew what they were rioting about in Detroit, but how in the hell do I know what everybody's rioting about in Washington, Memphis, Atlanta, Kansas City or even here? They expected us to be authorities on the subject all of a sudden. I always thought of riots as being 2000 miles away.]

When an elite is asked such questions as, "Why are you going to riot?", the questioner implies that all black people are identical. He wipes away the very difference that some elite Negroes try so hard to establish between themselves and other blacks. The black students in this chapter are angry with whites who lump them with all other blacks because of their common skin color. The elite black believes he differs from other blacks in his values, goals and behavior.

[DEBBIE: Or they would say stupid things like, "You're not going to condemn a whole race of white people because of one madman, are you?" and things like this.

CAROL: It was pretty sickening for a while. These middle class white kids who mix with us normally all of a sudden acted quite afraid around us and wanted us to say that everything was all right, and that we could explain the whole thing to them, and that nothing was going to happen, and all that sort of rubbish. Well, we didn't know any more than they did.]

In a variety of ways, the elite Negro tries to differentiate himself from other blacks, and as one effort to this end, he says, "Martin Luther King meant nothing to me." Other Negroes resent such a lack of identification with blacks and with black goals. The elite black, in his turn, resents not having his individuality (and his difference from the "average Negro") recognized.

[AL: One of my friends at this time called and said that a militant group was coming in from Chicago, and they were going to shoot any Negroes who went to school. Well, the day that Dr. King died I went to school.

DEBBIE: I went to school, too, and Carol went to school. The following day it was real hell in there. All of the Negroes came up to us and asked why we went to school on that day. We got pushed around a little bit, but it was more talk than actual violence.

AL: It was the best day in the whole school. All of the trash stayed home, including white trash, who look for any kind of excuse to cut their classes. It was very quiet around the school, and the classes were really great.]

Al's obvious intelligence, alertness and characterological difference from the "average" black does not save him from the effects of the overt prejudicial behavior which a more extreme representative of the prejudiced white community may manifest. This is brought out as he relates an encounter with a white adult in which some of the students at Plains High defended their school against some whites who were trying to downgrade it.

[CAROL: Al wrote this fantastic satire about redistricting and presented it beautifully before the school board. A lot of Negro kids didn't understand what he was doing, though. They became very angry, the dumb fools. They thought he was knocking our race, but he wasn't. He was being satirical.

AL: Well, there was this one white lady who'd get up and say things in a derogatory manner about the Negroes, and then she'd turn to look at me and frown. I was ridiculing the area, and I'd frown back at her after I'd make a point. This lady even came up to me and kicked me in the shins, right in front of this public meeting. I thought the whole thing was amusing, particularly since we won. When she kicked me in the shins, I turned around and said, "Madam, you have a run in your stocking," and the whole place cracked up.]

Al deals with much unpleasantness by humor and denial. He feels the degrading situation he describes to have been "amusing," just as he thought it was "amusing" when a teacher called him a "cross-eyed pygmy." Amusement can perhaps help Al maintain a sense of superiority in a way that anger and hurt could not.

The following statement by Debbie illustrates the confusion about identity, the rootlessness, the mortification about where one stands, even in regard to one's fellows, the bewilderment with regard to whether it is better to be dark, light or medium. One is again struck by the detachment between the elite Negro and other blacks. From what we have seen until now, it appears that the responsibility for this detachment between subgroups lies both with the elite Negro, who tends to reject his blackness, and with the elites' resentful fellow blacks. Such comments as "The Negro kids really worry me," and, "You just don't know how to act in front of them," underlines the chasm which the elite considers to exist between himself and other blacks.

[DEBBIE: You know, the Negro kids really worry me sometimes. You just don't know how to act in front of them. They're very prejudiced about color. I'm a little bit lighter than a lot of Negro kids. Al is darker, and Carol is lighter. The darker ones are usually discriminated against. Yet, the darker ones also say, "I hope she doesn't think she's better than we are." Then there's the confusion about what to call us. Some say, "Call me black," some say, "Call me Negro," "call me colored," "call me Afro-American," "call me nigger." You just don't know what to say anymore.]

[QUESTION: What are the dating patterns like at the high school?

CAROL: Well, the white girls have much more of a range to choose from. There are probably from 50 to 75 attractive boys that they have to date. Myself, I have five, none of whom I like very much, but they're the only ones I can go out with. He has to be somebody my parents approve of—not from the South side; and he has to be Negro, and to boot he has to be lighter colored. They don't quite approve of Al because he's darker.

DEBBIE: Well, my parents always ask me how he is in school. This seems to be quite important to them. They mean, how's he doing academically. Of course, he has to be Negro—they'd never allow me to go out with a white boy, and there just aren't that many middle class Negro boys in school. He has to be Negro, but light skinned.

You know, white boys would be scared to ask us out anyway. The Negro boys will ask out white girls, but the white boys would never ask out Negro girls.

QUESTION: Why is that?

DEBBIE: Well, for a Negro boy to go with a white girl is quite an accomplishment. It also raises his status, even if the white girl is lower in social class than he is. All white kids are supposed to be better than Negro kids. So it raises his status, because he's dating a white girl. On the other hand, if a white boy dated a Negro girl, even if the white boy were one of the trashy kind and he were to date someone like myself, his status would drop.

They'd ask him if he were hard up or something that he had to date a Negro. In general, then, the white boys would be stepping down if they asked Negro girls for dates.

AL: My parents would be horrified if I went out with a white girl. I went out with this Negro girl, and my parents didn't like it because her parents thought they were better than most Negroes. They live here in the East side. Of course, I didn't really know what my parents were talking about until finally I had the opportunity to meet the girl's parents. All Negroes who live on the South side are supposed to be lower class. The Negroes who live on the East side think in those kinds of terms for the most part, and besides I'm dark, and that doesn't help much, either. I have a problem dating, also, because there're just not enough available Negro girls in the right social class.

CAROL: Well, that's the same with me, too—there just aren't enough available Negro boys in our class.

AL: There're some Negro girls I wouldn't be seen dead with. They dress wildly, and they're coarse. There just aren't that many middle or upper class Negro girls.

CAROL: There're more Negro girls in the upper class than there are boys.]

The dating patterns which these young people describe consistently reappear throughout later interviews. Negro young men date white young women, but white young men do not date Negroes. Our respondents emphasize that a Negro young man's status is enhanced when he dates a white girl. They do not, however, say that a Negro young woman's status would be enhanced if she dated a white man; instead, they point out that the white man's status would be lowered if he were to date a Negro. In other words, dating patterns seem to involve sexual as well as racial prejudices.

[AL: But I understand that white and Negro kids do dance together at school dances; but, the white kids can't really dance. The trashy niggers dance real good. The trashy niggers also dress like fashion magazines. The girls—you should see the girls. They wear wigs and silver shoes and dresses up to their necks. They're so dumb—they just want their education given to them. They work simply for clothes or for a Cadillac. Their houses are falling down—in fact, on the Cadillacs parked out in front of them. Take my father. He has 24 suits. We all have our own tuxedoes. They'd rather have beautiful clothes than eat. We have five cars; one for each member of the family. My aunt has a wig (it's about four feet high), 69 knit dresses, but she lives in a shack. It's the same way with us. I'm ashamed of my home. My cousin lives in the good part of town. I always give his address as my home, in case anybody drives by to see where I live. It seems to me that these Negroes are more interested in what people see. That's why they place so much emphasis on clothes and cars. You know, you can't carry a house on your back.]

Al becomes increasingly angry, and in his anger he becomes ever more disparaging of the blacks, whom he disowns and rejects. More and more obvious are attitudes which, if expressed by a white person, would certainly be characterized as "racist." The comments which follow further show how the elite black is located in a psychological no-man's-land—while he tends to reject and be rejected by other blacks, he is usually not fully accepted by the white majority either.

[CAROL: Well, it may have started when they couldn't buy houses, they could buy clothes and they could buy a car. In fact, anyone can buy cars. So many of them put down ten dollars and drive the car out, and then it's repossessed.

DEBBIE: We had a very hard time trying to find a house. It was pitiful. We wanted a house in the better part of town. My father was in the Army at the time. We'd call up first, and the house was available, and then we'd go out to look at it; and sure enough, once we got there, it had just been sold. We finally got a place, though, and it was really something when we first moved in. Our neighbors across the street would sit on the porch and just gawk at us. In fact, it was like a movie; sometimes they'd sit out there eating popcorn. After a while, my sister and I would make faces at them and put on a performance. Our church is quite different from Al's church. Al is a Baptist, and they really swing out in his church. In our church our minister expects us to be very passive. He wants us to sit and absorb our religion. He doesn't want us to move. You know, some of these Negro spiritualists are quite moving, and you just like to swing. Well, he doesn't permit any of this.

AL: Well, most Negroes are Baptist—it's the easiest religion to get into. In our church, we really move with the music. They really make some joyful noises to the Lord. You know, that soul music is actually music from the church. It's religious music speeded up with drum beats. This is what the black Africans brought with them. They took the spirituals and the religious songs of the white men and speeded them up to drum beats. If you want to become a Baptist, just come to the church and tell them you want to be a Baptist, and they'll half drown you in water, and there you are—a Baptist. Then you can make joyful noises to the Lord, too.]

Although Al works to reject his blackness, and although he tries to maintain a distant, "amused" attitude toward the whole racial situation, something happens occasionally to remind him of those very things he is trying to forget and trying to deny.

[QUESTION: Are there any situations in the school which produce stress for you, other than the fact that you have to watch what you say and take the jibes of other Negroes who call you Uncle Tom?

AL: Well, I don't get embarrassed any more, if that's what you mean. Let me tell you about something that happened to me—nothing else could embarrass me any more than that. My uncle came to school in his awful hat and funny clothes one day. He was looking for somebody that he knew. My uncle is an alcoholic. I was coming down the hall, and I noticed him, and I proceeded to run to my class because, you know, I've tried to maintain an image of myself in the school—getting away from those people. I work, and I buy my own clothes, and I study hard. In fact, I have all "A"s in my classes and I'm in many of the white activities, like Speech—the only Negro in the whole group. He saw me and yelled out "Al, Al," and everybody looked at me. I was so mad I started crying. He was drunk, and I ran up into my class, and I was just crying and crying. Then they sent for me, but I wouldn't go. I just kept sitting in class, crying. The teacher didn't know what was going on, nor did the other kids. All of a sudden, he came crashing through the door into my class and started making speeches in front of my class, that I shouldn't be embarrassed, that he had raised me, and that I was his nephew. I was mortified. I had tried to present a different image of myself. In any case, I had to help him downstairs to find his friend and help him find his way home. I stayed away from school a whole week after that incident. The only other thing I fear is the toughies at school. I don't argue with them at all although sometimes it's hard because, if you try to avoid an argument, they say you're conceited.

DEBBIE: In order to avoid these people, very often Carol and I talk in Spanish so that they don't know what we're talking about. For instance, if we want to say something which we know will cause them to become angry, we always speak in Spanish.]

To speak Spanish, of course, is the same as rubbing others' noses in the fact that they are less "intelligent," less "educated," and different from the elites in other ways as well. These people may not know what is being talked about, but the very fact that it is being said in another language is to say, "You're not smart enough to understand what we have to say," and is bound to increase the already fragile relationship between the elites and other blacks.

Often the teachers, counselors, and administration are seen as trying to maintain the status quo more or less subtly. It is hard to know how many of the students' accusations are accurate or fair. While some of the accusations may be entirely just, others may reflect the usual resentment of adolescents undergoing a rebellion against adult authority, while clothing the rebellion in a socially acceptable uniform. It will become increasingly apparent later how certain resentments, which probably have little to do with racial matters, are turned into racial issues, apparently in order to make the original resentments more "just." At the same time, teachers, counselors, and administrators, as representatives of the older generation and of the way things have always been done, tend to want to see things continue the same way. Any basic change in social interaction, doing things very differently from ways they always have been, is often highly threatening. For this reason, persons who have been around longer than adolescents, persons whose lives have been lived a certain way, and who, because of their age, tend to change less flexibly, try hard to maintain the status quo. A new way of organizing racial relationships is threatening because the changes that are involved are so profound.

[QUESTION: How do the teachers react to interracial mixing?

AL: Well some teachers pressure kids to remain separate. The counselors, particularly, impress on you separation of the races. There was this Negro boy who was dating a white girl. He was on the basketball team—in fact, he was the star basketball player. The counselors knew how they could really get to him. They went up to him, and they told him that if he didn't stop seeing that girl they were going to get him thrown off the team. Well, he stopped seeing the girl.

DEBBIE: That boy was really loyal to the team, and he didn't want to see the team lose. So they did stop seeing each other. The girl is also a very brilliant girl, and the counselors would tell her that if she didn't stop seeing him that she wasn't going to get a scholarship, and they would see to that.

AL: I don't think there's anything wrong with interracial dating. I think the teachers are wrong. If these kids want to see each other and go out with each other, it's their business. My own parents wouldn't like interracial dating. I'll tell you something else the counselors do: they don't want Negroes to apply for scholarships to white schools. As a matter of fact, they won't even give you the forms. They tell you about the Negro scholarships that are available.

DEBBIE: I also find that the counselors very often misadvise Negro kids. They do this all the time and it's not just by mistake. They'll send Negro kids into a biology class after half the term is over, and you really can't make it unless you have the first half of the class. They always try to give Negro kids business courses or physical education courses. They don't want them to take Music or French or some of the more academic courses.

AL: They told me I was too dumb to go to one of the state universities. I was told this by a counselor. He said that I should go to some junior college. Of course, I was accepted at the state university, and I'm going there. I was also accepted at some other colleges.

DEBBIE: I got pressured into taking a math course that I didn't want. They wanted me to take the course. They don't advise the white kids to take this course—it's really tough. I almost flunked out of it. In fact, I would have flunked out of it if I hadn't been permitted to drop the course. I think that very often the white teachers think that all Negro kids are stupid. They see us all as if we were Al's uncle. Sometimes I feel that I'm being used by the counselors and some of the white teachers. They point to me and say, "Look at Debbie. Look how well she's doing." They use me for an example. They never point to the other 250 Negroes who're doing rather poorly.

CAROL: I really got mad at Mr. Scott one day. He came up to me and said, "Why, didn't you run for student government? You would've made it. All the Negro kids would've voted for you." I didn't like this at all when he said the Negro kids would've voted for me. If I were going to run for office, I would hope that the kids would vote for me because I was qualified, not because I'm Negro.

AL: I'm trying out for a scholarship now in Speech. I'm not going to major in Speech, but it's a Speech contest in which I can win a scholarship. I won first in the district and second in the state so far. It was kind of fun—there were only 3 Negroes out of 2000. Sometimes I like being the only Negro in a large group. It's a distinction.]

These students accuse the counselors of a number of racist attitudes and actions: of trying to hold the black student back by not treating him as an individual, by lumping all black students together as lazy and stupid. These young people feel that the counselors do not want or expect to see them succeed, that they advise them along paths which reflect the preconception that the Negro can probably not make it. Once again, the elites complain that the counselors treat them as though they were the same as all other blacks, while other blacks treat them as though elites were no longer part of their race.

Carol ends the interview pessimistically. Her pessimism, however, may be more appropriate to the situation into which some elites have become wedged than to the possibility of an improvement in the interracial situation.

[QUESTION: In general, what do you think of your experience at Plains High School? What has your experience taught you about racial matters?

DEBBIE: I didn't know anything about race until I came here. My father was in the Army and we lived in quite a few places. We lived in Vermont before we came here, and there aren't many Negroes there. I was scared when we came here. I think I'd have to say that I learned about Negroes by coming to this high school. ·

AL: Well, I live in the middle of the Negro district, and I don't even know them or how to deal with them. As far as Plains High School is concerned, that's the first place in which I was put down. I always went to Negro schools and I was used to being in the front and on the top. However, I wasn't going to let them put me down. I decided that I'd try even at Plains High School to be in front. I think I've succeeded somewhat. They hate me for it, the Negroes hate me—if you want to pull yourself up as I do, they call you Uncle Tom.

DEBBIE: When I first came here, I was no naive that I'd always raise my hand in class when a question was asked, and I'd recite, and then the Negro kids would always ask me if I was trying to make them look bad.

CAROL: Well, one thing I learned was that there're all kinds of Negroes and there're all kinds of whites, and I'd say that it isn't going to be very easy for all of us to get together.]

The Black "Elite"

Part 2

The second group of black elite high school students (four young women) is more actively concerned with being part of a prejudiced-against group than the group of elites in Part 1. The present young women seem more identified with the injustices that have characterized white attitudes towards blacks, and they are more active in trying to do something about them, albeit in a less direct way than black militants. Again it is apparent how groupings are made for the convenience of theoreticians, and how people within a particular group are, at times, no more identical to each other than is one total group to another, even when it is called by the same name. Each of these adolescents is trying to find principles which will organize his own particular life. In trying to decide who he is and what he wants to do about it, each person finds his own solution, and for each individual the solution is unique. These young people are at an age where they are very much concerned with themselves, so that "pressures" often do not involve feelings for persons other than themselves. A concern with "self," however, is understandable and characteristic of most adolescents who, after all, are trying to organize their futures. In spite of this age-appropriate need for self concern, the four young elite women in this section demonstrate their active concern about racial justice, even when this does not involve them in the most direct fashion.

[QUESTION: What pressures do you feel from attending a desegregated school?

MARGARET: Well, when I was in junior high school, I was an all "A" student. Just before going over to Plains High School, my counselor in junior high called me in and said, "You know, you've made some pretty good grades here, but when you go to Plains High, things won't be the same. There're a lot of bright kids at Plains High School, and you probably won't do as well as you have here." But, I found out that I *can* do as well. I've been here for two years now and have been receiving the same kind of grades as I did in junior high school. I don't find the kids are any brighter than I am, but this counselor told me that I'd probably find the competition tough. In the junior

24

high school I attended, the majority of kids were black. I do as well as anybody else at Plains High School. I'm taking accelerated classes. In most of my classes, there aren't more than two or three Negroes. That's another pressure. With only two or three Negroes in the class, you feel that you have to do extra good to measure up to the other kids. Take my English class. I'm particularly good in English; this is my favorite subject. If the teacher asks a question—there are only two Negroes in that class—if she says, "Margaret" and calls me to answer a question, the kids know that I'm good in English. They'd watch to see if I'd get the answer wrong. Usually it's no problem in English, though. I don't have much trouble showing them up. Math is something else. I'm in a special class. I'm not very good at math, and I never did really like it. I'm getting by, but I'm not getting the kind of grade I'd like to get.

QUESTION: Do you mean the kids are actually waiting for you to fail?

MARGARET: Well, some kids don't care whether you fail or not. But sometimes you feel they're just waiting to see if you'll measure up. The first place I felt this was at Plains High School. I went to Jackson Elementary School. Of course, it's easy to get all "A"s in elementary school. Anybody can. Well, I take that back; if you have the ability, you can. I always had "A"s in junior high. Of course, in elementary school you're little, and you don't know anything anyway. Also, in elementary and junior high school, the teachers have always taken a liking to me. Some of the white mothers would call my house and complain. They'd say things about my being the teacher's pet. I also went to Emerson for a while. There were more Negroes there, and I was still at the top of the class. I've always liked school, so that's made it easier for me. Where I went to junior high, I liked it a lot. I always did anything I wanted to do. I was cheerleader, I ran for offices, I was involved in everything. I find this to be a pressure, too, because, at Plains High School, if you're a Negro, you just can't run for cheerleader and get it. There're so many whites, and the whites usually win.]

One of the greatest pressures which blacks feel, particularly black elites, is a pressure from other blacks which comes in the form of the message, "You think you're better than we are." The black elites, for whom "success" is so important, find themselves in a difficult position. If they do "succeed," they are resented by most other blacks—if they do not, they lose prestige among other elites, their family and their white friends.

Pat says that when she succeeds it means success for black people and not just for her. Yet she is painfully aware that striving for success in academia involves an uphill battle which has rewards primarily from the white community (particularly from white teachers) and only rarely from blacks.

[PAT: I felt the greatest pressure from members of my own race. I'm an all

"A" student; I'm always on the honor roll; I'm in Madrigals, and so on. Because of these small accomplishments, there's a tendency for the Negroes to think that I'm better than they are. They think I'm boasting. Take Nancy—Nancy ran for office, and I've heard other Negroes say, "She thinks she's so good." I don't think of it this way. These small accomplishments that I've achieved aren't just for me, but they're to help the Negro cause. I do things for my race, not just for myself. Most of the time, though, I don't pay too much attention to these kids. It's just a small percentage of Negroes, anyway, who're the trouble makers, and they resent the fact that I'm doing something, and they aren't.

BETTY: Well, if you run for office and your own race degrades you, it makes it very hard for you to try to achieve this position. I've heard it so many times—Negroes'll say, "How come she's running for office? Does she think she's better than we are?" After a while, you don't want to try. I think a lot of Negroes don't try for these offices for this reason.

NANCY: Well, I knew that there'd be some Negroes who'd say, "She's trying to be better than we are" when I ran for office. But I ran anyway because I also knew there'd be some Negroes who'd appreciate it, who'd know that I was doing this, not only for myself, but for my race.]

The elites must walk a thin line if they are to be popular with both whites and blacks. Even the person most popular among blacks is jeered by other blacks when he becomes too popular with whites. He must pay for his popularity and for his office by seeing to it that other blacks get a benefit. Even then, he is disliked if he knows too many whites.

Margaret is torn between two ethical values. She wonders whether she voted for a school candidate because of his qualifications, or because he is black. Racial loyalty obviously represents a very strong value, a value which sometimes competes with other values in ways which cause mental distress.

[QUESTION: Is it true, then, that any Negro who tries to achieve a political position in school is automatically downgraded by his race?

BETTY: No, that's not true. Jeff, for example—he likes people regardless of race. He ran for class president, and he made it. He's going to be the class president next year, and he's Negro. But everybody likes him. If it had been someone who said things that were bad about Negroes, then I think that the Negroes would reject him for having achieved that office.

MARGARET: Well, it's not just that. Jeff has a large white following as well. He's a nice boy. Everybody likes him. I voted for him because he's a Negro. Well, I guess he was also qualified. He was as qualified as the other kid who was running. I should've voted for the most qualified person. It's not right for me to say what I'm saying. But I'm sure that I really voted for Jeff because he's a Negro, and I wanted a Negro president. I think a lot of the other Negro kids voted for him, too, because they wanted a Negro president. This was our chance.

BETTY: Actually, Jeff is just a real average boy. He doesn't think he's better than most people. But some people think he's real special. I think more Negroes dislike him than white people. I think Jeff has more white friends than he has Negro friends. I've heard some Negroes threaten him, now that he's president. They'd say things like, "He'd better do things for the Negroes, or else." Charlie, you know Charlie Baldwin? He's another Negro who was active in high school. He was in everything. Because of this, he was called an "Uncle Tom," but Charlie is actually real nice. A lot of the kids don't like him because he knows too many white kids.]

Being an "Uncle Tom" has many possible meanings. To these elite girls the term signifies someone who "goes too far to the other side," "somebody who goes along with the establishment," "somebody who is successful in the white world." But the meaning is obviously always derogatory. Pat becomes extremely literal when she says that people who use the word "Uncle Tom" have not read *Uncle Tom's Cabin*. As the interviews in this book continue, it becomes apparent that the term "Uncle Tom" has almost as many different meanings as does the term, "Black Power." Both terms mean different things to different people and tend, particularly, to have specific implications for a white or a black point of view.

[QUESTION: What does "Uncle Tom" mean?

BETTY: An "Uncle Tom" is a Negro who goes too far to the other side. By the other side, I mean other race.

MARGARET: We've had a lot of trouble at Plains High School about cheerleaders. We didn't get a Negro cheerleader last fall, so a lot of kids wanted the football team to boycott, but you know, it wouldn't have really worked. The coach would've gone ahead and played without the Negro boys. Charlie and the other Negro boys didn't agree to boycott. You know, Charlie is a football star. Because of this, they called him an "Uncle Tom." He was the only one out of the Negro boys on the team who was called an "Uncle Tom," although the other Negro boys also didn't agree to boycott.

BETTY: Well, his dad is also supposed to be an "Uncle Tom." I don't know why. They're very nice people. Do you know Mr. Baldwin? He was recently in the paper.

PAT: Well, the people who're calling him this don't even know the meaning of the word "Uncle Tom." There's a tendency for certain Negroes to degrade other Negroes who succeed at something. I don't believe most of the people who use this term even have read the book, *Uncle Tom's Cabin*. A lot of these Negroes are living in a different era. They think that you can isolate yourself from whites, but you can't. You have to come into contact with them.

MARGARET: Well, my great grandfather told me something once which applies here. I'll tell you about this. He said, "The Negroes can be just like a bunch of crawdads in a bucket. If one tries to get out, they let him crawl all the way to the top of the bucket. Just as he's about to go over the edge of the bucket, another crawdad reaches up and pulls him down." Now take our group; we have our own group; most kids have their own groups. You just don't like all Negroes if you're a Negro; you just don't like all whites if you're a white. We don't really try to exclude anybody, but I guess we do exclude some people. There're just some girls we don't have anything in common with, so we don't hang around with them. Because of this, we're called sedits. How could I be a sedit? I'm poverty-stricken. [All the girls laugh.] Another thing is that white people think all Negroes know each other and hang around together. Well, that's not true. We don't know all Negroes because we don't associate with all of the Negroes. Our group decided we were going to get involved in things at school, and we did. We all go to the varsities. A lot of the Negro kids don't go to the varsities or to the parties. We all went out for Honor Pep, and we made it. We tried real hard last year to rack up enough points to get into Honor Pep. With the exception of Betty, the three of us are in Honor Pep next year. Because of these things, we're called "Uncle Toms." There's this one Negro, Shirley, she's from Florida. She calls us "Northern Negroes" and says if we knew what it was like where she came from, we wouldn't be so friendly with the whites. She doesn't like us. She says we're too friendly with white kids.

BETTY: I'll tell you of a situation in the cafeteria. One morning we were sitting at this table. We always go early in the morning, sit at this table, and do the last minute things that we haven't done in our homework. Don, who was the white president of the Senior class last year, was sitting at our table one morning. Shirley got up and left; she wouldn't sit there. Later she came back and said, "You aren't going to sit there when he's there, are you?" She's really something. Then she has a white fiancé, but she says he's different. He's got soul. She says we get too involved with the white kids. We're sedits.]

Carefulness about what is said, particularly whites' carefulness about what they say in front of blacks, is a recurrent theme which most young people stress during these interviews. But not only do whites feel they have to be careful about what they say in front of blacks; certain black subgroups, such as the elites, feel they must be careful about what they say in front of other blacks. This "not wanting to hurt the feelings of others," for a variety of reasons, is very typical of all these young people whom we have interviewed. The elites' resentment about being expected to know everything about blacks comes up again; this resentment is probably largely associated with an awareness that many, if not most, whites consider all blacks to be alike. The elites, however, as has been apparent, are trying to distinguish themselves from other blacks and to emphasize their wish to be known as "individual persons," rather than as Negroes.

[QUESTION: Do you ever have to watch what you say to other kids?

MARGARET: Well, there's this one white girl, Donna. I've known her since grade school. I can say anything to her, and she can say anything to me. But with some kids, you do have to watch what you say. I think more important than that is that you notice that the other kids are always watching what they say to you. It's really funny to watch the white kids being so careful. They're just ridiculous.

BETTY: Yes, they'll sometimes say something, and then they'll say, "Oops, I shouldn't have said that," or they'll look up the wall and turn the other way or do something equally ridiculous. Sometimes we just laugh amongst ourselves when they do that. They're oh so careful not to say anything which might offend us.

NANCY: It's funny how a lot of the white kids think just because we're Negroes, we're experts on everything. In this history class where we had some pretty good discussions, there were two Negroes—another girl and myself. They'd ask us all kinds of questions and expect us to know everything. They'd ask, "Why do Negroes riot?" or "Why do you burn things? Are you going to burn Center City?" and all kinds of stupid things like that. How do we know?

MARGARET: I'll tell you another thing which is kind of funny. They really do expect us to know everything. This one white boy, in all seriousness, came up to me one time and said, "What's it really like, living in the ghetto?" Well, I've never lived in the ghetto, so how do I know? I told him, "Baby, your ghetto is just like mine. You tell me."]

Betty's comments, which follow, show an ability to go beyond the self-centeredness of the adolescent, mentioned previously. She is able to put herself in the position of the person who has not had her advantages.

[BETTY: The Negroes who've lived here in this city all their lives just don't know the hardships the other Negroes have suffered. How do we know? We've gone to integrated schools throughout our schooling. We've grown up with white kids. When we get out of school, we'll still associate some with whites. Shirley and some other Negroes in the South just don't understand what it's like for us. She's gone to an all-Negro school before, with all-Negro teachers, but we never have. Maybe it's easier in an all-Negro school; maybe there aren't as many pressures. Certainly you don't have to be worried about being called an Uncle Tom for associating with whites. Everybody in an all-Negro school is probably in one accord—all striving to learn.

NANCY: I went to Thoreau Grade School. There were only two Negroes in my class up to the time I was in the third grade. Then they integrated Thoreau. When that happened, there was a Negro boy who came in from one of the other schools who made "B"s. I was shocked to find that there were some Negro boys who were smart, because the other two kids who went to Thoreau with me, before it was integrated, were Negro boys, and they were kind of stupid.]

Here is another kind of evaluation of an all-black school, different from that given by Al in the previous interview. While Al thought that scholarship was high in such a school, Pat feels that it was not. There were, however, other advantages, about which both Al and Pat agree.

Again, we hear how there need be no whites around for a black person to be called an Uncle Tom. In Nancy's opinion, any black who does better than the average is considered an Uncle Tom. This feeling is consistent with that expressed by the previous group.

[PAT: I lived in a suburb of Detroit for two years. It was an all-Negro community. The junior high I went to was 99% Negro. I think there's a great difference between an integrated and segregated school. I regard the school in Detroit as segregated. In a segregated school, there weren't any pressures. We all did the same thing. We all liked the same things. I didn't learn as much. There was so much noise. Also, in this all-Negro school, they resented the other races, and they never really knew what the other races were like. But even in that all-Negro school, I made all "A"s. I was in the accelerated math course and some other accelerated courses, and again I was called an "Uncle Tom" and "conceited." I had a Nebraska accent. They'd say to me, "You talk like you're white." I never knew the difference.

QUESTION: Well, how could you have been called an "Uncle Tom" when there weren't any whites for you to associate with?

PAT: Well, it isn't just associating with whites.

NANCY: No, any Negro who actually does better than the average is considered an Uncle Tom.]

The examples of "integration" which these girls discuss take place on an individual level, are of short duration and of low intensity. There is an attempt to break down racial barriers and act in a friendly and companionable fashion with whites, but much of the "integration" that does take place seems to be little more than an expression of "the thing to do," rather than an outcropping of genuine feelings. Genuine integration seems to be less characteristic of high school than of elementary and junior high school.

[QUESTION: Have your relationships with the whites changed any from the time you were in junior high school?

MARGARET: Definitely. I feel there's a greater barrier between whites and blacks in high school. I feel that I was closer to white kids in junior high, but we've grown further apart in high school. We talk to one another, but we're not really friendly.

BETTY: I'll go along with that. At Plains High School, it's different. There're some Negroes who can get along with white people. And then there're some Negroes that all you have to do is mention the word "white" to them and they're ready to kill and to burn. I know this white girl; I met her at Plains High. I really didn't know that she was that close to me. But she is. She's a real nut, and everybody likes her. One day she called me on the phone. I was really surprised, because no white kid ever called me before except for business. She just called for pleasure. Then she called again, and another time, she came over to my house when I wasn't there. She came over, sat on the floor, sang "Happy Birthday" to my mother because it was her birthday, and when I came home, I saw her sitting there on the floor with her shoes off, just making herself at home. She always calls me and comes over.

NANCY: That's the exception. Most of the time, whites and Negroes don't get along that well. When I was in grade school, for the first few years there were only white kids there so I had no one else to play with but white kids. I always played with them, and thought nothing of it. I even had this white boyfriend. I used to go over to his house, and he'd come over to my house. I really liked to go over to his house because he had the neatest tree house. It was really great. I still know this boy now, but we've grown apart. We say hello to one another, but we're not really friendly. Now I hang around with Negroes mostly.

QUESTION: Is this by choice?

NANCY: Yes.

MARGARET: I'm generally more friendly with some white kids, but then there's some others—like Barbara, for instance. I can't get along with her at all. She doesn't like blacks. There're some white kids who'll accept us just because we happen to be acceptable Negroes. We get involved. Then there are some kids like June Baxter, who'll just turn up her nose. I refuse, though, to let them not accept me in school. Out of school, I don't care. I don't want to go to their parties with them. As long as I can have the same job without fighting, then it doesn't matter to me. The ones I really dislike are the ones who are so fake about it. Some put on a show. They come up and say, "Margaret, I just love you." Well, that's a lot of baloney.

NANCY: There's this girl, Sherry, I always thought she was a fake and putting it on. But I guess she isn't. At a basketball game one time, she came up to the section in which all the Negro girls were sitting. She said, "I'm going to integrate this section." She sat down. But I know a lot of the kids at school just try to be liberal because they think that's the thing to do. But they're not really liberal.]

Interracial dating represents a major threat to those who want to keep things going the way they have always gone. It may also represent a vital path toward true integration. Gordie, a black athlete, and his romance with Jean, a white fellow student, is brought up over and over again in these interviews. As will be apparent, black young women (even the elites) are against interracial dating. For one thing, they feel their reputations will suffer if they go out with a white boy—"He'd only be interested in one thing."

[QUESTION: Where do you find the most integration?

MARGARET: Sports. If you can play basketball or football, they just love you. Mostly basketball. I go with one of the boys on the basketball team. A lot of white girls have walked up to me and said, "Do you go with Jack? I think he's so wonderful. If I could go with Chuck, I'd be so happy." That's another player. They say, "Gee, if you could go with Chuck, why don't you go with Chuck? If I had a chance to go with him, I really would." That's how foolish they act. Charlie Baldwin, for example, he's got it made. He's acceptable. The girls all love him because he's involved. He's in sports, and he's really involved in the school. Gordie—that's another basketball player. He went with this white girl. They called him down to the office, and made it real rough for them because they were going together. That's where I really got mad. I think that that's their business, not the school's business. She was crazy about Gordie, and he was crazy about her. They went to Plains High to get an education, and that's what the school should be concerned with, giving them an education. Instead, they threatened Gordie, told him he wouldn't get an athletic scholarship. I felt this was entirely wrong for the school to interfere with this. It's not the school's affair to concern itself with whether or not the students have companionship, and with whom they receive this companionship. It's their business to teach. Now this Gordie and Jean—they're not the only couple at school. There're other interracial couples, too. Jean was a class officer; she was somebody. This other couple I know, the girl is just "white trash." They don't say anything to this couple. She's not as important. It's the important ones they want to "save."

QUESTION: How do the Negroes feel about this relationship between Gordie and Jean?

BETTY: Some of the Negroes said to Gordie, "What are you doing with her? You're an Uncle Tom." But this didn't bother Gordie at all. I think most of them knew Gordie wouldn't care what they said.

PAT: Some of the Negroes said, "How come you picked an outsider? What's wrong with us?"

BETTY: Jean and I would talk after school a lot. She told me Miss Deane was really against her. Miss Deane is a counselor. Jean said her mother was worse than her father about it. Her mother said she couldn't go with Gordie; she wouldn't tolerate it. She went to all kinds of extremes to get out and meet Gordie. She told me once if she ever had another fight with her parents, she just couldn't take it. She wouldn't make it. They tried for a time not to speak to each other in school, so as not to get the administration upset. Gordie could do it, but it was Jean who couldn't. Jean was telling me it was just too hard to walk by Gordie and not say something. If you're a low white person, the administration could care less, but if you're a higher white person, they're worried that you might be dragged down by a Negro. That's why they interfered with Jean and Gordie.

PAT: I think the school is afraid of its image. They're afraid that outsiders will say, "Look at the integrated couples at Plains High School. We can't have that."

BETTY: That's right. The parents would call and cause trouble.

NANCY: They're always trying to build up a certain image on how great Plains High is interracially. I can say that I'm honestly proud to be here, but there's definitely room for improvement. I hope when I leave Plains High School, I can say that I helped improve it. My brother has said that it almost seems like a fad for white girls to want to date Negroes nowadays. There're an awful lot of them who'd like to.

BETTY: Some of the Negro girls are really angry with the Negro boys who go out with white girls. My cousin was a football star. He was going with this Negro girl. He said his girlfriend would get mad because when they won games, the cheerleaders would come out and kiss the football players. She didn't like this at all. The colored boys, when they win a game, they just prep themselves up for the white girls to come out and kiss them. It's really funny to watch them.

MARGARET: You should come to one of the games when the cheerleaders run out and kiss the boys. Some of the parents just sit there at the end of their seats and glare.

PAT: Well, you know it's hard not to run out. They're all just excited, and you just want to go out there.

BETTY: I know that certain people on the basketball team would say, "Move out of the way now, so this girl can run out and kiss me. I want that one to move out and kiss me."

QUESTION: How do the boys feel about interracial dating?

MARGARET: Well, Gordie used to go with Doris, who was half Mexican and half white. The boys would call her the "red light," which wasn't very nice. But for the most part, for the guys, it's okay. Most of them don't really care, but I think the boys get along better, anyway. Negro boys and white boys go out together. They drink beer together, and they're seen together more often. But this isn't so with white girls and Negro girls.

NANCY: You know white people think it's worse to have their girls go with Negro boys than to have their boys to go with Negro girls. But it's funny, I don't know of one couple at Plains High School where a white boy goes with a Negro girl. In high school, it just doesn't happen

QUESTION: Suppose a white boy asked you out. How easy would it be for you to accept?

MARGARET: Any white boy that asked me out, I'd know what he wants. For a Negro boy to have a white girl is some sort of a status symbol. But if a white boy asked me out, it would be a step down for him, so I'd think he wanted something, and I'm not about to give it to him.

PAT: I think it would be hard for girls to accept dates from white boys anyway, because girls have to worry more about their reputations. The boys don't have to worry about this, but the girls do.

MARGARET: Also, if I were asked out by a white boy and accepted, my parents would pitch a fit. My father would say, "If another Negro man isn't good enough for you, that's too bad, then you get out of my house." It would really be something.

PAT: My parents don't feel that way. They usually say that it's the couple's business. We've talked about interracial dating. It's nobody else's business but theirs.

NANCY: I think my dad would think more about the character of the person. That's what he's always thinking about.

BETTY: Well, I can tell you that my parents wouldn't like it. There was this white boy that I got to know, and I liked him. I remember I was a sophomore. I came home and I told my mother there was this boy that I met and that I really liked. I said, "He's white," and she said, "Oh, no." Then she said, "Quit fooling around, Betty." She knew I was fooling because I knew that I couldn't really get serious about him. So I was fooling. We're still good friends. He's very friendly with me, and always says hello and talks to me when he sees me.]

The generation gap is described with understanding. Again, a drift toward increased acceptance of other races is described. This time, however, the situation is somewhat different because of the role of unusual family members.

It is interesting that Margaret expresses a concern that whites think they are better than she is. Previously these elite girls complained that they could not stand out scholastically because of the "average blacks'" complaint that the elites considered themselves "better." Margaret expresses the same concern about white reactions to her. The thought of being looked down on by persons who think they are "better" appears to be a prevalent and deep-seated concern.

[QUESTION: What's the generation gap like? Do you think you're more liberal than your parents?

BETTY: We're definitely more liberal than our parents. That's because we've never experienced some of the things that they have. We'll never go through the things that they had to go through. My mother remembers real discrimination and talks about it. For example, in buying a house, it always costs more for the Negroes. Take our house. We paid far more for it than what it's worth. We bought it from a white person. Also, they jack the taxes up on us. They're going to get us one way or another. With my grandparents, it's even worse. They never mix with whites. They act friendly, but they don't mix. I'd say we're more liberal than either our parents or our grandparents.

NANCY: My great grandmother was half Negro and half Indian. She never spoke against white people. She never told the kids not to mix.

MARGARET: Well, my grandparents on my mother's side are real religious. I never heard them speak out against white people. My great grandparents, I think it was my great grandmother, was white. But, you know, everybody's a little bit mixed up anyway. I know my mother has always told me to be proud of my history and never to be ashamed of it. My great grandparents were slaves. When they were released from slavery, they wanted to get away from the white person who owned them. They came out of Mississippi. Most of the slaves took the names of their slave owners, but not my great grandparents. They decided they wanted to leave that all behind. So they selected the name Watersham. My mother always told me, "If you ever run across any Watershams, you're related, because that name started here through my great grandfather." She's always told me to be proud of what you are, "Never be ashamed, or I'll disown you." And I am proud of what I am, and nothing makes me angrier than to have someone think that they are better than I am. I won't permit this. I won't permit them to think that they're better than I am.]

[QUESTION: Earlier, you hinted that there were some areas of improvement needed in the schools. What are some of these areas?

NANCY: Well, the cheerleader elections, for one. This year, when the results of the cheerleader election came out, we were really angry. We really expected a Negro to become a cheerleader. We got out a petition, but then when you sit and think about it, you realize, well, it was a vote by popularity. If they didn't get the votes, there isn't anything you can do about it.

MARGARET: Our own kids didn't register and vote. It was partially our fault. The four of us in this room tonight, we really worked hard to get a Negro cheerleader elected. We solicited kids to register and vote. We didn't run for cheerleader ourselves because we wanted to help get a Negro elected and worked on that aspect of it. So we helped in the selection of someone to put up as a candidate, and then we worked hard to get that person elected. I think aside from the fact that a lot of the Negroes didn't vote, another problem was that the procedures weren't exactly clear. The elections took place during Dr. King's death; also, there was a change in the hours in which voting took place. Although these things were read out during the first hour bulletins, a lot of the kids don't pay any attention to the bulletins. The thing that makes me mad is why should we have to go out and solicit the votes? If the best person were elected, then we wouldn't have to go out and solicit the Negro votes, because at least one of the girls who was elected was elected strictly on popularity, but she's lousy as a cheerleader. And I know that at least one of the Negro girls who was running was a lot better than she is. This has really made me mad, because Plains High School has always had good cheerleaders. They may have been all white, but they've always been good cheerleaders. This year I'm just going to laugh, because they elected this white girl who is really lousy.

BETTY: The death of King threw everything out of whack. There were two Negro girls who made it through the primary, but they weren't elected in the final. So part of it, too, was the Negroes' fault because they didn't vote.

PAT: That's right. There weren't enough Negroes who registered in the first place.

MARGARET: Well, the whites didn't support them, and neither did the Negroes support them. In order to win, you need the support of both. I think the cheerleaders should've won on their merit, not because they're Negro or white. But the cheerleader elections are a popularity contest. I don't care whether it's racism or not. Electing this white girl this year is a case of deterioration at Plains High School.]

The foregoing comments illustrate how this group of elites both identifies itself with and at the same time separates itself from other blacks. These elites work to get a black cheerleader elected, but at the same time they complain about having to go out and solicit the Negro vote. Again, they find themselves in the competitive value dilemma of whether to support someone because she is the most qualified or because she is black.

The girls in this chapter complain of incompetence among school administrators, counselors, and teachers, but they do not complain that these persons express anti-black attitudes. Non-elite blacks, on the other hand, attribute racist motivations to many of these same white adults. Perhaps the present group of elite adolescents does not attribute racist attitudes to the administration, counselors, and teachers because they identify more with such whites than with "average blacks," or perhaps it is because they are less emotionally involved in such situations. Certainly not to be ignored is the fact that the elites expect help with their career goals—going to college—from the counselors and teachers. When such help is not received, it is small wonder that their appraisal of such personnel is that of incompetence.

[QUESTION: Are there any other areas in which you think you've experienced discrimination?

MARGARET: Well, we haven't ourselves. But I've heard from kids who aren't in the acceptable class who talk about discrimination in the classroom. Ourselves, I can't say anything about it, because I haven't experienced it.

QUESTION: How about counselors? How do you think the counselors treat you?

NANCY: I hate the counselors. When I was in junior high, I waited for the counselors to call me in to talk to me, and they never did. When I got to high school, I waited for them to call me in to talk to me, and they never did. Finally, they called me out of class one period, which was dumb. They're not supposed to call you out of class. Also, I found that they don't really know their business. They don't really advise you, because they don't know how to advise you.

BETTY: I went to the counselor when I was failing geometry. I told him I wanted to get out of that class because it wasn't for me. He said the teacher didn't say anything about it; the teacher's supposed to send a letter. There's all kinds of red tape. I tried to get out of that class all year, and I never did. I first went to him after I'd been in class only seven weeks. But, come June, I was still in the class.

MARGARET: I was in this advanced math class. I'm not so good in math. I made a "C" the first nine weeks, the only "C" I've ever received. I don't like making a "C" because you can't get on the honor roll. I went to a counselor and said I wanted to get out. The counselor said, "Oh, I don't know. You better stay and try." They just don't help you at all.

PAT: It's really a laugh because Mr. Ewing, the principal, gets up there every year and tells you to get involved in the school. He also tells you if you have anything that troubles you, go to your counselor. But, if you go to the counselor, they never know anything. You ask a question; they don't know. The best counselor up there is Mr. Gage. He's a good guy.

BETTY: I don't know. He's the one who wouldn't let me out of that geometry class.

QUESTION: How about Mr. Ewing?

PAT: You hardly ever see Ewie.

MARGARET: Ewie walks up the hall and doesn't even speak. It makes me kind of angry. The junior high principal would talk to everybody. He'd ask you a question, he'd ask you how the class was. I really didn't like him either, but he was still nice because he did ask you how you were getting along. But not Ewie.

PAT: I'd say the home room teachers and the counselors, both of them, just don't care. In Detroit, I was just a number, too. But I was called to the counselor's office twice while I was there. He still didn't know my name after that, but when he saw me in the hallway, he'd say "Hello." At Plains School, they don't even talk to you.

NANCY: You just learn that you don't go to the counselors for anything. You learn after a while that when you need something or have a problem, you go to a favorite teacher, and talk it out with the teacher.

QUESTION: Do you discuss race in class?

MARGARET: In some classes we discuss race, but for the most part the teachers aren't open about it. They might touch on something which has come up in the newspaper. They'll touch on it lightly. They'll do the talking and won't permit any class discussion on it. If you raise your hand, they ignore it. If you interrupt, they say, "We have to go on," and "We'll talk about it later."

NANCY: In some classes you do discuss things. In my history class, this other Negro girl and myself did a report on the black protest. The teacher gave us two whole periods in which to do it; which was more than any other group. The kids asked us a lot of questions. I really liked it. When Dr. King was killed, there was some open discussion, too.

MARGARET: I have one pretty liberal class; it was in Psychology. He likes to talk. Sometimes it gets kind of comical though, because the kids don't really have anything to say; they just talk to hear themselves talk. In American Literature, where I thought we'd get into something, we never did. You know, we never even studied any Negro literature.

BETTY: In American History, we went into race a little bit, but not much.

MARGARET: I took World History during the summer, and that was a good class. If you got an "A" the first semester, you didn't have to take an exam the second. You could write a term paper. So I wrote a term paper on the Negro in the Civil War. I had never done any research on Negro history. It was really great because I learned a lot of things. They don't teach Negro history at Plains High, you know. They try to skip over it.

PAT: Well, they don't want to touch on it.

NANCY: Mrs. Taylor touched on it now and then. She broke all of the rules in the blue book. She laughed at the blue book, but they're getting rid of her now. She's going to junior high school.

MARGARET: You know, when I was first in school, all we ever heard about was George Washington and Thomas Jefferson. I never read anything about Negroes. I always used to think, "Gee, what's the matter with us? Haven't we ever done anything?" I was so glad to learn that there were some Negroes who had done something.

NANCY: In history class it wasn't part of the textbook, but a supplement. There was something about this Negro who had planned the city of Washington. It said how this French designer wanted too much money to plan it, so they got this Negro who planned out the city. It was just on the side, though; it wasn't really a part of the class. Not much else has ever been mentioned at school about Negroes.

BETTY: Mr. Caldwell, the science teacher, wanted me to go to Upward Bound at Taylor College, but our income was too high, so they wouldn't let me. He was telling me once that he'd fought for years to try to get Negro history at Plains High. He also told me about the problems they had in trying to get an Upward Bound program at Taylor. The college administration didn't want 50 Negro kids on their campus. You know, one of the sorority houses wouldn't let the kids use their house this year. This Mr. Caldwell, he's a big Black Power man. He doesn't like the NAACP. He says they're always asking, "Can we walk on this street?" He said, "To hell with asking, we should burn it." I said, "Burn what? You aren't going to burn my house!" It might be all right for the Negroes in the slums; it might make more sense to burn the slums because it's just trash they're burning. But I don't like this when they say, "just burn."

NANCY: You know, it's funny. A lot of white kids at Plains High really want to know about Negroes. I think they'd like to have a Negro History course. They're always asking us about Negroes. You know, what I think has brought the Negro and white together more than anything else? Soul music. I'll tell you something else. If the colored kids have a fad, it won't be long before the white kids catch it. Take a new dance. Just as the Negroes are giving up that dance, you'll notice the white kids start picking it up—or slang words, or clothes. They're always about a month behind.

QUESTION: How about at the dances? Do the kids dance together?

MARGARET: No, not really. The whites dance in a line, and the Negroes dance in one part of the gym. Every now and then a couple of Negro boys will go in just for fun and bust up the line.]

[QUESTION: What has your experience at Plains High taught you about race relations?

PAT: Well, it has taught me about other races, ethnic groups, and religions. Through my experience at Plains High, it's a little bit easier to get together with people from other races. We don't get up tight, but I think I've learned to understand whites better. I think I've gotten more broadminded by going to Plains High; I try to listen to both sides. Also, it's taught me to notice the differences between people. Some are distinct, some are subtle. The differences in the same race is what I'm talking about. It also has taught me to learn and distinguish who is sincere and who is phoney.

NANCY: I'd say, the thing that I've learned most is to learn about other religions. Most Negroes are Baptists. If they're not Baptists, they're either gone one way or the other—Holy Roller or Methodist. But I've never really known a lot about other religions, until I went to Plains High. I never ever really knew anything about Jewish people, for example, until I met Ruth and talked to her about Jews. Or until I was in Mrs. Thaler's class. She's real sweet. I think she's a little eccentric, but she's real good. Also going to Plains High School has taught me something else. All we ever get is the white person's history. We never get anything about the black man's history. So how are the white kids supposed to know about us? They don't learn anything about Negroes in school.

BETTY: I think you learn how to face life at Plains High School. In elementary school, you just don't know any better. You don't feel any difference. But at Plains High, you experience dislike from the whites, and you also experience dislike from the Negroes. You learn and experience how you can be united or separated. I've also learned at Plains High School that there'll be some whites and blacks who will never mix. When I first entered Plains High School, I never thought I'd ever have any close white friends, but I was wrong, because I do have some. You think the whites will turn up their noses at you, but this isn't true. Some of them may not speak to you, but they'll always smile. I never have felt rejected because I'm a Negro, at Plains High. Sometimes you feel there's a fakeness, but not a rejection. I've also learned that there can be togetherness. You can get along just as well with white people as you can with Negroes.

MARGARET: After two years at Plains High School, I guess you can say I've learned a lot. I've learned I can get along with white kids. But one thing I've learned is to be bitter. That's right—bitter. The first discrimination I've felt was at Plains High. After three years of junior high school, where I sat on top, and the majority of the kids were Negroes, there was a rude awakening to go to Plains High School. Even though you have the merit to back you up, merit is not enough, and I've found that out at Plains High. I've learned that you have to try to get along with the white kids. They don't know us as well as we know them. They live in white neighborhoods, and they go to white churches. I've learned that I have to try to understand them, and give them time to try to understand us. Things could go faster. I also know that they don't have to discriminate against Negroes. If I have the capability to do things at Plains High, I should have the chance to do them. This is a fact of reality. I've had to learn to face this reality at Plains High for the first time. There were things I couldn't do because I'm a Negro. Of course, it was a bit unreal when I was in junior high because I could do anything I wanted. We were in the majority then. I've also learned at Plains High that I can be accepted, not by being an "Uncle Tom," but because I'm capable. I want what should be rightfully mine. Being Negro shouldn't be a handicap, and I won't let it be. Plains High is like a world in itself. I've learned to be proud of what I am. I've got as much dignity and integrity as any of them. I've gotten involved at Plains High, so I can say that I'm doing something good for Plains High. If you're a Negro, you have to try extra hard, and I have. But I've learned that involvement is the only way to better yourself and to better your race. I'm still a student at Plains High, and I know at Plains High color will make a difference. This is reality. But I also know that they have got to learn to live with it, and so do I.]

One would expect to hear many cliches and generalities in response to the question, "What have you learned at Plains High?" On the contrary, however, although the responses do begin in a somewhat generalized fashion (so that one first tends to suspect that these young people say what they think the interviewer wants to hear), the answers become more and more specific and concrete. The final response, by Margaret, seems altogether spontaneous and articulate. One has the feeling that Margaret is saying what is truly in her heart and on her mind. She expresses her deep resentment about the situation in which the black person finds himself, a resentment which never seems unreasonable or indiscriminate. One sees that these particular elites, as distinguished from those in Part 1, do not attempt to flee from their blackness. Even though they may feel somewhat different from the "average," they nevertheless cast their lot with their fellow blacks. If they reject other blacks, their rejection is based on the fact that they have little in common (values, goals, and so on), rather than on "blackness."

CHAPTER 3

The Black Militants

A major misconception of the white community, as has been said, involves grouping Negroes into one indistinguishable collection of people. Perhaps this tendency constitutes part of a need to depersonalize, since it is easier to take the ugly posture of prejudice against someone who is not distinguishable and who, therefore, does not stand out. In an interview with avowed racists (see Chapter 4), we are told, "There's one class of Negroes; they're all black." We hope that this book will help to break down this misconception. The Negro community, just as the white community, is made up of different people who do not all share the same values, hopes, and dreams.

Most of the students with whom we talked identify the three students in this chapter as "black militants." Some call them "Black Power advocates." As we ask the members of our sample for a definition of "Black Power," many of the whites talk of "violence" and "black supremacy." Even some of the better-informed white students associate violence with the movement. The blacks, on the other hand, define Black Power as involving primarily *economic and political power.*

A number of students—both white and black—question the basic motivation of one of these militants, Tim Howard, whose outspokenness has been labeled "attention seeking," "crowd pleasing," "acts of a mad dog," and "personal aggrandizement." Many of the students were fearful that Tim might destroy the home of one of the authors, where the interviews were held. Those students said, "He's a wild man; you don't want to talk to him." In point of fact, however, Tim was one of the few students who addressed the female member of the interviewing team as "ma'm."

Perhaps these "militants" do play a different role at school. Perhaps they receive social recognition from their fellow students for playing the "militant" role. However, more than once we are told of situations in which the students who appear in this chapter prevented a fight which other students thought might have turned into a race riot. When the administrators, teachers, and counselors were impotent in the situation, a mere "cool it" from Tim more than once saved the day.

Unlike the Elites, these young blacks are not academic competitors for white students. They do not run for school offices, are not in accelerated courses, do not join school clubs and refuse to participate in sports. Although sports hold out the chance for college for the Negro male, these "militants" refuse to participate in sports because, they claim, the Negro is exploited by the school.

In this interview, we talk with three young black men, Phil, Tim, and Bill. Tim links the pressures he has experienced to his color, while Bill talks more of pressures which pertain to grades. He complains of the rigidity with which classes are run, but his complaint that attendance—not grades—determines whether you pass or fail is only indirectly relevant to racial matters, since white students are also expected to attend class. Bill's reaction probably reflects his special sensitivity to matters involving relations between whites and blacks. His feelings, although probably not particularly accurate, are nevertheless understandable.

[QUESTION: What kinds of pressures have you experienced from attending a desegregated school?

TIM: Since you're colored, we have to let you in by force, and you have to do what we say, or the Man is going to be right on top of you and kick you out. You're the underdog. They're always on you, and you got to watch out what you do.

BILL: You've got to put on certain airs to be acceptable to the teachers and students. To the students, you have to make good grades; and you have to make good grades for the teachers, too. If you cut up, and still make good grades, they don't judge you on the grades. They judge you on the fact that you cut up. I like to be myself. I don't like to fake it out. Your attitude has to be one of conformity. I don't like to conform. I like to be myself.

TIM: Your vocal expressions around the school get you into trouble. I'm always in trouble, because I speak up.

BILL: I only went to History nine times. I took the tests, and I got the notes. I made a "B" average, but I got kicked out for not going to class. I don't see why you have to go to class if you keep your grades. If you maintain a grade-point average that's acceptable, they shouldn't put you out. If you know what the subject is, you shouldn't have to go.

TIM: The trouble is that you're a Negro, and that's why you have to go. A white kid could cut class like that all of the time, and he'd get into trouble, too, but he wouldn't get kicked out.

BILL: That's true. This white friend and me left school the sixth hour the other day. Neither one of us wanted to stay in school, so we left. The counselors had me sign a paper saying I'd get kicked out if I did something like that again. This white kid, who's been in as much trouble as me, didn't have to sign anything, although he was warned not to do that again. We were both reprimanded, but I had to sign a paper saying that they'd kick me out if I did anything else.]

The black students at Plains High School agree that they should have a Negro cheerleader. Since most players, particularly in basketball, are black, both the black players and the black students feel they should have "one of our kind representing us." Aside from interracial dating, this was one of the most talked about issues.

[PHIL: The most discriminatory thing I can think of happened this year. The Negro students tried to elect a Negro cheerleader. Election was held the day of Dr. King's funeral. The Negro kids weren't there to vote. The primary election was on that day. The Negro cheerleader that the kids wanted to elect wasn't elected. I don't see any reason why the school had to have the election on that day. I think that's outright discrimination.

BILL: Well, the way they elect cheerleaders is pretty stupid anyway. You have to register for the election before you can vote. I mean, if you go to Plains High, why do you have to register beforehand? You know it's pretty hard to register 2500 kids in two or three days.

TIM: Well, that isn't the half of it. The way they pick the kids in the preliminaries—there's another act of discrimination. The cheerleaders are picked by Girls' Pep, Boys' Pep, and last year's cheerleaders. Girls' Pep, Boys' Pep, and last year's cheerleaders are all white. They usually pick white kids. The reason why Girls' Pep, Boys' Pep, and all the others are white is because it costs bread, and the Negroes don't have the bread to get into these organizations.]

However, if money were not a factor, the reactions of other Negroes might well be a deterrent to join Boys' Pep or Girls' Pep. Members of the black minority group themselves have an idea of the group's "average." Deviants from this average are labeled "white Negroes." Often the children of middle and upper-class Negroes are identified as "white Negroes." This term, however, is also used for those blacks who try to join such traditionally white activities as Girls' and Boys' Pep.

[PHIL: Well, the type of Negro that joins that type of thing are Negroes who look down on other Negroes anyway, and conform to the white ways. They wouldn't vote for a Negro themselves. They won't be individuals. Their idea is to get a good education and try to be as white as possible. They're what we call "white Negroes." They're not for the Negroes. They're for the whites. They've learned the white ways, and they want to be white and act white. Negroes don't like this kind of Negro.]

[QUESTION: Aside from the cheerleader incident, can you think of any other situations of discrimination?

PHIL: Usually the discrimination is kept at a minimum. However, you feel it; you know that it's there, and there's this feeling which is hard to explain. In junior high, it's not too bad, and in grade school it almost doesn't exist at all. The kids just seem to be friendly with one another, and just don't pay much attention to race. The higher you go in school, the worse it gets. As you get older, people pull away. After high school, it's even worse yet, unless you go to college. If you don't go to college, you're completely away. In grade school you play together, in junior high you play a little bit less; when you get out of school, you're completely away from one another.]

The students at Plains High often blame their parents, teachers, and the school administration for the racial cleavage that increasingly crystallizes with age—particularly with the onset of puberty. Yet, as we will see later, pressures from peers are often as devastating, if not more so than those exerted by parents and by the school. Because of the pervasiveness of the peer group in the lives of adolescents, its role in promoting racial cleavage should not be underestimated.

[PHIL: The parents are the ones who cause the discrimination. If you would raise five whites and five Negro kids together, they would be just like brothers, unless older people told them otherwise, told them to hate each other and discriminate against each other. It happens in the families. It's the parents—Negro and white parents both—because Negroes are told just as much as whites, by their parents, not to participate in things with whites, to stay away from whites, to look upon whites as all the same.

TIM: Well, the older you get, the more mature you are, and you start getting involved in social activities. I think it's the social thing which causes the parents to try to keep the races apart. They're afraid that a girl will get pregnant, and this will be very bad for the family. The kids listen to their parents; they get their mind tricked up. Dating is also a big fear; that's the thing now. Whites and blacks both fear this. You go to Plains High and you pay your taxes, so why don't they just leave us alone? We'll just take care of our own social life. I was going with a white girl at Plains Junior High. The teacher called the girl in and talked to her, told her she couldn't go out for cheerleading and all that, and that she would call her parents, so that was the end of that. Teachers always call in the girls, because it's a lot easier to trick up the girl's mind than it is the boy's. The boys don't listen as much. So everytime they want to bust up some interracial dating, they always get onto the girl. The principal got on to this friend of mine who is on the basketball team. He got the same thing from the principal. He was told he couldn't play basketball unless he stopped dating this white girl. I think this is all wrong.

You know who you want to choose for yourself, and you should be allowed to choose that person. You shouldn't be denied the right to choose somebody you like because of race.

BILL: I go to mixed parties all the time; I never have trouble. Young kids usually don't notice skin color. They could care less. If I had a daughter, I wouldn't care if she dated a white guy as long as he was good as a person. That's what I'd look for. I'd expect her to bring home the white guy, so I could look him over to see if he was all right. If he was all right, it wouldn't bother me one bit if she dated a white guy.

PHIL: Well, the teachers cause a lot of trouble. If they would only stay out of it, there'd be a lot less trouble. They're always trying to bust up things like dating. And they're always trying to separate the races. Most Negroes are prejudiced on white people. As soon as they see a white person, a whole bunch of ideas run through their head, such as, "Oh, there's a white person. He's going to look down on me, and he's going to exploit me, and if I'm not careful, I might be killed." They do this all the time. They just lump all white people together. I think the Negroes are more prejudiced than the whites, because prejudice means having a preconceived notion about other people. And if that's what it means, the Negroes certainly have preconceived notions about whites, without even knowing a white person. Negro kids get this attitude from their parents. The parents put pressure on the Negro kids to keep them separate.]

Earlier in the year, the Center City School Board decided to include some previously all white neighborhoods within the school boundaries of Plains High. The white parents in East Center City objected on the grounds that Plains High lacked adequate facilities and that the transporting of students would cause traffic congestion. Almost all of our student respondents—white and black—questioned such parental arguments. Almost to a person, they agreed that the white parents objected to Plains High because of the number of lower class and black students that are there.

[TIM: Look at this situation with East Plains High. Now there's something for you. The reason why they didn't come to Plains High School is that they said the facilities aren't as good. Well, that's a lot of baloney. The facilities at East aren't as good. They always use Plains High facilities for all kinds of things. They come over to use the pool; they come over to rent the auditorium; they come over to use the basketball court—all kinds of things like this, because at East they don't have these facilities. The people at East got big dough. They're afraid they'll be influenced by colored people, drinking wine, shooting craps in the back halls, and things like that—that's what they're worried about. I think that integrated schools are a good experience for kids.

I think, in fact, if you don't attend an integrated high school, that part of your education is missing because you never know that those people out there want to stay separate. They want their kids to stay separate. They're worried about us.

PHIL: I went to a segregated grade school. I didn't know anything about white people when I was in that segregated grade school. I think you have to live together to get to know one another. The majority of people in South Center City are non-white. They don't get the true picture. They don't know whites, and whites don't know them. And this separate but equal stuff, that was never true. There are many differences, like there's a white school out here right now in this part of town. What's the name of that school over there? Franklin. Well, my sister is in her third year of college. She's going to be an elementary teacher and, as part of her training, she's had to go to the various schools. She's noticed that over there, they have all kinds of fancy little things, electrical things that the kids can play with and learn from, all sorts of little machines and gadgets. They don't have these kinds of things at Lincoln and Washington, where the majority of Negro kids go. They're not separate and equal; they're separate and unequal. They're not equal at all, and the reason for that is that the parents in this part of town [East Center City] put pressure on the school board; that makes a difference, and they get what they want. A lot of the parents in the southern part of town don't even know what their kids could have. They don't even know about these things. They don't ever put pressure on the school board, city and things like that. They don't even know that they can. We built the country, I don't know why we can't have these sorts of things.

TIM: We built the country, so we'll burn it down, too. That will make a difference. If you're treated like a dog, the thing to do is to act like a dog. And that's what the Negro is going to do soon.

'PHIL: You can't survive in a place where you can see things and can't have them. Everything's going out and nothing's coming in. This is very bad.]

This generation has been dubbed "The mass media generation," so that Watts, Detroit, New York, and Washington are usually no further than one's TV. Some students at Plains High have visited these cities. In the preceding chapter, for instance, Al told of having seen the ghettos in Detroit. Because of this firsthand experience, Al, who did not identify strongly with the black man, could at least empathize with the Detroit Negroes who rioted. Here is what Bill has to say about Watts:

[BILL: I quit school last year in March and went to California, to Watts. They're always asking, "Why do you riot?" Well, if you could see Watts, you could see why they rioted. You should see the conditions out there. And the prices the people have to pay. They're overcharged for food, and are often given spoiled meat. The kids go to school in four-hour shifts. There are over 2000 kids in this one school. However, there's a new school two miles away, for white kids. And there aren't enough kids to fill it, while these Negro kids have to go to school in four-hour shifts. You always see the kids at home alone—seven or eight year old kids—while their parents work. The father works two jobs; the mother is working another job just to make ends meet. The kids stand on the corner drinking wine, smoking pot—I'm not kidding. Center City is a lot safer. That's why I came back. It's really bad out there. Here I can walk down the street at one in the morning, and I don't have to worry about anything. I just walk down the street as free as you can be. In Watts, you're always looking over your shoulder. You have to watch out. You never know what's going to happen. Hell, in Watts, I'd look over my shoulder at eight at night, not just one in the morning.]

At times, it is not easy to separate whatever genuine prejudice exists from a special sensitivity about racial matters—from a readiness to sense prejudice even when it may not exist. Referring to a black high school student as a "boy," for example, is perceived as prejudice by the black students in this chapter, even while they agree that teachers sometime also refer to a white student as a "boy." Perhaps this is an example of a readiness to sense prejudice where none is actually intended. On the other hand, since in the past the term "boy" has been used disrespectfully by whites with reference to black men, irrespective of their age or position, the overreaction of the black students to the word "boy" is quite understandable.

[QUESTION: How integrated is Plains High?

PHIL: Well, the clubs aren't too well integrated. The Negroes don't try to get into clubs. They feel they won't be fully accepted. Your clothes aren't good enough for one thing. They seem to judge on appearance an awful lot, not what's inside a person. Sometimes there's a little discrimination in some of the clubs. A lot of times it's just the things that you feel; it isn't the outward discrimination that's so bad. You just know that you're not going to be accepted, so you don't want to get involved in these kinds of things, because you don't want to feel bad.

TIM: Sometimes teachers lay it hard on you, and you know they're doing it because you're a "nigger." One thing about us, though, is that we lay it back on them. We don't take that much stuff, anymore, from teachers.

BILL: The Economics teacher, he's really prejudiced. Every time somebody's talking, or acting up, or doing something else—the whole class could be talking—he's always calling me down. I had a 93 grade-point average in that class, but I got a "D" on my report card. He's always laying it on me, because

I'm a Negro. I have this habit of holding my hand over my mouth; I've been doing it since I was five years old. I don't know why I do it, but I do it. When I complained to my mother, and she went up there to see this teacher, he said he even graded me down a little bit because I hold my hand over my mouth. Can you imagine that?

PHIL: The teachers can't show prejudice right out usually. They're sneaky about it. But they're prejudiced.

BILL: The way some teachers talk to you, that's one way you know. You're walking down the hall with friends, and this teacher will say, "Hey, boy, you're talking too loud." I don't like this; I don't like to be called "boy." The teachers are always doing this, so one day I broke it down to them. I told this one teacher not to call me "boy." He can call me "young man" or he can call me anything he wants to call me, but not to call me "boy." I don't consider myself a boy. You know why we don't like that word, don't you? Well, there's something wrong when teachers in an integrated school use that word.

QUESTION: Do they also call white kids "boy?"

BILL: Yes, they do, but there's a different inflection than when they call Negroes "boy." They may not mean it that way. Besides they shouldn't use that word, when they know that it arouses feelings in the Negro.

TIM: I'll tell you what the difference is. I've had them call me that, too. They put a little more emphasis on the *boy* when they say it to me, and I know what they mean, and they know what they mean. They're sneaky about it. This is their way to get at us.]

Although there is general agreement that sports are integrated, black and white students differ in their opinions as to why the black student is accepted in that activity. Many white students feel that the Negro has matured more quickly; others speak of a different biological endowment; still others consider sports to be the Negro's ticket out of the ghetto, so that he works harder in this area than do white athletes. However, in spite of the widespread belief that one way out of the ghetto is through sports, Tim and Bill have "quit playing for the white man." They would prefer the ghetto rather than to help the white man exploit black athletes.

[QUESTION: Where do you find the most integration?

BILL: The most integration takes place in sports.

TIM: I wouldn't say that. I wouldn't say that the most integration takes place in sports. All of the teams rely on Negro players a great deal. The Negro players are on the first team usually, and yet we can't get a Negro cheerleader. Basketball, for example, the most popular sport at school [four of the first string players on the basketball team are Negroes] doesn't have one Negro cheerleader. The white man wants us to break our necks, but they don't want to give us the courtesy to have a Negro cheerleader. I gave up basketball for this reason. I could be on the first string. I was on the first string in junior high, but I made a decision that I wasn't going to play for the white man anymore. The white man can go to hell. I'm tired of breaking my neck out there, working hard and sweating.

BILL: They only accept the Negro for his physical ability. That's the only time that color doesn't seem to enter into their minds. Or maybe it does, because they expect all colored people to have this physical ability.

TIM: You're accepted on physical strength. It's traditional from the time of slaves. The Negroes were laborers. They didn't sit behind desks. They had big muscles. They could lift hundred-pound bales of cotton. Even now they put you on a broom. You don't have nothing. You work for less than the going rate, and it's always physical work. If you're a Negro, you're supposed to have physical strength. You're not supposed to have any mind.

BILL: Sports in school is just another form of exploitation. You're accepted through the basketball season, or through the baseball season, or through the football season, but not after that. One time, in school, when I was on the football team, this white boy told me plain out, he said we couldn't have a Negro girl out there as a cheerleader. Well, I really wanted to lay it into him, but I couldn't. I was already in trouble, and if I'd laid it into him just one more time, I'd have been thrown out of school. And where would I be without no means of getting an education? They threaten us with this all the time. If you want an education, you toe the line. Because if you don't, you're out. They don't give you a chance. The white boys have more chances. I quit football in my junior year. I decided I wasn't going to run my tail off anymore. There aren't any Negro cheerleaders. If we don't have any of our kind out there to make us real proud, they weren't going to run me anymore.]

Tim and Bill tell how they feel that the teachers are responsible for racial separation. Bill also tells about some pranks pulled by him and a white friend to upset two teachers. This friendship between Bill and Frank is unusual because it is not limited to school or to the playing fields as most other black-white relationships are. Bill describes a kind of joking which he explains to be limited to friends. Phil then explains that Bill's relationship with his white pal, Frank, is exceptional.

[TIM: It's a lot more integrated when the teachers aren't around. For example, we go into the john and we all smoke, white and black, all together. When the teachers come in, we split up. Negroes go in one section; whites go in another section.

BILL: Kids who are with white friends—the teachers don't like it. I got this one white friend. He's a real crazy guy. I'm the only Negro in this one class. He's real funny. We went into the class and we were sitting up front. This kid turns around (he can pull this because he's a friend of mine), and he said, "We can't have this. Go to the back of the room." Well, the teacher sent him to the office. It was really funny. Another time, we were walking down the hall, leaving school fourth hour one day. We didn't feel like staying anymore, and there was this teacher. She was real young. We didn't even know she was a teacher. We got up real close to her, and I said, "Let's lay it on her." He said, "Get out of here, nigger. You're not supposed to be near me," and I said, "I'm going to burn your house down, man." This teacher had a fit. She just couldn't belive it. We do things like that when we're friends.

TIM: A lot of times the kids are friendly in school, but they're not after school. You see white kids you know, who you're friendly with in school, then you see them downtown, and they're with their parents—they won't even speak to you. He's afraid of what his father'll say.

BILL: We were having chitlings for New Year's. This white friend of mine said he'd never had chitlings, so I said, "Come on over to my house." He did and had chitlings and really enjoyed them. Then it wasn't too long after that when he called up one day and said, "Hey, Bill, come on over; we're having chitlings." Man, I was afraid. I didn't know what he meant. I went over there, and it turned out that his mother knew how to make them all along. We had chitlings.

PHIL: Yeah, though in most cases, you don't go to *their* house. And they don't come to your house, either. That's an extreme case where Bill and this white guy are real friendly and go each other's houses. You might be friends at school, but after school, you're separated. That's the usual case.]

[QUESTION: Which sex mixes best?

BILL: The boys have more informal relations with each other. We usually have a party every Friday night. It's usually integrated. After a while, they accept you. I don't try to change myself to suit them, and they respect you more for this, so I get along real well. In junior high, you try to fake it out, and that's when you end up an Uncle Tom.

TIM: That's the guy that's got nowhere to go; he's worse off than anybody. Uncle Toms compromise with the system. If and when we ever really separate and get down to the wire, he isn't going to have any place to go, because the Negroes are going to jump on him, and whites don't really accept him. In fact, the Negroes and the whites may even team up together to jump on them.

QUESTION: Can you give me a definition of an Uncle Tom?

BILL: If the Negroes wanted to walk out of school, the white people would tell an Uncle Tom what they wanted him to tell other Negroes to get them to stay. He would help the white person to get the Negro kids to stay. He's also a person who sucks up to the white people all the time. He helps white people get their prestige. He'd rather drive a white person to California than take a Negro across the street. There's a kid at school who's an Uncle Tom—well, quite a few kids at school are Uncle Toms. I'll give you an example that might give you an idea of what I mean by an Uncle Tom. All of the Negroes got together, and we had this big plan that we were going to walk out of this assembly. It was a demonstration that we were going to have. We weren't going to have any trouble; all that we were going to do was to walk out and boycott this assembly. Well, this Uncle Tom told the principal what our plans were, and the principal canceled the assembly. You can't walk out when there isn't an assembly; that killed the whole plan. That kid is an Uncle Tom.

QUESTION: Do you know who did it, and what happened to the kid?

TIM: Yeah, everybody knows which kid it was. Nothing happened to him. I, myself, I really felt sorry for this guy. Nobody bothered him. We were upset that our plans were broken, but most of the Negro kids just felt real sorry for him.

BILL: Well, a lot of the kids—like football players— I know, we had planned to use this kid's name on posters. We were gonna put these posters all through the hallway, naming this kid as an Uncle Tom, to shame him in his own race and also to shame him among the white kids. But we never did it.

TIM: I think most kids feel like I do about it. They feel sorry for this kind of cat.]

Tim was arrested once by a black policeman whom these students claim to be an example of an Uncle Tom. Tim and Phil think that the policeman's motive for arresting Tim was to look good among his fellow officers. The sharp bitterness Tim and Phil express toward the policeman is an indication of how much contempt they have for blacks whom they consider betrayers of the black race.

[PHIL: The police officer that arrested Tim last year, he was an Uncle Tom. He's a Negro. Tell him about that, Tim.

TIM: Well, we were driving down First Avenue, where they were having a lot of trouble, and there were cops all over the place. So we pulled up in this car and I yelled out "Soul Brother baby, Black Power is here," and we parked the car. This Negro policeman came over, and he said, "Listen to me—I don't want you saying that kind of thing in front of me anymore." I said, "I can say anything I want to say. It's a free country. As long as I don't say anything about wanting to overthrow the government, or things like that, I can speak my piece." The cop said, "I don't want to hear you talk that way." I said "bushes," so he arrested me.

QUESTION: Why did you say bushes?

TIM: Oh, that was a thing that was going on at that time. Instead of saying "bull shit," we'd say "bushes." This cat thought I said "bull shit," but actually I said "bushes." He arrested me, put handcuffs on me, whacked me on the head once with the billy club, and he stuck the club in my ribs. I was arrested for resisting arrest, for using profanity, for inciting a riot, for all kinds of things.

PHIL: I went to the police station. I was actually trying to help them, because they put him in the cooler with all the adult prisoners, and he was only 16 years old. He was a minor, he could have sued 'em, so I said to the man at the desk, "He's only 16 years old." He said, "Out, get out!" And I said, "Well, I just want to help you, and I want to tell you that this kid you just arrested and put in the cooler is only 16 years old, and his name is Tim Howard." Tim wouldn't even tell them his name. He said, "Out, out, I told you to get out!," so I started to walk out. I was standing on the steps, and there were about three or four cops there, and they said, "Out, we told you out! Get going." I said, "Oh, drop dead!" so they arrested me, too. Tim was sent to Juvenile Division, and they dismissed him right away. But I ended up going to court 'cause I was older, and it cost me $30. In court, they really lied. They said I was drunk. And I wasn't; I hadn't had one drink. They booked me on loitering. Loitering! Just because I stood on the steps and paused for a minute—that was loitering.

TIM: That Negro cop, he arrested me to show the white cops that he wasn't afraid. It was part of a front.

PHIL: After I got into the elevator (they were taking me up somewhere), I had this cigarette, and I dropped it on the floor. This one cop said, "You shouldn't drop that on the floor." I didn't bother saying a thing. I was really afraid then because you hear all kinds of things about when they get you in jail they beat you half to death, and what have you—and they say you fell down the stairs, or you had an accident. But they didn't beat me.

BILL: I'll give you another example. My brother was outside our house, he's my older brother. He was right outside of the house. He was drunk, and he was coming up to the house. I was sitting watching TV, and I wasn't about to get up to help him at all to get into the house. Well, these cops came over, and there he was home, and he was telling them, "I'm home, and I'm going into my house." They said, "You can't be drunk on the streets. Into the car." He started raising a little hell, so they clubbed him and pushed him into the car. He was just outside of our house. Well, when I saw this happening, I said, they can't be doing that, so I went out to help. They hit him in the stomach, and I started yelling and really laying it on 'em. Well, they took me in, too, and we were both arrested.

PHIL: Well, hell, I was just trying to help Tim, 'cause he was a minor. They had him in the bull pen. I used to think cops were really something special. I thought they were the kind of people who were supposed to help little old ladies across the street. My parents always told me to respect the police and all that sort of stuff. Well, I can't respect them after this experience I had with 'em. They even lied in court, can you imagine? They told the judge all sorts of things. They had all kinds of stories made up beforehand, and they all agreed.

BILL: I was in Minneapolis once. The cops said, "Get off the corner, you might cause trouble," but we weren't doing anything. But, of course, right after that, we started breaking windows. I didn't get caught that time, and I'm glad I didn't, but you see they kind of started by suggesting we get off the corner before we started trouble.

TIM: This fall I was leaving school. It was kind of bad then, you know, the cops were following us all the time. They'd follow us everywhere we went all week; they'd even follow us back home. These two kids were gonna have a fight. They were two Negro kids, so I decided to go down and see what it was all about. Well, this big dumb Negro cop, he hauled the kids in the car. I tried to help the kid they were picking on. They were just picking on kids. Well, I got arrested again that time. They took us to the station. They put us in a line, threatened to beat us and everything. I didn't tell my parents, because they feel like the white people are right. They're afraid of white people. To tell your parents you're picked up and mistreated by the police, they say you must have been doing something. You can't really tell your parents. It's pretty much the same with school, too. If something happens at school which is really discrimination, you tell your parents and they're so afraid of the white man and the power structure that they just say it's your fault. My real parents live in Louisiana. I live here with my aunt. Last summer I went back to Louisiana for a visit. I was walking down the street. I acted just the way I act up here. I saw these two white girls and they looked kind of nice, so I whistled at one. She looked real queer at me. My parents said, "That's all for you brother; you're going back up north. We're not going to get killed over you." So, they shipped me back.]

Most of the black students tend to agree that non-white parents fear the white "power structure" and that they fail to support their children whenever the children confront the "white man" and his institutions. Most of the students also agree that black and white young men get along better with each other than do black and white young women, and that most physical fights take place between black woman students. We also learned that sometimes a fight is called "racial" when the original bone of contention is actually not racial at all. This tendency to attribute racial meanings is probably a smaller-scale reflection of the more general cultural anxiety regarding racial matters.

[PHIL: In general black and white boys are hanging around together more than black and white girls. The girls, they don't have as much in common. They aren't as friendly, not even in sports—although there are Negro athletic girls and white athletic girls, but they're not like the boy athletes. I think it's because women just don't get along together, in general. Also, the white girls, I think, are afraid of the Negro girls. The Negro girls are rougher. If something gets started, a Negro girl would fight. A white girl doesn't want to fight. Also, a lot of white girls don't want to associate with Negro girls, so you don't see as many girls together as you do boys.

QUESTION: Are there many fights at school?

BILL: Oh, you don't see very many fights. I think the girls fight more than the boys. I'm a senior now, and all the time I was in high school I had one fight, when I was a sophomore, and this was in the pool. These three white boys, they dunked me, and they kept me under a long time. My teammates, who were all Negro, they were on the other side of the pool. When I came up and yelled for help, they came in. I got this one white boy, who had me under, and I held him under too long. Bubbles started to come up, and all that. When I let him up, he had to get out of the pool and lay on the side of the pool—the whole bit—and he was really mad. He said to me, "Come on, boy, I want you in the pool." I said, "Hell, no, man, wait 'til I get some clothes on." I wasn't about to get drowned. All these Negro kids in the locker room were saying to me, "That white boy's going to whip you, that white boy's going to whip you." Now this really wasn't a racial incident; it didn't start out to be one. We were just in the pool and were horsing around. Well, the white boys were with this white boy on the other side of the locker room and they were saying, "That Negro boy's going to whip you, that Negro boy's going to whip you." Well, sure enough, it turned into a racial thing. We got into the hallways, and man, oh man, did we have a fight! And it was racial, when it shouldn't have been. It was really a bunch of guys horsing around in the pool. That's what it started out to be.

TIM: That's another thing I don't like about school. Everything that happens between Negroes and whites is called "racial." When I was on the basketball team in junior high school, the referee kept overlooking the fact that I was getting elbowed, and all kinds of things were happening during a game. It was just a game. This happens anytime someone can get away with it. However, I was getting mad, because this guy was never calling the shots in my favor. He let me be elbowed, and all sorts of things. Well, I finally took this as long as I could, and I really got mad, so this white boy and myself started to get into a fight. The referee came along, and he pushed me clear across the court. Well, I fired on him, too. I was kicked out that day. I just lit the cat up. You know, you take it as long as you can, then you retaliate. It wasn't racial, but it was interpreted as racial.

BILL: You know, when you get people working for the same goal, they forget their color. When we were in football, one time one kid on our team was busted under the face guard, and his jaw was broken. We were really mad, and in the huddle we were talking about how we were gonna get this one guy who did this. It wasn't a color thing. We weren't saying "I'm gonna get him, because he's black," or "I'm black, and I'm gonna get him 'cause he's white." The whole team was after this guy 'cause he hurt one of our players. You depend on each other on the team. There's less of this racial stuff.

PHIL: Well, women don't have anything like this together, and that's why they're more separate. The girls are far more separate than the boys. They don't have this kind of team spirit, or this working together, like you find among boys.]

None of the students knows of a single case at Plains High in which a Negro young woman is dated by a white young man. Many black young women resent such a state of affairs, since the Negro male athletes, who have "gone over" to white young women, have not been replaced as potential dates for black female students. Some Negro young women feel white young men would lose prestige were they to date blacks; others feel sure that Negro young men do not want white boys to date blacks and would "beat up" any white young men who tried. While the students in this chapter do not openly oppose interracial dating in which the male is white, they report their shock the first time they saw this particular black-white combination. The shock they describe is quite similar to that which many whites experience in similar situations.

[QUESTION: Do you know of any interracial dating in which white boys date Negro girls?

PHIL: Well, at the state colleges, you do see Negro girls with white boys. But you know, it's a funny thing now that you mention it, you never really see Negro girls with white boys at Plains High. Not at all. I've never seen that. You see Negro boys with white girls.

BILL: Well, you know I was in New York once, now that you mention that. It's kind of funny. I saw this Negro girl with a white guy. I was shocked. You know, I looked, and it just seemed kind of funny to me. I mean, you see white girls with Negro boys, but you never see a Negro girl with a white guy, and it's kind of shocking at first.

TIM: It's more common for Negro boys to date white girls. I think the other is just too much of a shock at first. I don't care; as far as I'm concerned, if they want to date each other, that's fine. I don't know of any boys that I hang around with, anyway, who put the press on the Negro girls not to go out with white boys. It still kinda shocks you, though. But as far as I'm concerned, I don't care either way.

QUESTION: How do Negro girls react to interracial dating?

TIM:, Well, at Plains Junior High, the Negro girls resented the fact that I went out with a white girl, and they really got after me. They feel inferior. The white girls got all the guys. Some hostility between the Negro girls and white girls comes from this. The Negro girl kinda feels left out. She doesn't have white guys to date, and she doesn't have Negro guys to date. She says, "Hey, gal, you dating that Negro guy, and I can't even get a date with him." This kind of builds up a resentment in her and hostility, and she becomes very aggressive towards the white girls. I think the white boys don't like it also, but they're scared to say anything about it. They're afraid they might get in trouble if they say something, so most of them don't say anything.

BILL: This friend of mine, Frank, this white guy I was telling you about earlier, he's a real screwball. He decided to fix me up with a blind date with this girl from East High School. He didn't tell her I was a Negro. He told me she was white, but she didn't know I was a Negro. When we got to where we were picking up these girls, he said, "This is Bill; he's your date." Man, her jaw just dropped, but later on in the evening, we had a real nice time together.

TIM: Some Negro boys just don't like white people, period. It doesn't necessarily follow on skin color. I know a very light Negro, who could actually pass for a white person; he hates whites worse than some of the real dark Negroes.

BILL: Well, my cousin, he's light, and he makes good grades in school, and he hates whites. He says, "Leave me alone—I don't wanna fool with any whites."

PHIL: Well, there are differences in every race. There are Negroes who're different; there are whites who're different. Everybody isn't the same. Negroes think that all whites are giddy and silly and soft. And whites think that all Negroes are stupid and dirty, but that isn't true. There are some Negroes who fit that, and there are some who don't. Sure, there are some whites who're giddy and silly, and there are some who don't fit that stereotype. And once we stop thinking in those terms, we'll be a lot better off.

BILL: When I was in English class one time, we were talking about the racial situation. I'm the only Negro in that class, and this white girl said, "Well, I don't want any Negroes moving into my block, because they wouldn't keep up their property." Now here's a stereotype for you. How the hell are people going to keep up their property when they're barely existing? They can't keep up a yard and all that when they're working two or three jobs.

TIM: They don't even have bread for a lawnmower, anyway, so the hell with the lawn! This is why when you go out to South Center City, you don't find any lawns, you find a lot of weeds. People just can't keep them up. Then there are the white kids in the same category as the Negroes. They don't have too much bread. They're afraid you'll get ahead of them. They're worse than a lot of the kids. The poor white people are afraid you'll get something better than them, and they discriminate. I'll show you how they categorize people. I started school this fall, and I just didn't give a damn. I'd wear the tackiest things to school, raggedy clothes, and they had me pegged. Then they had a dress-up day, so I wore this new suit that I got recently, and I had this shirt laundered, and what have you. Well, I came to school all dressed up, and this girl said, "That can't be you, Tim Howard, is it?" They didn't expect it.

BILL: My father bought me a Mustang last year, and I had it parked out at a teenage hangout—a lot of kids at East Plains hang out there. I was in there, and I was having a great time. When I came out, on both sides of the car—in big black letters—some kids had painted the word "Nigger." That really got me mad. I don't know why they want to do that.]

Bill and Phil talk of the importance of being oneself. Bill is angered by blacks who try to "play it white," as well as by whites who try to "play it black." A number of whites told us they liked blacks because of their "soul." By this they mean that blacks are "cool," that they are good dancers, and that their music is fine. The present group of "militant" blacks does not share this definition of "soul."

[BILL: There are a lot of Negro kids, too, who think they're better than other Negro kids. These are usually the Uncle Toms. They scratch their name off the black man's list; they don't want to be called black. There was this colored boy I know who spoke to one of these Uncle Tom, uppity Negro girls in the hallway one day; she just turned her nose up at him. She lives out here in this part of town. Take some of these white kids who try to fake it, who try to talk the way we do, and things like that. I don't like these guys at all 'cause they're putting on airs. They're putting up a front. I don't like people to put up fronts. Be yourself. They try to put on this "soul" stuff. They don't even know what the hell "soul" is. "Soul" is just being an individual, but they come out with all this stuff. "Man, I like you 'cause you got soul," and that sort of stuff. They don't know what the hell they're talking about.

PHIL: You know the Negro kids do talk differently. My music teacher says it's more varied, and the tone qualities are a little bit different. Some of these white guys try to impersonate us, because they're trying to suck up to us. They're not too well liked for it.

BILL: We were in this restaurant and this white guy put on a Ray Charles record one time. He kept saying how good it was, and he was trying to put on all this "soul" stuff. But he just couldn't make it. For example, you'd know right away if a Negro was trying to fake it as a white person. Well, we know white persons who're trying to fake it as Negroes.

PHIL: Sure, there are a lot of Negroes who try to fake it as white people; they try to tuck in their lips and dress white. These guys will never make it, whether they're Negro or white, because they're known as fakes.]

The black students in this chapter express a dislike for the school administration. While, at times, they consider the administrators racially prejudiced, at other times the complaints are not really "racial" but resemble complaints voiced by all students, white and black. As an example of this latter type of complaint, the young men being interviewed express their anger toward the administration because it does not allow students to experience things for themselves and because it does not support them in their attempt to change such situations as having to stay in school for lunch or wearing the clothes they wish to wear. Although such complaints are not racial, they are presented in a racial context.

[TIM: The principal, we don't like him very much. He discriminates an awful lot. He's a real loser. We wanted a club to discuss racial issues. It wasn't just for Negroes. It was something that would be open to anybody, but we wanted to specifically discuss racial problems, something we were interested in. He said, "We have enough clubs. We don't need another club." Every time you try to put a question to him, he beats around the bush. He never gives you a straight answer. We just don't like him at all. Plains High would be better without him.

BILL: Mr. Johnson, a psychologist, used to come to talk to us at school. We talked about our problems. I talked about the cafeteria and the problem with the cafeteria. We were going to change it. We wanted to be free to leave the school at lunchtime. We had a plan to talk to the principal about it. We were going to try to put it up to a vote among the kids, and if the kids wanted it, we felt the school should allow it. Mr. Ewing, the principal, talked to us while Mr. Johnson was there, and said, "Well, in Roseville, when they let the school out at lunchtime, there was a lot of stealing, so we can't allow it."

TIM: You see what I mean? He's always talking around things. What the hell does Plains High have to do with Roseville? Just because some kids in

Roseville were let out, and started stealing, this doesn't mean that the kids at Plains High are going to start stealing at some drug store. They always do that; they don't give you a chance to find out for yourself. That's what I really hate about school. I broke it down to a couple of counselors. I told 'em what it was all about, but they can't help us very much. A couple of 'em are on our side. They dig us, and we dig them cats.

BILL: Conrad, he's good. He'll tell you what he thinks. He's real open. I'd rather have someone who's open about it, someone that you can count on, who'll lay it to you without beating around the bush. He's all right.

TIM: For example, we called the press one time, because we were going to have this big meeting in the cafeteria, and we wanted them to come along. They were all set and were going to take pictures and everything. Well, the photographer called up the school, and the Assistant Principal told him, "Well, I don't think this would be the kind of meeting you would be interested in," so they didn't come. We wanted to express ourselves. They had no right deciding whether it would be a good meeting for this fellow to come to or not. They don't give us much air—that's one of the problems at Plains High. There are two classes of kids up there. There are the upper class with the good grades. Many of them are teachers' pets. They can say things, and they can get things done. Then there's the lower class. They have no air. They put you in the guard house. The Man is after us all the time. It's a big prison.

BILL: You can't wear bermuda shorts. If you're dressed funny, they won't allow it. Now why can't I wear bermuda shorts, or dress the way I want to dress? I'm not going to wear anything too screwy 'cause the other kids will make you feel funny. The group will make you feel funny, so you don't go too far out. They won't let me have a beard. For example, I'd like to have a beard like yours [the interviewer's]. I had one once, and I looked real good.

TIM: We have a student congress, but they're just big figureheads. They wait for Mr. Ewing to say something, and then they put it down. He won't allow any pantdresses at school. He's 99 years old. What does he know? Students don't have a voice. Why can't we smoke in school, or right as soon as we get out of school, on the school grounds? I smoke at home, and it's all right. I'm not going to burn anything down. They say we'd throw cigarettes on the floor, but we don't have any ash trays in the wash room. One time a whole bunch of us brought in ash trays, and there wasn't one cigarette butt on the floor. But then, they confiscated the ash trays. This is a different group and age. Let us try; let us experience things. Don't restrict us, and always tell us what's going to happen. We've got to experience things for ourselves. We can't learn from something somebody else does. We're always being told; you should have the right to experience some things for yourself, even though the tuition might be high.

BILL: A dentist came up and said he didn't want Coke in the machines because it was bad for your teeth. They took out the Coke machines. Right after we get out of school we go and have three Cokes, so what's the difference? I mean, I'm going to drink Coke if I want to drink Coke. But, we can't talk out too much, because if I don't get an education, I'll be sweeping the floor, and they're always threatening us with throwing us out.]

[QUESTION: What has your experience at Plains High taught you about racial matters?

BILL: Well, it's taught me that you can't judge somebody by his outward appearance. In junior high school, I wouldn't have anything to do with this one guy, but I've learned since then that you've got to look at the person and what he is, and not just how he looks.

PHIL: It's taught me to be yourself. You've got to be yourself to get along. You can't put up a front. That's the problem with a lot of kids who have trouble. They try to put on airs and try to put on a front. You can't do that, 'cause the kids see right through you.

BILL: I want to be an individual. Don't tell me I'm always wrong. I like to try things.

TIM: The one thing I hate about the whole situation is the people, for example, who came to this country to start it. Supposedly, they came over here for religious freedom. Then they try to make one religion. They came to get a dictatorship. They won't recognize that people are people. All people are created equal except Negroes, Mexicans, Puerto Ricans, poor whites and a whole bunch of other people: Chinks, Spics. Nobody is equal. Love and respect are the answers, I think. You don't try to force people; you have to see people as themselves. The Golden Rule, in my book, is the answer.

BILL: America, for example, we learn in history, is supposed to be a great melting pot. I'll tell you how good a melting pot it is. The ingredients won't blend. I don't think it'll work.

TIM: Abe Lincoln; they're always telling us about Abe Lincoln and how much he did for the slaves, and how he freed us and all that. Well, that's a lot of baloney. Abe Lincoln had as many slaves as the other guy. He was forced by his party to do what he did. He didn't do nothing for me. If anybody has done anything for us, I think it's Presidents Kennedy and Johnson. These are the only Presidents who have really taken a stand on the Negro issue and have tried to do things.]

Both white and black students feel that their generation, at least the students at Plains High, is moving toward greater racial equality. They consider their parents and grandparents to be far more prejudiced than they—at times, to the point of being a little embarrassed about them. Often a white student will say, "I was shocked. I always thought my parents were liberal." The Negro student is in a better position to accept his parents' and grandparents' hatred for the white man, by pointing to the many indignities blacks have had to endure in this country.

[BILL: Every generation sees more and more racial freedom. In two or three generations, it might be pretty good, providing we're around that long.

PHIL: The older Negroes, they hate and they fear the white person. My grandparents actually hate white people. You have any great grandparents around, it's even worse. They can't abide white people at all. My parents also hate white people, but the younger people, they get along a little better, so I think things are improving. Integrated schools have helped do this, and I think if we can continue along these lines, in time we'll get along.

TIM: The older people have the attitude of, don't do nothing against the white people or you'll get killed. They're afraid. They'll take an awful lot. But we're not gonna take an awful lot in the younger generation. We're gonna give back as much as we take, and we'll retaliate.

BILL: My brother who goes to the State University brought a white girl over to my grandpa's. We were having a family gathering. My grandfather came into the room, and he saw this white girl, and he yelled out, "Take that white girl out of here, or we'll all be hanged!" That's the kind of attitude the older Negro has, not the younger Negro. We always tease my grandfather about this. We tell him we went out and beat up some white boys, and he's always telling us they're going to take us to jail, they're going to beat us with hoses, tie us up with barbed wire, bash our brains in, and bury us where nobody will ever find us.

PHIL: Well, you know, he's only telling you what was true for him during his time, and it *was* true. These things were happening then, so they're very much afraid. Their friends were hanged, because they looked at someone, or someone just wanted some excitement. But the younger generation isn't as afraid as this older generation.

TIM: We waited 150 years; we're not going to wait any more. I tried talking, I tried marching. I'm gonna do like it's been done to me. You treat me like a dog, I'll act like a dog. If it takes burning, I'll burn.

BILL: For example, you pick fruit in somebody's orchard, you know you want some. That's what it's like.]

[QUESTION: Are the schools helping to promote better race relations?

BILL: Well, they thought the Negroes were ignorant. Now they find they're pretty smart, so the schools help break it down somewhat, because they've made it possible for Negroes and whites to see each other in action, to find out that all Negroes aren't stupid.

PHIL: It's the only thing that'll help. Each generation, as we go through these schools, will try to force less and less segregation on their children, and it'll get better. The schools are helping. The younger ones don't fear the whites, and the white kids don't fear the Negroes. It's the older ones, the older Negroes fear the whites. Although there's something quite different that's happening now. I don't know if you've noticed it. But in general, I'd say this is what the situation is like. In the white community, because the younger people have seen more militant Negroes, it's the younger people who fear Negroes, so it's just the reverse.

BILL: Some of these younger kids don't understand what's going on, either. For example, I was talking to this one white girl at school, and I said something about Black Power. She really became afraid. She said, "Why do you want to kill me?" She doesn't know that Black Power is social and economic power.

TIM: They always say to try to do things peacefully. Try to do things by asking, but you don't get anything by asking. There was this window at school that was all busted out, and it was there for a long time. One day we decided to take the whole window out. There was this broken towel rack, and half the time there weren't any paper towels in it, so we ripped that off the wall. The next day when we went to school there was a brand new window there, and there was a brand new towel rack. Now, what do you mean, we're not going to get anything if we break it down or burn it down? It seems to me that we did that time.

BILL: You know you can be violent without killing somebody. You come as a group, and you apply yourself to the problem. That's the kind of power you need, manpower, not necessarily killing power.

PHIL: If every minority person didn't go to work tomorrow, and if everybody didn't go to school, and if everybody turned off their lights for a whole week—in the Negro community—that would sure set the community back some. Even the power company would feel it, with the lights.

BILL: If anybody steps on my toes, I'm going to push them off. That's the way the young person feels. That's the difference. I don't want to go into your restaurant; I mean if you don't want me in your restaurant, I'll stay out. But I want to have the choice. If I want to go in, I want to go in. If I know I'm not wanted, I'm not going to go in.

PHIL: For example, when I was in class as a young kid, we always said the Pledge of Allegiance to the Flag. Now the Negro boys went over to fight the Germans. The Germans were trying to kill them—trying to kill other Americans. And Negroes and whites were fighting side by side. I'll tell you what's really bad. The Negro soldiers came back and found out they were second class citizens. Any of the German soldiers, who were killing Americans, could have immigrated here after that, and could live anywhere they wanted, and would have been eligible for any kind of job, 'cause they were white.

BILL: I think it's kind of stupid in Viet Nam right now. Here we are trying to uphold the Civil Rights of Vietnamese, when the Negroes don't have their rights right here. They could be doing things here. It seems kind of stupid. If I came over here to clean your house and left my own house dirty, I should clean my house first.

PHIL: You know, I used to get all jazzed up about the Space Flights and going to the moon and things like that, because I like science. But now I think it's all kind of stupid to spend all that money going out in space, when our own house isn't cleaned up, when there are a lot of people starving, a lot of things that could be done here.]

Discrimination is told about as it occurs outside as well as inside school. In one interview, a black young man said, "I don't hate white kids in my generation; it's the older whites that I hate." Phil, Tim, and Bill tell of prejudicial experiences they have had which fan their hatred of adult whites. In school, Tim thinks that a portion of the discrimination has to do with discrimination against the "have-nots," of whom many are black.

[TIM: You know, I have a band, and we're all Negroes, and we're damn good. We're probably the best band in this area. They call us "The Angels." We went to this place to audition, and we were real good. We played about an hour, and everybody enjoyed it. Finally, I went to the man and said, "What's the story?" He said, "Well, you know, I can't really have an all-Negro band because it would attract too many Negroes. I'd lose my white customers." But, yet, a lot of the Negroes go over there anyway to hear white bands. But that's all right. He wouldn't let us play there.

BILL: I went over to this place one time, and I was in my levis, and the guy said, "You can't come in 'cause you're in levis." So, okay, I went home and changed and came back. When I got back, there were five white boys sitting at the bar in levis. I didn't say anything, but I let him know that I knew. I don't know whether it embarrassed him or not—maybe it didn't.

TIM: We were playing in a small town out here. It was a real small town out in the back woods, and the people really acted wild. They came in, and they were calling us niggers, and they were spitting on us, and they were throwing things at us, and they were doing all kinds of things. Well, we didn't fight back, because you can get killed out there. We were alone. But that's the kind of stuff you have to put up with if you're a Negro.

BILL: We had some trouble in one of these small towns one night. They ran me out. The following night, I went back with 15 Negro guys. It was different then. The guy with the big mouth, I went right up to him, and he didn't say a word.]

[QUESTION: How is it at Plains High?

TIM: Well, at Plains High you see people as more equal. It's pretty much always been mixed, and the kids have always been in mixed schools, so they watch what they say, and it isn't quite as bad.

BILL: Well, the East Plains High kids will have some trouble when they come to Plains High, if they look for it, because they haven't been used to mixing with the races. But they'll probably hang around with the white kids, because that kind always does. Then they won't have any trouble. The best way to get along at Plains High is just to be yourself. Don't try to put on a front.

PHIL: When I was a sophomore, we always sat on the fourth floor; that's where all the Negroes hang out, you know. We joke around a lot. There's a Mexican kid we know; we call him Taco Bender. The Mexicans call us Cornbread and Chitlings. There really isn't that much trouble at Plains High 'cause the kids are used to mixing.

QUESTION: Are there times, at Plains High, when you're made to feel you're Negroes?

BILL: Yeah, in my Economic's class, I feel like I'm a Negro. There's this teacher who tries to prove he's not prejudiced, and he's always saying, "You all know I'm not prejudiced." Well, as soon as he says that, I know I'm a Negro, and I know he's prejudiced. And they're always saying things like, "You know the fields the Negroes excel in are sports and music." Well, that's another way of telling us who we are and keeping us in our place. He makes me feel like a Negro all the time. In English class one time we were reading "Huck Finn" and the teachers, you know, are always cute—they always call on the Negroes to read the Negro parts. That's another time when I feel like I'm Negro. He called me to read this one part in a real Negro dialect. I couldn't read it, so I told him, "I can't read that, man. You read it."

TIM: In junior high school this teacher called me aside. I was working like a dog in sports and doing all I could, and he called me aside and said, "You're supposed to do better, man." And I said, "What do you mean I'm supposed to do better? I'm doing as good as anyone else, and the best I can." He said, "Well, you're a Negro, and you're supposed to be better in sports." This thing that's going on at Plains High School, in addition to the racial things, it's "Green Power." Not Black Power or White Power, but Green Power: money power. It's a social class thing. There are those who have it, and those who don't have it. The ones who don't have it are at the bottom, and you're made to feel that you're at the bottom.

CHAPTER 4

White Racists and Conservatives

Part 1

In the preceding chapters, we emphasized that lumping people together on the basis of such superficial characteristics as skin color or hair quality is a foolish oversimplification. Because a person is black, he does not see the world around him as do all other blacks. This, naturally, is just as true for the white person who, as the Negro, varies immensely in his actions and perceptions of the world in which he lives.

In this chapter we will first present an interview held with three whites who, more than any other group of interviewees, were openly prejudiced. We have called them "racists," for they were identified that way by some other students. Aside from their prejudicial attitudes, these young men were "low" academic achievers, not involved in any extracurricular activities, and constantly in fights. More often than not, their fights were with Negroes. Each young man has a history of being suspended from school, and each has a police record. Their offenses have included driving without a license as well as auto theft.

Two themes dominate this interview. First, these students are blatantly anti-Negro; and second, they are preoccupied with fighting.

In Part 2 of this chapter, the students also express anti-Negro attitudes. Their prejudices are more subtle, however. They surface only toward the end of the interview, when the young woman respondent expresses her hatred of rioters and unionists. Less pronounced reflections of prejudicial attitudes may be seen earlier—for instance, when one of the boys suggests that "white girls wouldn't want to slow-dance with Negro boys;" or when all three talk about cultural differences between whites and blacks. "They're [blacks] easy going. They just like to have a lot of fun. They don't think about the future and things that are important, like getting a job or supporting a family."

It is this more subtle prejudice which, in the long run, is more harmful to the prejudiced. It is easier for the Negro students to cope with the overtly prejudiced respondents of Part 1 of this chapter. The coping may be primitive, such as "dotting their eyes," but it is direct, swift and relatively uncomplicated. Such direct action indicates to others what may happen to the person who is not willing to keep his prejudices in check. For the members of the minority group, open discrimination may be cathartic in that it legitimizes swift retaliation; simply beating on "Whitey" without provocation, on the other hand, may reinforce the aggressive stereotype of the Negro which is held by some whites.

The names of the three young men in the first part of this chapter are Jerry, Paul, and Ed. All three are juniors at Plains High.

[QUESTION: What are some of the pressures you face from attending a desegregated school?

PAUL: Well, if you mean socially, there aren't too many that are bad, because there aren't too many cliques to tell you what to do. If you're talking about race, and integration-wise, well you have to watch your mouth because most niggers are pretty hefty. You say "nigger," and you may end up on the floor. But they can call us "honkies;" it makes me mad that I can't call them "niggers." That's what they call us. They call us "honkies."

JERRY: Well, not too long ago, you know what happened to me. I said "nigger" and ended up on the floor. Somebody asked me what I thought about King. I said, "He's pretty good for a nigger," and somebody hit me. All I said was that he was okay for a nigger. I said this to a white guy. I didn't even know that there were any niggers around. But there were a bunch of niggers behind me. I turned around and jumped on the first guy I saw, and I hit back. They kicked me around for awhile; then they let me go.

QUESTION: Do you get kicked out of school for fighting?

ED: Well, the teachers won't even do anything in a fight. The teachers aren't very good anyway. In English, we had this teacher who'd let us discuss things, but she wasn't really much of a teacher. You couldn't say what you wanted to, because you'd get stomped. It's hard to talk in class because of all the racists, and you don't know how it's going to be taken. I could never voice my true opinion in class, because I was afraid that one of the niggers there would take it back to one of his bunch. Then they'd beat me up.

QUESTION: Do you talk about racial matters among white kids?

JERRY: Oh, you can do anything among white kids, and you can say anything around white kids. You can also say anything around some colored kids, but not many.

QUESTION: Who are the black kids you can say anything around?

PAUL: Well, there's this one black kid. He's as black as coal, but he thinks he's white. Guys like that, you can talk to them. If you think a Negro's doing something wrong, with this kid, you can say you don't like what this nigger is doing, and it's okay. You don't have to worry about getting stomped.

JERRY: They don't even like for you to say "Negro," if you're saying that they're doing something wrong. It doesn't matter so much if you say "nigger" or "Negro" or "colored." If you say that they're doing something wrong, they don't like it. They don't like to be criticized.

PAUL: For example, one time I was in the hall talking to Dave, and Dave said, "Some of those Negroes just don't have it." Three Negroes came up and said, "We hear you've been talking about us." We said we weren't talking about you, but Negroes in general. This guy said, "You want me to knock you down, or you want me to slit your throat first?"

JERRY: The guy that said this is the kind of nigger who's as black as night. He has yellow blood, and little slits for eyes. If I had a choice between hitting a white guy and hitting a nigger, I'd hit the nigger. There're some whites, too, who're pretty tough.

ED: It seems to me that the colored can get away with an awful lot. They can get away with anything, but the whites can't. Like bringing food into the cafeteria. Colored kids brought food into the cafeteria for awhile, because they didn't like the food in the cafeteria. Even this one teacher said to me, "If the whites had done that, they would've been suspended." But they let these colored guys do it.]

For these students, the reluctance of white teachers to correct Negro students is interpreted as "discrimination against whites." They say that Negro students can get away with things because the teachers are afraid of them. This attitude is shared by other white students who find themselves in classes with a large percentage of Negro students. Some of the other students, however, do not talk so much about the teachers' fear of bodily harm, instead they emphasize the teachers' fear of organized protest from the community.

[PAUL: The school is mainly white, or, at least, the staff is; and they're scared of the Negroes and Black Power. They won't do anything to correct the Negroes.

JERRY: I've seen it a number of times. If a white kid gives the teacher trouble, the teacher jumps on him pretty hard. The colored kid doesn't get the same heat. I've given the teacher trouble, lots of trouble, and I've gotten suspended. In fact, I was suspended all this year. But the colored guys don't get into the same trouble if they do the same thing.

PAUL: There's no question that most of the teachers are afraid. Take Ewing, he's had a knife pulled on him three times by niggers.

JERRY: There're some teachers who don't take anything from anybody. Glass—this gym teacher who's quitting now—he'd say, "Come on cat, I'll knock the color right off of you."

ED: Yeah, one time Tim Howard was down in the locker room. He was getting the niggers all riled up. Glass went down to break it up. He's not afraid of them. He just walked into them, and told them to disperse. Most of the teachers are scared to death, and I really can't blame them.]

In the following exchange, Jerry sees the problem as one which could be solved easily if the whites would stick together. Several times in the interview, he tells how the white students, who are numerically in the majority, could "keep the Negroes in line" if they would only stick together. He also complains that if you fight one Negro, you have to fight them all. We suspect that Jerry and his friends use this accusation as a rationalization because, as a matter of fact, they often lose their fights with Negroes.

[JERRY: I'll tell you the kind of things that get me mad. I'm still mad at the white kids for not banding together. If they had any hair on their chests, they'd band together and wipe them out. I was just standing there, talking to them of Martin Luther, and bam, I got it from nowhere from behind. The white kids don't band together like the niggers. If they only would, we'd wipe them out. You know there's more of us than there are of them.

PAUL: Once you start fighting a Negro, the other guys will jump in. You have to fight all the Negroes.

ED: In the restroom where we smoke—you know that's the only place you can smoke at Plains High—I've had them threaten to jump me, because I wouldn't give them a cigarette or money. They're always trying to get something out of you.

JERRY: I'd like to put a cigarette right between their eyes when they try to shake you down for a smoke or money.

QUESTION: Do you fight often in school?

ED: Well, I haven't had many fights at school with colored, but I've had some out of school.

JERRY: Whether or not you fight depends on whether you keep your mouth shut. It's okay if you take a lot of shit, but if you're not willing to take this shit from niggers, then you're going to have to fight.

PAUL: There're even one or two Negroes that the other Negroes won't help. If you get into a fight with them, you don't have to worry about the rest of the niggers jumping you. Usually these are guys who're pretty inept. You know, most Negroes can really dance and run, and they're good in sports. It comes natural to them. Well, the guys who're poorly coordinated, or can't dance—there're some Negroes who can't dance or play basketball—these are the ones that the other Negroes won't help. They don't have any of the qualities that the other Negroes have.

ED: Actually, you know, I get along with quite a few of them that I got to know from junior high. I went to Adams Junior High School. There're a lot of them at Adams. About 50% of them is black.

PAUL: Yeah, you can get to be friendly with some Negroes, but the minute they find out you hit one of them, they're not your buddies anymore.

JERRY: When it comes to black and white, they're pure black.]

[QUESTION: Are there situations in which whites and blacks get along fairly well at school?

ED: Oh, there're one or two who date niggers, but I think this is more for attention than anything else. There's this girl, Mary, who dates Jackson. He's a Negro, she's white. But I think she does it for attention on her part.

JERRY: I don't know if it's attention or not. You know, he's getting her an engagement ring. I think she's hung-up on him, and he's hung-up on her. I think it's for real.

ED: Well, there aren't many who do this, but I think it's getting started. I think we'll see more of it.

JERRY: Most of these white girls who go out with niggers aren't too clean. You know, "cool," man.

PAUL: Well, this white girl who's going with Jackson, she's pretty decent to look at. In fact, she's the only decent one I've seen, who's gone out with a nigger.

JERRY: She's pretty nice, too. She's always pretty nice to everybody. Jackson, well, he's the nicest colored guy you could meet. He's probably cleaner [more "cool"] than I am. He dresses well. He's pretty acceptable. I say if any white girl has to go out with a nigger, it should be someone like Jackson.

ED: Financially, too, he's pretty well off. Some Negroes, you know, live in houses that are falling down and only worry about cars and clothes. They don't care about these other things.]

Most of the students, including Jerry, Paul, and Ed, do not know of a single case of interracial dating in which the young man is white. However, unlike some of the other respondents, who talk about the pressures from society, other students, or their parents, these students, as is characteristic throughout their interview, reject interracial dating as part of their general prejudicial attitude. Thus, they say that Negro women students are tough and start fights. Perhaps the young Negro women they know *are* tough. A number of other students report this quality among black female students. In looking at the young women in Chapter 2, however, it is difficult to think of all black women students as tough and as starting fights.

[QUESTION: Do you know of any cases in which white guys have dated Negro girls?

JERRY: I'd rather have a bad-looking white girl than a good-looking colored girl.

PAUL: I've never found one that I liked well enough to date.

JERRY: I don't like them at all anyway. They're the ones who start most of the fights up there. They'll come up and say, "Say, white boy, you've been bothering me," and before you know it, this big black sucker comes out of nowhere. He's her boyfriend, or her brother, or her cousin, or something, and he's after you.

PAUL: Yeah, a lot of them are real tough. You may be talking to one of them, and she slaps you. You turn around, and you tap her on the face lightly just to let her know. Then you turn around and get punched in the face by someone standing behind you. One thing colored girls like is a fight.

JERRY: They fight with themselves a lot. It's really keen to watch colored girls fight. They scratch and bite, and they really tear after each other. They've these real long fingernails, and they slash each others' cheeks. Before you know it, someone has a big gash, bleeding all over the place.

PAUL: I'll tell you one thing. I'd rather fight a colored boy anytime, before I'd fight a colored girl.

JERRY: I'll tell you something else I don't like about colored at school. I had a pretty good-looking girl. A lot of the colored guys would ask me if they could date her. I don't want a colored guy dating my girl. They're really doing this just to bug you. There aren't too many colored kids I suck up to much, so most of the time I end up fighting them. They don't bother me too much about my girl, anymore. They did at first.]

Thus far, we have heard of one major anti-Negro reaction—fighting. Ed now discusses joking as a way to avoid fighting. He tends to use the joking strategy first, and to fight only when it does not work. A similar strategy has been noted in the past among some blacks who allowed themselves to be the object of jokes as a means of "conning" the white man out of a handout. For Jerry, joking is "sucking-up," so he is more apt to fight. Jerry is very candid about how he has avoided being expelled from school because of his fighting.

[ED: Well, the thing is that nobody will back you in school on your opinion. You can't do nothing, or you'll get kicked out of school.

JERRY: A couple of times I've been in fights with niggers, and I'd have to go down to the office. I'd just say, "Oh, come on Ewie, you've been smashed by those niggers. You're not going to kick me out for a nigger, are you? You know what the scoop is with those niggers. Let me sneak in, or pretend that you kicked me out or something."

ED: A lot of times you don't have to fight. You can joke your way out of things. Joking seems a pretty good way to get out of it. At a varsity not too long ago, two colored guys came up and said, "You know what we do with little sophomores like you." I said, "Yeah, you bust them up, and you eat them for breakfast." They started laughing. Or another time, I said, "Now you better be careful because I bleed an awful lot, and I'll bleed all over you, or if you punch me, I'll puke on you." This kind of joking goes over pretty well with the niggers. You don't have to fight them.]

[QUESTION: Do the students integrate at a varsity dance?

JERRY: No! At a dance, the colored dance over here, and the whites dance over there. They don't mix.

ED: No! They usually bring their own dates. There's very little mixing. Another thing that bugs me at these dances is that they're always trying to shake me down for money. As far as white guys dancing with colored girls, I don't think that would happen because there aren't very many white guys who care much about Negro girls.]

[QUESTION: Does dating a Negro make a white girl less acceptable to white boys?

JERRY: Well, I'm not dating no white girl that went out with a nigger. I don't care if a girl goes out with a nigger if she likes him, but I'm not going out with her. Another time at one of these dances, a nigger cornered me in the washroom and said, "I've got a bottle of booze here for you to buy." I said, "Well, I don't want any booze." He put the switchblade up to my throat, and said, "You either want some booze, or you're not going to have a throat." I said, "I want some booze." So I bought it.

ED: It's the same with cigarettes. A lot of times they'll come up to you and say, "Look, man, you need a pack of butts?" You say, "No, I've got some. I just bought some." He'll say, "Well, you need another pack." And you're forced into buying them.

QUESTION: Do you generally fight when such situations arise?

JERRY: Well, you either joke your way out of it, or you fight. I don't run. I'm too proud to run. Besides I'm too slow, and they'll catch me anyway.

ED: That's right. They push you into it. If you don't fight, you're a chicken, and that's worse.

JERRY: A lot of times they'll get at you when your girl's standing around. You've got to fight. You're not going to look like a chicken in front of your girl.

PAUL: About dating a white girl who's dated a Negro, I'm dating a white girl now who dated a colored guy before. So I wouldn't say that all of the guys would refuse to date a white girl who's dated a Negro. But I think I've gotten more liberal this year, and that's why. As far as fighting, if I think there's a chance to run, I will. One time these six guys cornered me. I said, "Is there any way I can get out of it?" They said, "Yeah, you can lick my shoes." I said, "Cram it, nigger." When they finished with me, I had six cracked ribs.

JERRY: It's worse if you run. If you run from them, they'll rile you. When I stand up to them, I don't get riled anymore. One time this nigger said to me, "I won't hit you if you give me a buck," I said, "If you expect to get a buck out of me, you'd better start hitting." One thing I don't want to do is to put up with any colored kid trying to jew me out of money, or make me look bad before any woman. I tell you I'd like to send all of them back to Africa. I don't like 'em.

ED: I just feel that I don't trust them. I've had so much stolen all through junior high school. They've stolen all kinds of things from me. They'll cut the brass buckle right off your belt. In gym class in junior high school, you put your clothes in these wire baskets. When you came back from gym class, you'd find some of the wires spread apart, and all your stuff would be gone. I just don't like them at all. I've had too much stuff stolen; I can't trust any Negroes.

JERRY: The thing that really riles you up is to see some colored guy wearing your shirt. You say, "Hey, man, that's my shirt." He'll say, "That's not your shirt." You don't get any help from the teachers either, because the teachers say, "If that's your shirt, why's he wearing it?"]

Most of the students agree that white young women who date Negroes are no longer dated by white young men. Yet Paul—who is open about his racist attitudes—dates one. This is surprising, for even white liberal students have a tendency to reject a white young woman who has dated a black. Equally puzzling is Jerry's account of a friendship with a Negro, formed after having fought with him daily. Perhaps this is because Jerry confers status on others for their willingness and ability to fight. Later he speaks of two black students with some deference. Both have reputations for being good fighters.

[JERRY: There's only one colored guy I've ever liked. His name is Zack. From the first day I met him—I was just a kid—I looked at him, and thought, that guy's different from me. He's black, and I'm white. I fought him. We'd fight every day. We got to be friends through fighting. We'd fight every day we saw each other. I liked him because we enjoyed fighting, but I don't like niggers in general.

ED: I can get along with them if I have to, but I still don't like them.

PAUL: You know, I never knew what a Negro was until the fourth grade. I lived in Elwin. There weren't any Negroes. Then we moved to Center City in the fourth grade, and that was the first time I came across a Negro.

ED: Oh, I knew Negroes from way back. I had one who used to babysit us. They lived right down the street from us. We played with their kids when I was little. Then we moved here. Ever since we moved, I've had things stolen from me, and I just don't like them.

JERRY: Well, you just have to get along with them if you can, because if you hit one of them at high school, you'll have the whole damned town on your back.]

[QUESTION: Paul, you said you're more liberal this year, what do you mean by that?

PAUL: Well, by liberal, I mean not looking too much at the color of a person's skin. I've gotten to where I look inside people a little more. I can't stand being around stupid people, or mentally retarded people. I just can't stand it. This year I learned that if you get to talk to them that there're some of them that are pretty smart. They're not all retarded. There're two of them that I work with out at the VA Hospital. I get along with them fine. We can even talk about things intelligently.

JERRY: I've found that you just can't say what you want to. You can't say it in class, or some colored boy will get you. Some of the girls say what they want to, but the boys can't because they'll get killed. This girl, Susie, almost got me killed one day. This colored guy put his arm around her, and she said, "Get your hands off me, nigger." I said, "Come on, Susie, let's go." She said, "Wait a minute; I want to cuss this nigger out." She just wanted to cuss the nigger out. She could've gotten me killed.

ED: A couple of the teachers say what they want. Mr. Willis, my English teacher, he said what he wanted, and Mr. Glass, the gym teacher, used to say what he wanted to. But that's why Mr. Willis isn't there anymore, because he talked up.

QUESTION: Suppose you didn't have to watch what you said, what would you say?

PAUL: I'll tell you what I'd say. I'd like to say to those damned niggers to know their place and keep it. I don't mind them being equal, but I don't like them thinking they're better than I am. Up north, in Wisconsin, they run things. In Florida, it's quite different. In Florida, I've seen a nigger go into a theater, and some white guy would yell, "There's a nigger in here," and all these white guys would go looking for him and this nigger would go running out of the theater. In Wisconsin, they [the Negroes] run you out of the theater. It's getting that way here. I like for them to keep their place.

ED: They're always yelling Black Power. They always want to yell Black Power, so that's an excuse to hook you ["hook" means "punch"].

PAUL: They have a lot of Black Power movements at school. They're quite organized. Even though they don't admit it, they're organized. You see them outside. They have these black arm bands, and they're talking up Black Power all the time.

JERRY: If I could say what I want to say, I don't even like them being equal to me. I'll tell you one thing; I hate them trying to think they're better than I am. I really like them being lower. That's the way I feel about it. If I had my way, I'd rather have them being lower than me. It's all right if they want to be equal, but they'll never be better. And if they try to be better, I'll fight them every day. Also, I want them to leave me alone. I don't even like to look at them in the hallway.

PAUL: Well, I don't like anybody trying to be better than me, or trying to push me around. Last night I was thrown in jail, because I was driving without a license, but I won't crawl to nobody. Those cops, they think they're better than you are. Another thing with that Black Power, there's too much of that Black Power stuff. It's just an excuse for power to burn and kill.

JERRY: If we'd get the white guys to stick together, we'd run the place, and we'd be running high. There's more of us than them. There're a lot of white guys like myself, who don't like flying with the niggers. Then there's a lot of PW's.

QUESTION: What's a PW?

JERRY: That's a kind of punk who will shine your shoes to keep you from hurting him. A lot of white guys are this way. It's because of the PW's that we can't stick together. I don't consider myself particularly hard, but I don't consider myself a punk either. A lot of these colored guys would say, "Kiss my feet." I say, "You kiss mine first, and then we'll take turns."

PAUL: Now you take one nigger alone. He ain't gonna do nothing, but you get them in a group and it's a different story.

JERRY: It's a fact, you know, that colored guys mature a lot faster than we do. But that doesn't bother me none. As long as I know that cat feels pain, I don't care. So far, I've always been able to walk away from a fight. There was this one time I was beat pretty bad, and I said, "I'm not going to lie here in front of this nigger," so I got up all of my strength to get myself on my feet, and I did. Then he walked away. Right after he was out of sight, I fell to the ground and laid there for about two hours. I was hurt pretty bad that time. But I don't care, because I know when I get into a fight, I'm gonna hook with the other guy, and I'm gonna try to get him bad. I don't care if I lose, just as long as I know he felt some pain.

ED: Well, if you let them know you can fight, they won't bother you as much.

JERRY: That's right. That's the whole thing behind it. At least a colored guy will say, "Well, I know this white guy who hurt you." Then he might hesitate.

QUESTION: Do you ever gang up on a Negro who beat you up when he was with his pals?

ED: If I get whipped by a nigger, and these two guys [Jerry and Paul] want to help me jump that nigger when we caught him alone, I wouldn't want them to help me. I'd want to get revenge on that one guy myself. I wouldn't mind having these two guys around just to see that no one else jumped me, but I wouldn't let them jump in. We're not like the niggers.

JERRY: There's nothing that satisfies me any more in life than being able to beat up a guy real good, at least once, no matter what he is. I don't care if he's white, black, Chinese, or what.]

As far as a socializing among races is concerned, Jerry, Paul, and Ed do not think their school is "integrated." Ed, in fact, thinks, "It's like putting a tiger and a lion together in a cage." As a way of almost justifying racial cleavage at Plains High, the three young men speak of Negro rioters who flout the law in front of National Guard troops. The rioters were seen on TV and lived in places like Detroit, Washington, and Newark, rather than in Center City, which had no riot by the time of the interview.

[QUESTION: How integrated is Plains High?

PAUL: I'd say Plains High isn't integrated. They're together because they're in the same building, but they don't mix.

ED: It's like putting a tiger and lion togehter in a cage. They aren't going to mix. Riots are just an excuse to steal. White kids hate them for it. You know the National Guardsmen don't even have bullets when all these people are stealing. If I had my way, all of those guys would have bullets. They'd cut those niggers down. I don't blame them for going out there and rioting. If I was a colored kid, I'd probably go to a riot to steal. If I thought I'd get something out of it, I would. And that's exactly what they're getting, because they won't shoot them.

JERRY: You know, there was this black girl who ran past this National Guard. I saw it right on television. She said, "I stole this, shoot me." And he didn't. If that had been me, there would've been one dead nigger.

ED: Well, I'll tell you something. My dad's in the National Guard, and they're going to do something about it. They're mounting weapons on helicopters, and when they start this sniping stuff, they're going to snipe back, and they're gonna get them. It's not just niggers; any sniper.

QUESTION: Can you think of one situation in which white and black students mix?

ED: Well, at the low-water bridge parties there's integration. We have these parties out in these rivers by the bridges. The water's pretty low. That's why we call them low-water bridge parties. These are pretty mixed. Everybody's happy at these bridge parties. There's plenty of beer, and everybody's kind of drunk. They all have booze and are boozed up, and they have their girls. There you find mixing. I think you find the most mixing there.

JERRY: Yeah, at one of these parties, the niggers even joined us in this game we were playing. We were trying to find frogs, and you weren't considered *hard* unless you ate a frog. They say you've got to be pretty drunk to do it. You take a slug of beer, then you pop this frog in your mouth and swallow him. A little later on, you can feel him jumping in your stomach.

ED: At one of these beer busts, if an outsider comes in, the whites and niggers band together. We were out there one time, and everybody was jumping off the bridge. Everybody was daring everybody to jump off into the water. These six college guys came over. Now, these are the guys I really don't like. I never did like any of the college students. Anyway, they were being real nice, sharing their beer and what have you. But then one of them was talking about raping this girl who was with another guy [this other couple was black]. Before you knew it, one of the guys said, "Well, that's my girl," and bam! He hit him. The whole bunch of us joined in, beat up on these six guys. Whites and blacks joined together.

QUESTION: Why did you join forces that time?

ED: Well, that's Harry's girl. Everybody from Plains High, white and black, joined together. Harry could do whatever he wants with her, but nobody else has the right to touch her.

PAUL: Another time we get together is when the kids from East Plains High play us in a ball game. After the ball games, when they come over to start riling us, then the Negroes and whites band together. Nobody's going to rile us about Plains High. That's when we fight.

ED: Yeah, we went with some niggers one time looking for some East kids to fight after a game. One time it was pretty tough. We played at Greenwood. There're a lot of niggers at Greenwood. After the game, you didn't know which guy to hook. You didn't know if he was a Plains High nigger or a Greenwood nigger. You had to ask him first. You said, "Are you from Plains High?" If he said, "Yes!" man, you didn't hook him. If he said "No!" you hooked him.

PAUL: I'll tell you one thing. We ain't having no kid from East riling no Plains High kids. It doesn't matter whether you're black or white.

ED: Those East kids really think they're something. They say, "Man, you go to Little Africa or Harlem High," because it has mostly niggers in it.

PAUL: As I said before, no one cuts on Plains High. If they cut on it, they're going to have a fight. This isn't true at some of the other high schools. Some of these other schools, you know, you can criticize the school, and nobody'll do nothing about it. But not at Plains High School. You cut on Plains High, and we're gonna gang up on you.

ED: Well, you know, we cut on the school ourselves, and there're a lot of things we don't like about it. And we say it, but nobody else can cut on it. If you're from Plains High School, it's all right; but if you're not, you'd better not cut on Plains High.]

The Mexican-American students at Plains High constitute another minority group. Most of the students, including some Mexicans, agree that the Mexicans stick to themselves, and are seldom heard from. Jerry thinks they should wait until "the whites and niggers killed each other," and then take over.

[JERRY: The Mexicans don't come in at all at school. If they say anything, they're dead. If I was a greaser, I'd just wait on the sidelines and wait until all the whites and niggers killed each other. Then they could take over.

ED: I know of no taco bender who doesn't carry a knife. Myself, I don't carry a stiletto—I carry a metal comb. I only use it when a guy pulls a knife on me.

PAUL: Well, I can use a knife. I learned how to use one years ago, but I ain't gonna use one until someone else uses one on me. Then I'll pull one.]

For the most part, the students at Plains High recognize that there are different classes of white and Negro students. Sometimes the classification is no more refined that upper, middle, and lower. At other times, the classification is sophisticated and contains a number of refinements. Usually, the students, both white and black, identify the greater number of classes among white students. In what follows, Jerry resents the fact that he is not accepted by his richer fellow students, although he tries to justify the situation. Unlike the other respondents, he does not categorize blacks into any subgroups at all.

[QUESTION: How many classes of students are there at Plains High?

JERRY: There're real rich kids, middle class kids, the poor kids, and the dirt poor. Now take us. We don't have any money at all. We're in the poor class. We're not dirt poor, but we're poor. But I can run around with any of the rich kids that I want to at Plains High. I'll tell you why I can run around with them—because I have clothes, and I've got hair [Jerry wears his hair long]. But I can't go to their parties. They never invite me to their parties. I can talk to them at school and get in with them, because they're jealous of me. I've got one of the nicest girls up there. It doesn't matter so much if your girl is from the upper class or rich. She can be dirt poor, if she's "built" and good looking. Then all these rich guys want her too, and they want my girl.

PAUL: Well, I don't know. Money plays a big part in things at Plains High School.

ED: You know, generally I look like a bum, but that's because I like to. Now, take tonight, I got all dressed up—normally, I look like a bum. [All three had on jackets and ties.]

JERRY: The big percentage of us is dirt poor or just poor.

ED: Well, I wouldn't say we're dirt poor. We're just poor. We don't have no money in the bank, but we get along all right.

PAUL: The main thing is, if your parents have money or not, and our parents don't have any money in the bank. That's why we're in the poor class.

QUESTION: How many classes of Negroes are there?

JERRY: There's one class of Negroes—black. They always band together. Then there's a class of Negroes I guess nobody wants. There's a group of whites that nobody wants, too, and these whites and blacks band together.

QUESTION: If there's a class of Negroes nobody wants, aren't there two classes of Negroes?

JERRY: No! There's only one. They're all black.

ED: I agree. They're all black. You get into trouble with some of them. Suppose you get into trouble with one of these niggers nobody likes. A lot of the other niggers don't like it. They'll jump you.

PAUL: Well, sometimes these other niggers don't like these niggers either, and they won't jump you. They'll jump them. My third day in junior high, for example, I was leaning against the fence scraping my shoe. This nigger said, "Get out of my way." I said, "What did you say, black boy?" He said, "I said, get out of my way." So I cracked him right in the mouth. This kid, he's a Negro—him and me are up tight like this now—went up to this nigger and smacked him around. He said, "I told you not to do that, nigger." This kid was the toughest kid at Plains Junior High.

JERRY: Paul and me both went to the same junior high. You don't have much trouble there like you do in high school. At first I let them push me around, until I hooked two or three of them. I get along pretty well as a rule, though, because when I went to school in South Town, I was on the wrestling team. I met this same guy Paul's talking about at a wrestling meet. He was the hardest guy in school. Then when I went to Plains Junior High, the Negroes saw me talking to him. He was the only guy I knew there. They thought I must be something if I knew him. Also I started going with this cheerleader. That put me in good. But a lot of guys hated me, because they wanted to date her. When I first went to junior high, I have to say that the colored guys are the first friends I met. But slowly I began to move away from them and back to my own group. I got to hate them more and more every day.]

[QUESTION: What do you think of some of the Black Power people at school?

ED: Well, you take Tim Howard, he's like a mad dog. One day he likes the whites, and another, he's all for Black Power. You should see him in the bathroom. If there're whites there, he's pro-white; if there're blacks there, he's pro-black.

JERRY: He wants a big sign on him that says, "Look at me, I want to be noticed." He's a good guy, though. He runs around with a lot of the bad guys. He can hook. Next to this other guy, he was the best hooker in junior high. I'll say one thing for him, too; he don't really want to hurt nobody.

ED: When he gives his speeches in the smoking room, people really crack up.

QUESTION: What is your definition of Black Power?

JERRY: Black Power means "niggers."

PAUL: It's a bunch of niggers who want to cause violence.

ED: You know, when a bunch of white kids want to cause trouble, we go to a nigger neighborhood and we yell out "White Power" or "white backlash." I'd say, though, a lot of the colored kids don't really care about Black Power. A lot of the kids who use this phrase "Black Power" use it to cause trouble.]

The assassination of Dr. Martin Luther King, Jr., occurred as we started our interviews with the students at Plains High. Various students we talked with focused on this day as meaning different things to them. For some students, Negroes were cheated out of a black cheerleader, because primary elections were held on the day when most Negroes stayed home to watch the King funeral; for others, the school was peaceful that day because the Negroes and the white "hoods" stayed home; for still others, the assassination meant a genuine loss, a felt hurt, a time to hope more violence would not occur. A number of white students were afraid of the possible black reaction. One white girl said that she became aware of her whiteness for the first time. For Jerry, Paul, and Ed, the death was also a loss—not because a true prince of peace had been cut down but, rather, because Dr. King's nonviolent philosophy would have made it possible to say whatever they wanted to the "niggers," without the risk of a violent reaction.

[JERRY: The day King was killed, I was everybody's mother and dad. I called up to say so-and-so wouldn't be to school. I had a bunch of niggers and whites at my house who were drinking beer on that day and playing cards. Jackson was there, and he brought Cicero and a couple of other friends. They were all right. I liked them. Then there were a lot of other guys there that I didn't know. I didn't like them too much, because I don't like a bunch of niggers around me. But what could I say? I couldn't say, "You niggers get out," and let Jackson and the others stay. I wasn't about to say, "Hey, man, you're not the same color as I am—out!" So I let them stay. We got along pretty well.

ED: Well, we put on a big act, pretended like we were pretty busted up over it. We wanted to get out and have some fun. Personally, we don't care if he kicked off or not. As far as the memorial service at school that they had for him, we didn't care whether they had one or not. We went to it because we missed fifteen minutes of class.

JERRY: I didn't go to that service. I skipped out. I heard enough of King. I don't want to hear any more about him. I didn't care whether he was killed or not. This teacher, she saw me coming back in after that, but she was a clean head. She didn't say anything.

PAUL: The day after a lot of kids would come up to you and say, "Did you cut school to see King's funeral?" I found out that you'd better say, "Yes," or you were in trouble.

JERRY: Well, I wasn't about to say yes. I could care less. I'm not going to be chicken in front of anyone. As far as King is concerned, he was colored, and that puts him down, because I'm prejudiced as all hell. But I'll say one thing about King. If you got to have a colored, he was okay. He didn't like violence. He was a good guy, but he was colored. I was really for him, because I thought he'd make it so I could walk around and say anything about niggers that I wanted to say. All this nonviolence stuff, and they wouldn't fight. As far as I'm concerned, they killed the wrong nigger. It seems to me that he stood for all the right things. I think he stood for the things that I'd like to stand for. But I'm not going to, because I'm too prejudiced now.]

[QUESTION: What's your solution to the problem at Plains High?

JERRY: I've got a solution. Ship them back to Africa.

ED: I've got another solution. The white guys should band together and stomp them.

PAUL: Once they know we're on top, they ain't gonna do nothing. Once they know we're banded together and ain't gonna take this crap, there wouldn't be any trouble.

ED: This is true. If we'd band together and stomp them, there wouldn't be any problem.

JERRY: I really get a big kick out of some kids at East who ask me, "Is it true that whites are on one floor, and blacks are on another floor?" Man, I cracked up when I heard that. Hell, you can walk on any of the floors.]

The foregoing attitudes of "Ship them back to Africa" or "Band together and stomp them" do not prevent these three young men from supporting a basketball team which is four-fifths black. They want their team to win and feel that if black basketball players win games, then let them play. School loyalty in sports apparently outweighs considerations of prejudice. However, although a black girl may be qualified as a cheerleader, they nevertheless prefer to look at a white cheerleader. Few schools, they argue, have ever won recognition for a team which ended up in last place but had the best cheerleaders. It seems that these young men are willing to accept the Negro athlete, although, at the same time, they hate *all* Negroes. Perhaps, this represents the kind of exploitation of the black militants to which Tim and Bill refer in Chapter 3.

[QUESTION: How do you feel about supporting a basketball team which is mainly black?

ED: I don't care if they're all white or all black. If they play good, that's what matters. If a white kid isn't doing as good as a colored kid, I say pull the white kid out and put the colored guy in. As long as we win, I don't care who plays.

QUESTION: How do you feel about having a Negro cheerleader?

PAUL: Negro girls just don't qualify with their grades to be cheerleaders. Besides that, the colored boys don't vote for them. We had colored cheerleaders in junior high. But at Plains High, the colored kids don't vote for them, so they don't get in.

ED: That's right. That's the case. The colored kids don't give a damn. They wouldn't go to vote, so colored kids don't get in.

JERRY: I don't know. This Harmony Blake, she's real good. She's a nice colored girl. I like her. She has a nice voice, and she can really jump. But the colored kids didn't vote for her. That's why she didn't get in. She could've made it.

QUESTION: If she's so qualified, why didn't the white kids vote for her?

JERRY: Well, a white boy would rather see a white girl in there than a nigger. Besides, it's a popularity contest. Personally, I'd rather look at a white girl than a colored girl out there. But this Harmony Blake, she's really qualified.]

[QUESTION: Do you notice any differences in your racial attitudes with those of your parents and grandparents?

JERRY: My grandparents, when they were young, it was different. A colored person would even get off the sidewalk if a white person was walking down the sidewalk.

ED: As far as I can remember, all of my relatives have hated niggers.

PAUL: I think more white people accept Negroes, but back in my grandparents' days, everybody hated them except for a few radicals.

ED: Myself, I don't see anything wrong with colored persons. It's just what he does and how he does it that I don't like. Like stealing from you. You can't trust them.

JERRY: There're a lot of white guys I don't like, too. There's one guy in particular I hate. He's a white guy. I asked him to fight three times. He wouldn't fight.

Jerry and Paul tell with nostalgia about the "good old days," when everybody hated Negroes, and the Negroes would get off the sidewalk when whites approached. Actually, the extreme position of these three young men regarding racial matters is probably no more acceptable today than its opposite (favoring civil rights) was in their grandparents' day.

As with all students that we interviewed, we asked these young men what their experience at Plains High has taught them about race relations. To say their answers are unexpected is to put matters mildly.

[PAUL: It's taught me that the races can get along if they would sit down and reason and think about it. But if they want violence, the hell with it. We'll be violent.

ED: It's taught me that they can get along if they stay in their own place. This stuff with white girls and colored boys shouldn't go. They can be friends, but colored are for colored, and whites are for whites. I think we've got to learn to get along together, though, because the way it's going now, it's worthless. One group will eventually annihilate the other.

JERRY: Well, it's taught me that no matter what color you are, you can get along, if you try. But if I had my way, they could all go to Africa.

QUESTION: When you have children, will you send them to an integrated school?

ED: I'd send my kids to an integrated school.

JERRY: I would, because I don't want my kids to be a nigger hater. I want him to respect niggers as human beings, not like me. I want them to get along with them as equals, not to get along with them as being better than they are. I want them to judge a person for what they are, not the color of their skins. It's too late for me. I'm prejudiced as all hell, but I want my kids not to hate niggers.

PAUL: I want my kids to go to an integrated school, because I want them to know what "nigger" means. If my daughter brought a clean nigger home, that would be okay with me. But if he was grubby, or even a grubby white guy, or stupid, I'd kick him out. I can't tolerate stupid people.

ED: I'll let my kids know where I stand with them. But I want to teach them to respect them for what they are, not the color of their skin. That's why I want them to go to an integrated school.

QUESTION: Where do you think you got the opinions you have of Negroes.

JERRY: I got my opinions from socializing with them. I didn't really mind color until I got to junior high. They then tried to be better than me, and I can't stand any colored trying to be better than me. Then I started listening to the news and all this stuff about riots. I think they've got more rights now than I'll ever get. That's what started me on hating niggers.

ED: Well, I know my old man hated them. He always has hated them. When they started hurting me, they changed my attitude. When I learned what they were getting away with, like violence, stealing, and looting, I really got mad. Take the National Guard. They had guns with no ammunition. A bunch of them were arrested, and they were let out in ten days, out free. We're too free on them. Rap Brown, he ought to be put away.

JERRY: Rap Brown, he ought to be killed. In a way, I kind of envy Rap Brown, though. I'd like to be able to get on a mike and say what I want to say. Look at Rap Brown. He gets up there on a mike, and he gets a lot of those Ubangis dancing, and they go wild.

PAUL: They really do get away with an awful lot. Take in study hall—they can get passes to leave the room any time they want. They can do whatever they want. White guys can't get any passes to leave the room. We had this one study hall teacher. He's scared hell of the Negroes. He lets them do what they want. I have to go up to him and say, "Give me a goddamn pass, or else," and then he gives me a pass to go to the libary. But if I don't get mad and ask, "May I have a pass?" he says, "Sit down." But the niggers can get one any time they want.

JERRY: I like to get away with things, too. Nothing excites me more than to get shot at by the police. They've shot at me.

PAUL: Yeah, but they don't shoot at you. They just shoot over your head.

JERRY: Yeah, but I like it. It's real fun to run from the cops. It's exciting.

ED: Well, I don't like the cops. Once you get a record, they're always on you. You know, I've got a police record. We stole this car one time, and they always hold it against you.]

White Conservatives and Racists

Part 2

The following three white students are not as obvious as the preceding group about their racial prejudices, but the prejudice is there, if in a somewhat disguised form. As the interview unfolds, these "conservative" students say things which reveal their anti-Negro attitudes. Most of the time, however, their answers fall into the "socially desirable" category. If we talked to them for a short time only, we probably would have been forced to conclude: (1) that they suffered from selective perception, (2) that they were naive, or (3) that they told us what they thought we wanted to hear.

A number of Negroes has suggested that subtle prejudice is the type with which it is more difficult to cope. It also represents the type of racism which must be overcome if civil rights is to become more than a slogan. The type of racism which appears in this part of Chapter 4 is what we most often encounter. Jerry, Paul, and Ed's racism (Part 1) is too outspoken to attract many converts, while Rock, Mike, and Sally's represents a sort of "Gentleman's Agreement."

In what follows, we invite you to share a talk with two boys and one girl: Rock, Mike, and Sally. The three are juniors at Plains High.

[QUESTION: What are some of the pressures you face from attending a desegregated school?

SALLY: Well, I don't see too many differences at all. The only thing you have to watch for is a few of the tough Negro girls who might get after you. I'd say there really aren't any differences at Plains High as opposed to East Plains High School, or some other non-integrated school.

ROCK: There's no real differences. You do have to avoid serious slips, though, such as calling someone a nigger. You can call someone a nigger if you're kidding about it, and he knows you're kidding. This happens all the time. Some of them will call me, "Hey, white boy," and I'll call back, "Hey, black boy." But we're friends. I'd say that there really isn't any pressure or problems because you can be friends with Negroes just as easily as with whites.

MIKE: There's a difference between white and Negro kids. The Negro kids hang around in big groups. They dance in the hallways. But white kids don't hang around in big groups. They only go together in maybe fours or fives. It's a little hard to get used to seeing big groups of kids such as the Negroes. They seem to be more cliquish, and they seem to have a lot of fun, too. One thing I noticed is that the Negroes don't seem to care what other people think, like dancing in the hallways. You'd never see white kids dancing in the hallways, because they're worried about what kind of image this would present.]

Mike's idea that Negroes are different because they hang around in large groups and dance in the hallways, triggers Rock into this line of thinking. Rock says Negroes *are* different ("You can get killed if you call one a "nigger"). Although Rock does not say so, his assumption is that if there were an equally degrading term for whites (i.e., a "nigger" equivalent), whites would react much less violently. He agrees with the students in the first part of this chapter, too, that to fight one Negro embroils you in a fight with all Negroes. Both assumptions rule out the possibility of individual differences among Plains High's black students. Note how Sally thinks "soul" is exactly that to which the "militant" students in the preceding chapter object.

ROCK: You know, white people who listen to all of this civil rights stuff believe that whites and Negroes are the same. Well, they aren't. You can get killed if you call a person a nigger. They're really different in that respect. You can usually say anything if you smile. But, if you don't smile, you'd better watch out. Also, if you fight a Negro, you have to fight his cousins, his brothers, and all the rest of them. They're not like the white boys. They'll gang up on you.

SALLY: One thing about the colored people is that they got soul. They wear necklaces. They're cool, and they're fun. They have a cool you don't find in most white guys. It's a nice difference. I'd say Plains High has it much better than other schools because of the blacks. We have the cool black kids—the kids with soul. That really makes a difference. They add a lot to it. It's real nice because we always associate with the Negroes, particularly in class. Before or after school, it's a little segregated. The kids go home together [blacks with blacks and whites with whites], and they don't really see each other after school. But in school, we see a lot of each other. Also, there're three Negro boys that I know of who're always at the white kids' parties. I don't think I've ever been to a party where these three kids weren't there. They're real cool and liked by everybody. There's one of them, though—his name is Lester—he thinks he's white. He's a big cutup.

QUESTION: What do you mean by "He thinks he's white"?

SALLY: Oh, I don't know. It's kind of hard to put into words. He just doesn't think of himself as a Negro. I guess one thing that I can think of is that most Negro kids wear silk socks. The white kids never wear silk socks. Well, these Negro kids who're always with the white kids, they dress just like the whites. They don't wear silk socks either.]

Rock, Mike, and Sally are guilty of enunciating a myth we are trying to annihilate here—namely, that blacks are all alike. All Negroes are no more alike than are all whites. Rock suggests that all Negroes are belligerent and will gang up on a person in a fight. Sally can tell a "white Negro" from the others, because they do not wear silk socks the way all other Negroes do. The failure to perceive individual differences in members of another race is one of the most frequently expressed subtle prejudices. Mike next moves us into the topic of interracial dating to show how well the races get along. This turns out to be a poor choice of topics, however, because the incidence of interracial dating is low, and few students—whether black, Mexican-American, or white—accept students who date across racial lines.

[MIKE: I think the kids mix real well. There're some white girls who go with Negro boys. At first, the kids kind of stare and laugh a bit. But after a while, they accept it.

SALLY: Well, there're some who say, "Isn't it awful?" but I think it's usually their parents who influence the kids who say that.

QUESTION: Which kids stare and laugh at students who date interracially?

SALLY: Well, it's usually the girls. The girls will at first say, "Oh, I'd never do that," or they'll say things like, "I couldn't even touch them."

ROCK: The white boys don't seem to resent this at all. I don't really see it too much. I never hear the white boys talking about a girl, if she dates Negroes. Besides, it's none of our business. I think this is the way the boys react.

QUESTION: Once a girl has dated a Negro, is she also dated by white boys?

MIKE: Yes, if she's an appealing girl. If she's real attractive, I wouldn't care if she went with a Negro boy before, and I think this is the way most boys think about it. Most white boys will date a white girl, even if she's been out with Negro boys, if she's real good looking.

SALLY: I disagree. Some boys say, "It makes me sick to see this girl with a Negro." I think the white boys resent the fact that some white girls date Negro boys.

QUESTION: Do white boys also date Negro girls?

SALLY: No, the white boys are too proud to date Negro girls.

ROCK: Well, I don't think it's pride at all. The Negro girls aren't too good looking. They just aren't as pretty as the white girls.

MIKE: I agree with Rock. The reason I wouldn't date a Negro girl is that I just don't think they're as pretty. I haven't see one Negro girl at Plains High that I'm attracted to. I think it's just because they're uglier than white girls.]

Our respondents provide us with a variety of reasons to explain why white young men do not date Negroes. Their answers range from "that would be breaking down all the barriers, it's too far out" to "the Negro boys would beat them up." Rock and Mike say they would not date a Negro because she is never as pretty as a white young woman. Again all Negroes are lumped into one category—this time, one of "unattractiveness." For white young women wishing to date blacks, Sally says it is not "looks" so much as other "barriers."

[QUESTION: Is looks a criterion for girls also, and if so, are Negro men handsomer than Negro women?

SALLY: Well, some are cool and handsome as well. But there's a barrier. I'd like to date them except for this barrier. I can't really explain the barrier, and I don't know why I feel this way. On the other hand, if you start liking someone, it's hard to stop it. So I don't know. I'm a little confused on this.

QUESTION: Whose barrier is it? Is it the kids who set up the barriers, your parents, or is it within yourself?

SALLY: Oh, it's not my parents, except for dad. Dad would be very much against it. But he isn't home very much. He's a pilot. I could schedule my dates around his being home. I don't know if it's me or what the girls would think. I've thought about this, but it's very hard for me because I haven't been able to figure out an answer.

MIKE: I don't know about interracial dating. I've grown up not to think of Negroes as different. My folks aren't nigger haters. But somehow or other, I just know it's out of the question for me to date a Negro.]

In what follows, the students attempt to explain "the barriers" to interracial dating. They talk about cultural differences which impose a wall to this sort of activity, but the cultural differences of which they speak reveal that the youths in the present group accept the popular stereotypes of the Negro. To the degree that Rock, Mike, and Sally accept these sterotypes, they are less able to be fully aware of many Negro "elites," who certainly do not fit the over-simplified and erroneous image which is presented. It is the very acceptance of such a distorted image which partly helps to keep groups as the black "elites" less visable to white conservatives.

[ROCK: Well, there're cultural differences; there're different attitudes. I think that's what makes the difference. They're easygoing. They just like to have a lot of fun. They don't think about the future and things that are important, like getting a job or supporting a family. They're just out to have a good time. They do have a good time, I think. That's the cultural difference. They just don't emphasize these other things like we do. That makes it hard, because we don't have anything in common.

SALLY: I agree with that. It seems to me that the future and success just doesn't mean as much to Negro boys as to the white boys. So there's a difference, and I've noticed that. They don't ever talk about what they're going to do after they get out of high school, or going to college, or things like that. They're just out to have a good time. They like to dance and have fun.

MIKE: Some of the girls are smart, but you don't find too many boys who're that way. In fact, there're a lot of Negro hoods who refuse to abide by any of the school rules. In study hall, they throw chalk all the time. They won't cut their hair. They won't study. They never carry books. There's this one kid who's really a hood. He even smokes a pipe.

QUESTION: Are there white hoods?

MIKE: Oh yes, there're more white hoods because the white outnumber the blacks, in school anyway. These hoods smoke in the john, and they drink. But I think it's more than just smoking and drinking because most of the kids at school drink an awful lot and smoke. There's nothing really bad about smoking. It's more of a wild attitude, I guess.

ROCK: I think it's because they have to do things to prove that they're masculine. I think Negroes have a hard time proving their masculinity. So they try very hard to do these wild things to show that they're men.

SALLY: Well, I don't know. It seems to me that everybody at school is a hood. They all go to wild parties and talk a great deal about their wild experiences. They don't talk about ordinary things. It isn't dope or things like that; there isn't much of that at Plains High. I guess it's more drinking and doing things they're not supposed to do.

ROCK: I think Negroes do these things compulsively. They have to or they'll blow up. I agree with Sally; wild parties are booze parties.

SALLY: You know the kids really worry me in high school. There's so much drinking going on. I think a lot of kids, when they get older, are going to be alcoholics. The parents don't know about it. The Negro parents don't seem to care as much as the white parents. Negro girls come home drunk, and their parents just don't care. I've heard girls say that they've walked home completely drunk and when I ask them what their mother and father said, they say, "Nothing!" I'd say that the Negro kids are like hoods, but they have something more. A lot of the cool guys are Negroes. It's in the way they carry themselves. A hood is a different kind of person. He's not respectable. He looks for fights. I don't think most of the Negroes are like that. It seems to me that among a lot of girls, it's a status symbol to go with a hood. Some of them are cool, too. One thing about hoods, they do things that are disapproved of, and I guess that makes them hoods. It seems to make them more exciting, too.]

While Sally would not do such "disapproved" things herself, one detects a note of yearning in her for such "bad" behavior. The Negroes and the hoods are "cool;" they drink and smoke; they do things they are not supposed to do; they have *fun*. Sally sends a number of self-contradictory messages throughout the interview. At times, it seems as if she disliked certain groups of students for doing the very things she secretly would like to do.

When these young people were asked to describe the various classes of students at school, they told of a group which other students did not mention—the puds. Puds "are the kids who don't ever do anything." Puds also hold themselves apart and do not integrate. Puds seem to be primarily white; at any rate, our respondents can think of only a single black student who qualifies as a pud.

[QUESTION: How many classes of kids are there at Plains High?

MIKE: Well, there's puds. Puds are the kids who don't ever do anything. I only know of one Negro kid who's a pud. Most of the puds are white kids. They're dull. They don't do anything at school. They don't do anything in extracurricular activities. They never get involved in anything. They just go to school, and they study; then they go home. They watch television, and then they go back to school.

ROCK: You don't find many Negro kids who're puds, because the majority of Negro kids are tough. They're athletic. They play games all the time.

SALLY: I think the reason why they're athletic is because they have extra muscles. They're built different from white kids. I read that somewhere, and I think that's why they're so superior in sports. The white kids have a disadvantage.

ROCK: I don't go along with that at all. I think this is the only way they can prove themselves. I think this is why they try hard and usually end up on the first string teams.

QUESTION: Are there any other classes of kids?

MIKE: Well, there's a very small group of Negroes that are tops academically. But these are mostly girls. These extra smart kids all hang around together. I think the most integration between Negroes and whites is among these academically top kids. But they don't really hang around with the top white kids. They're really just above the hoods, I guess, if you know what I mean.]

A frequent complaint among black students is that the teachers, counselors, and school administration show preference for white students. Sometimes black students report situations in which prejudice is obvious. Other times, it is subtle; and at still other times, prejudice seems to exist primarily in the mind of the person doing the accusing. White students' opinions also vary: some agree that the school favors white students; others think teachers overcompensate for skin color—discriminating against white students. The three students in this section maintain that there is some discrimination in what takes place between students and teachers. It is not the teacher who discriminates, however; rather, the black student, they feel, discriminates against the teachers.

[ROCK: The teachers treat the kids just the same. They don't discriminate against Negroes or whites. In fact, they go out of their way to be very fair to everybody.

SALLY: But the Negro kids treat the teachers differently.

ROCK: Yeah, they do all kinds of dumb things in class, and they don't pay as much attention to what the teacher asks them.

MIKE: Yeah, they lip off to the teachers all the time. For example, we were coming out of assembly hall the other day, and there was this little shrimp of a Negro who was fooling around. This white teacher got ahold of him to straighten him out, and this Negro kid turned around and grabbed the teacher by the shirt and started yanking at the teacher and yelling at him. Well, none of the white kids would ever do that. But those Negro kids seem to rebel more. They don't care who they're talking to.

ROCK: There's another Negro kid who really pulled a sweet one at school. There was this attempted rape of this white girl in the hallway. This white girl thought it was this Negro boy. So the assistant principal grabbed him and threw him out of school. The kid said that he hadn't done anything, and it wasn't him. In any case, they called the police, and they took him to the police station. He took a lie detector test, and it showed he wasn't lying. He sued the assistant principal and was awarded five thousand dollars. The assistant principal is appealing the case. I don't think the white kids would've gone that far. But this Negro kid did. I think Negro kids just relate differently to the teachers.

SALLY: The Negro kids treat the teachers differently. They will fight back physically, even. White kids won't do this.

QUESTION: While we're on physical stuff, is there much fighting between black and white students?

SALLY: Well, I've never been threatened, but there's this Fred Trees who says he's a Lieutenant in the Black Power movement. . .[Sally is interrupted by Rock.]

ROCK: Yes, he usually tells us everything. He says there's going to be a riot the last day of school. I don't think there'll be a riot, because the kids aren't that fanatic. But he told us that we'd better go right home because he likes us, and he doesn't want us to get hurt.

SALLY: Well, the Negro girls use violence as sort of a joke, but they don't really mean it. For example, I was in the washroom the fourth period, when a Negro girl told this white girl that she hates her and that if she ever came into the bathroom again, or near her again, that she'd burn her house down. A lot of Negro kids kid about this. They'll say, "Your house is next."

ROCK: I don't think anything will ever really get started. It might get started in South Center City, where there're older kids to stir up the other kids, but I don't think anything will ever happen at Plains High.

MIKE: Well, there's something that goes on at Plains High that bothers me a little bit. The Negro kids will ask me for a dime, and you know it's bad not to give it to them. They talk you down and threaten you. One kid started telling me a sad story one day, and he asked for a quarter. He kept saying he hurt his leg, and he was out of work. They try to con you. I just got rid of him, and I didn't give him a quarter. But the other day, when I was in the lunchroom, a Negro shook me down for a dime. I just gave him a dime to get rid of him. You have to know when to give in and when not to. There's some threatening, but little actual physical stuff.

ROCK: Oh, there's lots of fights, but not necessarily among any group. Most of the fights are among themselves—Negroes fight Negroes, and sometimes a white guy is stupid enough to get into a fight with a Negro. But he has to be crazy, because when you fight a Negro, you don't just fight that Negro; you fight all his cousins and everyone else. They stick together.

SALLY: There's one thing that bothers me about Plains High School. A lot of Negro girls fight. I couldn't believe it when I first got there. I didn't think that girls fought. There're a lot of fights between Negroes and Mexican girls, too.

ROCK: The girl fights are more fun. Somebody will come running through the halls yelling, "Girl fight!" And everybody will go running out to see it.

SALLY: Well, I don't think it's funny. I think it's a shock.

QUESTION: Do the white girls also fight with Negro girls?

SALLY: Well, the Negro girls are different. They're better fighters, so usually, I think, the white girls try to avoid fights. You avoid it as much as possible, if you don't want to get hurt.]

There is little doubt in the minds of these students that the most integration takes place in sports. Among some students—not those in the college preparatory classes—the classroom is also frequently mentioned. In neither case, however, does "integration" go much beyond a physical proximity of the two races. It seems as if the definition of integration involves blacks and whites occupying the same building. This type of physical "integration" has been part of the Plains High scene for decades. An emotional integration, however, in which people genuinely relate to one another, has been conspicuously absent.

[QUESTION: Where do you find the most integration?

ROCK: Sports and in class is where you find the most integration.

SALLY: The girls in the bathroom are very integrated, too. I've been in there and seen them sharing cigarettes.

QUESTION: Are the black and white students as friendly when they leave the washroom?

SALLY: No. They split when they go out. They go off in separate directions.

MIKE: Well, in school, the kids integrate because they're thrown together. But after class, you don't call [Negroes] up and see them after school.

SALLY: There's one thing in which you see a lot of integration too, and that's in the political offices at school. If you're Negro, and you run for political office, you'll win. All the Negroes will vote for you, and some white kids will, too. But the white kids split their vote with the other white kids running, so they never win. [Authors' note: Two Negroes hold school offices.]

QUESTION: Why can't the Negroes get a Negro cheerleader elected?

SALLY: Well, after Martin Luther King's death, the Negro kids stayed home from school. Only the white kids were there, and that was election day for cheerleaders. There were a couple of Negro kids who were running for it, but there weren't any Negro kids there to vote for them.

QUESTION: What happened last year when they tried to get Harmony Blake elected?

SALLY: Well, Harmony Blake was the first Negro girl to get past the primary part of the contest. She was pretty, and she was good, but she really wasn't that good. I think she lost because she just wasn't that good. There was some trouble about that. I remember going into the washroom, and this Negro girl said, "Harmony got 100% of the student body vote, and the teachers won't let her be a cheerleader because she's Negro, so we're going to have some trouble about that." I told her, "I don't believe she got 100% of the vote; I didn't vote for her." This Negro girl said, "you didn't?" And then she got real mad at me and started yelling and screaming. But that's the way they are. They thought she got 100% of the vote, and the teachers were trying to keep her out. But that's not true. The white kids didn't vote for her.

MIKE: Yeah, they always try to twist what you say around. For example, I was in the hallway yesterday. There're two phones in the main hall. There was a Negro boy on one phone and he'd been on there for a long time, just yacking away. There's this other phone; there was a white girl on it, a Negro girl behind her, and I was behind the Negro girl, waiting in line. This girl wasn't on the phone very long, and this Negro girl said, "Hurry up, gal, let's go." So the white girl said, "Well, why don't you go over there and talk to him? He's been on the phone a lot longer than me." She said, "I'm not talking to him. You get off the telephone." That's what I mean. They twist things around all the time.]

Although the students agree that the most integration takes place in sports, there are some sports in which the Negro does not join—for example, golf, tennis and swimming. Such individual sports are usually associated with middle and upper socioeconomic status. Some white students maintain that the Negro's biological make-up does not suit him for these types of sport, but more pertinent, is that swimming and golf, for instance, require fees, even when the facilities are public. Further, for Negro young women swimming is a major problem since the slightest moisture will curl the hair that they often have worked so very hard to straighten.

[ROCK: The swim team isn't integrated at all. I don't know why, the Negro kids just don't seem to want to swim.

SALLY: You know, you never see Negroes try out for swimming. I can't figure that one out.

ROCK: Well, maybe it's because they don't have lessons when they're younger.

MIKE: Well, also, in order to get into the public pools, you have to pay. That might be why they're not very good swimmers, because they don't have the money to get into the pool as kids.

ROCK: You also find very little integration in clubs like the Debate Club. There was only one Negro girl last year.

QUESTION: How integrated are the school dances?

SALLY: Oh, at the dances you see a lot of integration. Negro boys will dance with the white girls. They usually stay in one corner, and all the whites are in the other corner. But all the white girls I know would rather dance with Negro boys because they're better dancers.

ROCK: Well, all except on the slow dances. I don't think the white girls would rather dance with the Negroes on the slow dances, because the white boys are just as good as the Negroes. It's the other dances where the Negro boys are a lot better.

QUESTION: What's the reaction of the Negro girls, when Negro boys dance with white girls?

SALLY: I hear they get real mad at the dances. They don't like it at all. Some of them dance with white boys, but mostly, they end up dancing with each other.]

Both black and white students tell of a change toward less racial mixing as the young become older. Racial mixing is more common in elementary than in senior high school. A variety of reasons are offered as explanations. Although fears concerning interracial dating seem best to account for most of this cleavage, white parents are not at all alone in their disapproval. On the contrary, the Negro student is often equally at odds with his parents and grandparents on the same issue. Rock, Mike, and Sally, however, have not noticed a change in their relationship with Negroes as they have gone from junior high school to their present rank as high school juniors. Perhaps this is because they have never mixed much with blacks, whether in elementary, junior or senior high school.

[QUESTION: Has your relationship with Negroes changed since you were in elementary school?

ROCK: Well, I don't think there're any real differences. The only thing is in junior high, particularly in your last year, you're on top of the heap, so you did what you wanted to do. But, when you first get to high school, you're at the bottom. You're kind of afraid of doing certain things. But I'd say that friendships between Negroes and whites just stay the same from school to school.]

[QUESTION: Sally, earlier you said three Negroes always attend the parties you attend. Do these boys bring dates?

SALLY: No! That's a funny thing. I've never seen them with a girl. They don't come with Negro girls, and they're never with white girls. This kid, Chauncy, who's always there, he doesn't think about girls. And there's this other kid, Grant. I think he plays up to the white girls. But he never seems to get past a certain point, because the girls don't pay any attention to him. They're just a lot of fun, and that's why they're at all the parties. But I think they know there's no hope of dating the white girls. Besides, I think it's more fun to go to parties without a date, because you're freer to do what you want to do.]

Although Plains High is a student body, 25% non-white, and in spite of Sally's statement to the contrary, its students rarely discuss racial matters in class. The problem of the black man in America is an avoided topic in most classes, even though the lid on classroom discussions was lifted at least temporarily at the time of Dr. Martin Luther King's assassination; courses in Negro history are nonexistent, and there are no clubs for the purpose of discussing racial issues. Even informally, the students avoid discussions regarding racial matters. While they may joke about race, they rarely go beyond joking. For many, the present interview is the first time racial matters have been discussed seriously.

[QUESTION: Do you discuss racial issues in class?

SALLY: Oh, yes, particularly in Public Speaking. There're these two Negroes in the Public Speaking class. One of the Negro girls, who never felt this way, after Martin Luther King died, said one day in class, "The Negroes aren't accepted as Americans, and that's what's wrong with this country." But you know, she's wrong. Even the other girl got up and said, "You don't really feel that way. Why are you saying that?" Now this other girl, I know her. She's real sweet, and everybody likes her. She even says there's no problem. There're no Negro problems at Plains High School. There're some differences, but the differences are ceasing to exist.

ROCK: I think in time that there'll be a great deal of intermarriage until there's no longer any difference at all.

SALLY: I think a lot of the time it's just because these Negro girls kind of like to feel like queens and have their say, so they'll push things. They'll tell you to do something, and if you don't, they'll be after you. Seems to me they're always preparing themselves for the worst and looking for the worst, so that they won't have to be on the bottom.]

The students give conflicting reports about the segregation of physical space in school. Some students believe certain floors are occupied by the whites and others by the blacks (they do not always agree on which floors). Other students deny this. The prevailing rumor in the community holds that the halls are segregated, that white young women are sexually assaulted by blacks, and that white young men are beaten and intimidated in the back halls by black students. There was no actual evidence for any of these statements.

[QUESTION: Are there any areas in school which are segregated?

ROCK: Well, the only place we can think of is on the second floor and main hall before school and between classes, all of the Negro kids seem to hang around there. This is a meeting place for Negroes, but you can walk through there if you want. And there's no problem. I walk through there all the time. I even stop and talk to the kids.

MIKE: I think one of the reasons why we can is because we know what to do and what not to do. I think maybe when some of these kids come in from East Plains High School, they might find themselves with some problems. But having gone to school with Negroes before, we just know what to do and what not to do.

QUESTION: Can you give me some examples of what you mean by, "We know what to do."?

MIKE: Well, for instance, at a basketball game, not too long ago—this was in another town—we were coming out, and the team lost, and some of the Negroes were really upset. This white kid from this other town went walking right through this group of Negro kids. He said, "Excuse me," and all that, but that's not enough. They beat him up. If I had been him, I would've just walked around those kids. I would've known not to go through there, even if I did excuse myself. The new kids from East are going to have to learn some things.

SALLY: I think one thing is that you have to learn to take a little more. For example, every day I get to school a little late, and there're always a bunch of Negro boys out there, and they make all sorts of cracks. But you just have to learn to take it. I don't even listen to them.

ROCK: Well, you know, if you give in a little, they do too. Then everything is just fine. The new kids'll be a little scared at first; they'll try to show that they're not, and there might be a little bit of trouble that way. But I think they'll find out how to act.

MIKE: You know, Plains High School has the same percentage of Negroes as the city. You have to learn to accept this and get along. I think it's a good place to learn it, because if we have the same percent of Negroes as we have in the city, we're going to have to eventually come to grips with this. It gives me a chance to see people I normally wouldn't see.

SALLY: At first, I was a little shocked to see so many Negro kids when I went to junior high. But I got to know the Negro kids, and I've never had any problem. One thing I've noticed, though, is that they act different when there's a whole bunch of them. When they're alone, you just don't notice it. They go along with you. But when they're in a group, they stand out, and it's a little bit different. They just feel a little more free, I guess, when they're together.

ROCK: Well, white kids do too.]

The following complaints these students voice about the school are not based on racial issues. They resemble the complaints of students throughout the country—black or white, college or high school. One complaint which appears in most of their interviews concerns the school counselors. Sally, for example, thinks the counselors are more interested in avoiding necessary bookkeeping than in her sister's career. The complaint that the school is a factory is the complaint of numerous college students at multiversities. In schools with some 45,000 students, one can understand why there might be an impersonal air in the encounter between students and the administration, but in a school with a total student enrollment of less than 3000, one wonders why this should be.

[SALLY: I don't see that Plains High has done any good for me at all. It's destroyed any incentive I ever had to go to college. I used to be dying to go to college last year, and my friends also feel the same way I do. The teachers aren't any fun. It just doesn't seem to do anything for me. The only thing I guess that it's done is that I've found that the Negro boys have soul. I kind of like that. That makes them cool. The white kids act sort of indifferent.

ROCK: Well, the high schools are a big mediocrity. They're just factories. They use the wrong methods for teaching. They always treat us as a group, and not as individuals. I don't see where they're doing any good. If you learn anything at Plains High School, you learn it in spite of everything.

SALLY: The counselors are horrible. My sister and I wanted to take Radio Workshop and Auto Mechanics, and they wouldn't let us. In fact, last summer my sister wanted to change a course, and she went to a counselor because this other course she was taking was a real stupid course. He wouldn't let her, because of the bookkeeping involved. He was going to make her stay there because of bookkeeping. Can you imagine that? Well, my mother called up and got it changed. The counselors don't care about the kids. I wanted to take Auto Mechanics, but the principal and the counselors wouldn't let me. They do some of the stupidest things. This counselor said, "Well, how would you like to go to the rest of your classes with dirty fingernails?" Now isn't that stupid? Also, they will grab you for clowning around and drag you to the office. And then other times, they just turn their heads when they see things, like in the lunchroom the other day, there was a fight between some kids. They just looked the other way and didn't stop it.

ROCK: Yeah, they're kind of erratic. You can't count on them. They're supposed to stop these things, but you never know how they're going to act. I'll tell you something else, too. Some of the teachers are a real pain.

SALLY: Yeah, like there's this German teacher, I don't like her at all. She's a dove on Vietnam. She's a far left radical. Yet she fights tooth and nail about Vietnam. I'm a hawk, and she's a dove. She always marks me down when I oppose her. She's kind of a nut. I can hear her yelling all the way down the hallway, about Vietnam and things like that. Then she's always bringing these pictures about how we're killing these poor kids. She just doesn't care about her country.

ROCK: You never know what you have to do to please them. They give better grades to kids who don't oppose them. There's no question about that.

SALLY: You know I flunked German because I opposed that teacher. That's the only class I ever flunked. I had a "B" average for a long time in that class. But when I started opposing the teacher, all of a sudden I flunked.

ROCK. Yeah, in general, I'd say whatever we learn, we learn accidentally.

MIKE: Well, you know, it's rated high academically, higher than a lot of schools.

ROCK: But my friends from East High tell me that more kids from there go to college than from any of the other schools.

MIKE: Well, maybe that's because so many of them are straight-laced.

ROCK: They really are. Mike and I were down at this drive-in not too long ago. We had some cigars and were clowning around. There were these kids from East High who started moralizing to us. I didn't like that at all. At East, the group decides what's cool, such as clothes, and you copy it or else.]

[QUESTION: Has your experience at Plains High taught you anything about race relations?

SALLY: I don't think that school integration brings the races together. It all depends on how you're brought up. I don't see where it helps a bit. If you're brought up at home not to dislike Negroes, you won't dislike Negroes. I don't see why we have to have integrated schools, or bus kids around.

ROCK: Well, it helps you to know what to do because I think you learn more about the Negro by being in contact with him. This might be helpful, particularly when the Negroes riot.

SALLY: If I ever went insane, I'd go to a riot or to a teamster's union, or the A.F. of L. or C.I.O., and I'd blow them all up. It just makes me mad for people to riot and join unions. Looting is just another name for stealing. They should be prosecuted. During the tornadoes, kids looted the stores. They don't think there's anything wrong with that. I think marches are ok, but riots, no.

ROCK: I can see violence, but not looting.

SALLY: If they're going to loot my house, I'd shoot them. I'd get a machine gun, and I'd mow them down. If they were going to loot my store, I wouldn't let them get away with it. After King died, there was a little bit of a difference. There were two or three attempts of rape—Negro boys tried to rape white girls. And then a bunch of Negro girls beat up a white boy at school. King was such an idol of the Negroes. I never knew he was before. I never knew he was so important.

ROCK: Well, I thought he was an "Uncle Tom." I liked Stokely Carmichael and Rap Brown better. Then I mellowed.

SALLY: I didn't like King at all. I never have and I never will. I just thought he was such a hypocrite. I don't see why they were so upset when he was killed.

MIKE: Well, I don't think the Negroes were upset. Nobody really felt bad about it. Nobody was touched by King's death. I didn't see one Negro kid who was touched by it. They were upset, but it didn't touch them. It's kind of back to normal now.

ROCK: This is when all of this stuff started about "Your house is next." But that's kind of just a joke, and there isn't even much of that anymore.]

If any doubt remains in the reader's mind that these students are prejudiced (albeit in a somewhat more subdued fashion than the three young men in the first part of this chapter), the interviewer's following exchange with Sally and Mike should help remove this doubt.

[QUESTION: When you have children, will you send them to integrated schools?

SALLY: I never would. I don't think you get enough out of it. If you bring them up right, you won't have to send them to integrated schools. It's kind of strange to force them to go to integrated schools. They can see Negro kids at the YMCA or someplace like that. You don't have to force them to go to integrated schools to see Negro kids.

MIKE: I agree with that. I don't see why integrated schools are necessary in order to learn about Negroes. If you really want to learn about Negroes, you can learn about them in other places as well.

CHAPTER 5

The Hippies

The next group of students to be interviewed consists of four white young women who are perhaps most aptly described as "liberals." As we hear them speak, we quickly recognize this bright, intellectual, rebellious, indignant group of young people. Undoubtedly, some readers have gone to school with persons very similar to them, perhaps mixed with them, possibly been one of them. The way in which they belittle the "establishment," rebel against the status quo and ridicule much of what exists (apparently primarily *because* it exists) may not be at all unfamiliar. Although they are rebels, these angry young women do not have many Negro friends. To explain their lack of black friendships, they make use of many of the same explanations as their less equality-oriented peers—i.e., "we don't share classes with Negroes," "we live too far from Negro neighborhoods," and so on.

The students in this chapter have been labelled "hippies" by their fellows. Their clothing (sandals, medallions, fishnet stockings, no makeup, sarapes) tends to set them off from other students at Plains High School and is similar to that worn by hippies in other communities.

A significant characteristic of this interview involves the "up and down" quality of what the young women say. Most of the time they express extreme indignation about the Negro's lot; at other times, however, what they say seems quite consonant with the attitudes of many who are either anti-black or uninvolved. One has the feeling that these young women have not solved many of their own inner problems yet, and that they tend to degrade everything about the "out there" because of their own insecurity and restlessness. One expects that, as they mature, their need for seeing to it that integration comes to pass will be acted on in a more consistent, more constructive fashion.

[QUESTION: What pressures do you feel from the fact that you attend a desegregated school?

AMY: Well, I don't feel any pressures. But one thing, the school is divided into so many strata. There's the college strata which all of us are part of. We only associate with white Negroes in the college strata. And for the most part, we only associate with white Negroes in the hallways.]

101

Amy is obviously dissatisfied with her lack of contact with black students at Plains High School, and she rejects as "white Negroes" (another way of calling them "Uncle Toms") those with whom she is in contact. At the same time, she rationalizes the situation by blaming it on a de facto segregation based on curriculum choice. Implied in her answer is the attitude that Negroes in the college curriculum are not "real" Negroes, for they are not the victims of social and economic deprivation. Such an attitude carries the belief that *all* Negroes are socially and economically deprived, which is as much a stereotype as thinking of all Negroes as socially and economically inferior.

[BLANCHE: I do feel a pressure. But the problem is the same pressures I'd feel in any racially mixed situation. There's the pressure to live up to what I'm supposed to be. As far as being unprejudiced, I'm really not unprejudiced. None of us are. You can't live in America without being aware of black and white differences, and without having some prejudices.

ERIKA: Well, the white Negro is more prejudiced toward Negroes than the white person.

QUESTION: What is a white Negro?

ERIKA: The white Negro is a Negro who doesn't understand Negroes. They're Negroes who have wealth and who're accepted by white people and then turn around and say, "Well it's not so bad." I think pressures come from the individual. If you believe in something, you're under pressure to live up to it. I think things are changing, also. My father, for example, teaches at the university. There's a new movement among Negroes in college. They feel they've been treated unjustly, and now they want to be treated better, although it might be unjust as well. Let me give you an example. What they say is, "You gave me an 'F' because I'm a Negro." Even if they don't come to class, don't study, don't take the exams, and things like that—that's what I mean by they want to be treated better. But that's unjust, too. They have to learn that they don't deserve special privileges. They've got to learn that they're not all lily white.

AMY: I don't really feel any special demands or pressures.]

One wonders, of course, why, if the "white Negro" is so prejudiced toward Negroes, these young women "only associate with white Negroes," at least "for the most part." Why do they not seek out black persons for whom they have more respect?

The statement that "They've got to learn that they're not all lily white" can have many meanings. One obvious meaning is that Erika rejects the idea that "black rage" should legitimately be translated into blacks expecting special privileges for themselves, or expecting that the rules of conduct in similar situations should be different for blacks and whites.

Pauline seems to be more consistent in her attitude toward blacks. Her points of view tend to be helpful, thoughtful, and one does not have the unsettling experience of being thrown in opposite directions within a very short period of time.

[PAULINE: Well, I talk to Negroes like I talk to white people. I'm not careful about what I say around Negroes. But, I do think that there're demands by the administration of the school. For example, the Negroes were planning to walk out of an assembly and the school got wind of it and called off the assembly. There's pressure from the administration on the kids. There was this one white girl that I know who was dating a Negro. The student counselors called her in. They told the girl to stop dating the Negro boy, who was on the basketball team. They said it wasn't nice for her to be seen with him, and if she didn't stop dating this boy, he wouldn't get a scholarship. It's this kind of pressure, I think, that exists at the school.

AMY: Well, I can be seen with Negroes and nobody ever says anything to me.

QUESTION: Why is it different for you than it is for this girl who was going with the basketball player?

ERIKA: They expect it of Amy and myself and those of us in this room. We've made so much fuss at school over these matters. They know we'll go to the Board of Education if we have to. I've raised a lot of fuss there myself in the past. Last year I had trouble with Miss Rhyder, the algebra teacher, and I took it to the higher ups. Miss Rhyder's a super patriot. This year I had to take a correspondence course rather than go to class, because I knew that I'd have difficulty. Occasionally, they've lowered my class standings. Of course, we turn around and always get it corrected. They've got to learn that they can't fool around with me. But if a Negro's parents went up to school to complain about something, they wouldn't even listen to them. That makes a big difference with us because they do listen to our parents. We don't let them get away with very much. Now, at Commencement, just recently, we had this speaker who was terrific—the office was flooded with complaints, though. They didn't like his talk. Tonight they're having graduation at East Plains High. They're so shook that they wanted the speaker to submit his speech beforehand, but he refused. The kids for the most part liked our Commencement.

AMY: Well, I wouldn't say that. This boy sitting next to me said, "I don't like what he's saying. I don't believe in welfare. I don't want to pay taxes to pay those bums," and things like this. There're all kinds of people at Plains High School. I wouldn't say that all the kids are liberal.]

These students are not afraid to speak up and take action with whatever powers try to control them. In a very real sense, they are "white militants." Unlike the black "militants," however, they know they will be supported by their parents, particularly if they are victims of an illegitimate use of academic or other power. The parents of black "militants" are more likely to believe "Where there's smoke there must be fire."

A brief interchange which concerns itself with the hopefulness or disenchantment that is felt with reference to the Civil Rights Movement takes place between the four young women. Erika is for giving up the effort to integrate, suggesting instead a separatist arrangement. In proposing her solution, Erika expresses the feeling that she has given up hope that any integration effort will work or be worthwhile. Pauline, however, disagrees; she feels that the effort to integrate should continue.

Blanche speaks up and says that she has made some "close Negro friends" at Plains High School, friends whom she respects and who appear more closely to represent the "average Negro."

[ERIKA: Well, I'm disenchanted with the whole Civil Rights Movement in town anyway. All we ever get in these civil rights groups, or out of their activity, is a bunch of laws. Nothing ever happens after the laws are passed. Negroes can't survive unless people change. I think it would be better to have a black and white state. Let the blacks have a separate state.

PAULINE: Well, I disagree. I've talked to many intelligent Negroes and some who're not so well educated. Most of the Negroes I've talked to want more communication between blacks and whites. They don't want to separate into different states.

AMY: Well, in segregated schools, the Negroes are failures from the first grade on up, and in high school it continues. They don't get the vocabulary in order to make it on the I.Q. tests. And that's all those I.Q. tests are, anyway, a test of your vocabulary. So they're put into a lower class in high school. By the time they get out of high school, their education isn't comparable to an eighth grade education. And yet they have a high school diploma. They have all these strikes against them. Of course, they can never get out of it. By the time they get out of high school, the difference between them and white people is great.

ERIKA: The militants would like to put whites on the same basis as they're on. My brother's best friend was recently murdered. He was shot in the face at college. He was considered the local Ghandi. He was loved by everybody. He was shot by a Negro one night and killed senselessly. For what? For no reason at all. Why him, and why not somebody else? There's a big division forming between whites and blacks. It's getting bigger all the time. You see it even at Plains High School. It's reflected everywhere. I'm supposed to be going to college this fall. But, I have my doubts as to whether the school I plan to attend will be standing after this summer.

BLANCHE: I've made some close Negro friends this year in spite of all the trouble that's been going on. These kids at school really hate white people. I've come out of school with a Negro fellow who's seen a white policeman standing there, and the fellow said, "I hate him! I'd like to kill him! I hate that white person!" And I'd say, "But I'm white." But he'd say, "You're different." They hate most whites. I feel a little more at ease with Negroes now. Before, I was afraid of them. I believed that they were different, but they're not really different.]

"Liberal hypocrisy" is severely attacked here. Over and over again in these interviews it is apparent how "liberal" parental talk differs from "liberal" parental action. Often the young people who are interviewed express shock and disappointment that their parents are not as their children had been led to expect, that the parents do not "come through" whenever a racial situation comes down to concrete choice behavior. Still, even the most radical student is not ready to have his own home destroyed. Blanche makes a sophisticated distinction between "understanding" and "accepting" violence.

[ERIKA: Well, this is the first year I've had to accept the fact that I'm white, and that I should expect to be scared, and that my home might be burned, and everything else. It's all phoney. The whites in Civil Rights are phoney. They work in it, but they still say, "I don't want my daughter to date one." And that's a big problem in itself.

BLANCHE: Well, this friend of mine, Fred Trees, is a militant Negro. He gets along beautifully with my mother, but not my father. He doesn't get along too well with my father. He senses this, too. He says that after meeting my father, that my father didn't like him. This is something new for me because my father and mother have always been liberal. Now that Fred has been over to my house a couple of times, my father is acting strange. I guess I'm learning something about him that I didn't know before.

PAULINE: Well, Fred is a violent person. I think it's his violence. Most people wouldn't like him. Maybe this is why,

BLANCHE: No! My father gave a different reaction than I've ever seen before. It's really quite different, and besides, Fred was very well behaved when he was at my house.

ERIKA: Well, the regular white liberals just can't understand violence. I can understand their movement because I'm a violent person myself. I used to applaud burning. I'd say, "Yea, burn some more! Get that building! Burn them all down." Now I don't anymore. All of a sudden I realized how I might feel if I were burned. I also realized for the first time that I'm white, and chances are very good that I'd be burned as well. I can't stand up there and say, "Hey, whoa, man! I'm on your side. I've been helping you all along." It just doesn't work that way. They're going to burn me out, too.

BLANCHE: Well, I think I understand this feeling within Negroes. They seem to feel "If we can't get out, let's burn it down. He's white and that's enough reason to want to kill him." I understand it, but I don't agree with it.

AMY: The Negroes at school have always been underdogs. For example, the Negroes make up the biggest percentage of our teams, and they can't get a Negro cheerleader. They've been trying to get a Negro cheerleader for years, and it's been impossible. Even this year, they weren't able to get a Negro cheerleader.

ERIKA: There was some token progress. Last year there was a Negro king and white queen. That was really something else, too. The administration called up the white parents to ask if it was all right that their daughter stand with the Negro boy who was elected king. You know, as part of the ceremonies, the king kisses the queen. So the administration called up the parents to ask if this was all right. Can you imagine that? As it turned out, the parents said that it was. But what if the parents had said, "No!"? You know they didn't call up the Negro's parents to find out if it was all right if he kissed a white girl. They were just concerned about the white parents.

BLANCHE: I'm in the group that's kind of a therapy class, with a psychiatrist there. It's for alienated Negro kids. In this group you really learn just how impotent the Negro feels. The Negro kids wanted a free lunch hour. They wanted freedom to leave the school. However, they weren't successful in getting this. Mr. Ewing just won't listen, and these kids think, "He's not going to listen to us anyway, so what's the use?"

PAULINE: I'll give you an example of how the administration reacts to things. It was during Dr. King's death. Two weeks before Dr. King died, we learned that a graduate of Plains High School was killed in Vietnam. The school gave two minutes of silence in assembly to honor this student who was killed in Vietnam. When Dr. King died, nothing was planned for him. I went down to Mr. Ewing's office and asked him if we couldn't show some recognition of Dr. King's death. Ewing said to me, "Well, you know, Pauline, people die all the time for all kinds of causes. You can't disrupt the schedule." Then he said, "Unless it's declared a day of mourning, we can't really do anything." Can you imagine? I agree certainly that it's tragic that a boy has to die in Vietnam, and I think it was marvelous that we had two minutes of silence. But I also felt that the school should've done something for Dr. King. After President Johnson declared a day of mourning, at the sixth hour a slip was sent out to all the teachers. The teachers read the slips, and there was thirty seconds of silence. But that was only because President Johnson declared it a national day of mourning. Mr. Ewing wasn't willing to disrupt his schedule, to take the initiative on his own. That's the kind of principal he is.

ERIKA: Well, I think that Negroes shouldn't go to Vietnam. It's preposterous for them to go over there and fight for freedom which they don't even have in this country. We're breeding a revolution in this country, and we don't even know it. We're more worried about revolutions in other countries than we are in our own.

PAULINE: Well, teachers discriminate a little bit, also. There's this teacher from South Carolina. She discriminates. I'll give you an example. There's this girl Patty Bernard. She's a militant Negro girl. She's in this art class with me. This boy tapped her on the shoulder one day. And this teacher said, "Keep your hands off her. Don't let her tempt you. They're all alike."

ERIKA: Most of the time, the teachers aren't quite so blatant because they're afraid of being beaten. If they discriminate outright the Negroes might beat them up. They're afraid of the Negroes. They don't control them at all. They just let them run wild.

AMY: There was an incident, not too long ago, which I witnessed which was kind of unbelievable. This white teacher was shoving this Negro boy through the halls. The boy kept saying, "Don't touch me, don't touch me." And he kept shoving him through the hallway. I think this teacher should've left him alone. There were white people in the hall, and they started following him down the hall. It was kind of sickening to watch this teacher shoving this kid down the hallway, and this boy didn't want to be touched by him. There's one thing about the Negroes, though. If one of them is in trouble, they all rally to his cause. So if one is going to have a fight, you find that there're many Negroes involved in the fight.

BLANCHE: Yes. The Negro group at Plains High is rather tight-knit when it comes to certain things.

AMY: I think the Negro students deliberately separate themselves to some extent.

BLANCHE: I'll tell you of another incident. There was this Negro and white boy who were going to have a fight. The whole school was upset. The word had gotten around. The counselors were very upset. They didn't know what to do. The teachers were upset. Everything was really incredible. Everybody was excited because they knew this might bring about a great deal of trouble. The white boy was a tough boy, and the Negro was also, and everybody was worried that there might be some sort of wide scale racial problem. This boy, Tim Howard, whom a lot of people criticize at school, who's rather outspoken, when all the teachers and counselors couldn't do anything, went up to these boys who were about to fight outside. He just walked right up to them and said, "Cool it, man." And they cooled it. He broke up the fight, when no one else could.

BLANCHE: I'll tell you another incident to indicate to you how concerned the people in the community are. Fred Trees and I did a survey on our block where I live. We went from door to door, and we talked to each of the neighbors. First of all, you should've seen the queer looks they gave us when they saw Fred and me together. We told them what the situation was in Center City. We told them it was going to burn. We asked them, if there were a meeting in our block, if they'd come. This one man said, "Well, if it concerned me, I would, but since it doesn't, I'm not interested."]

Here are some additional, and very negative, views of the school's and community's attitudes about integration. It is important to see how the same facts assume different significance, depending on the interpretations placed on them. For example, while some of the students see the blacks as "running in gangs" and "ganging up on you," the young women who are interviewed here see the Negro group at Plains High as "rather tight-knit" and "all rallying to the cause of another black student in trouble." It is interesting, too, to see how different students, depending on their orientation, interpret certain administrative decisions as reflecting racial prejudice, while it would not occur to other students to place a racial interpretation on the same decision, even though the administration's stand might be highly unpopular (e.g. students being required to stay in school during lunch hour).

[PAULINE: In general the kids in school are friendly, but out of class they usually separate completely. Blacks go one way, and whites go another way.

ERIKA: I've more sympathy for the common Negro than I do for the white Negroes like Nan Brewer. Actually, I think if you just confront them like human beings, that they'll respond to you as human beings. For example, one day I found myself in the basement, and there were a couple of lower class Negro kids talking to each other. I just walked right up to them and asked them for some directions. They were so surprised that I didn't run, that I wasn't afraid of being raped or something like that, and that I'd confront them as human beings. They answered me in a polite way and as human beings without any wise talk.

AMY: I think for the most part you use a little more discretion when you talk with Negroes.

PAULINE: Well, I don't think so. I think I talk the same way with Negroes as I do with white people.

BLANCHE: I think I do, too. Of course, I'm not a tactful person either with Negroes or whites. I say what I want to say. [All agree and say, "Yeah, Blanche, you're a little tactless."]

ERIKA: I agree with Amy. You just don't talk about anything as freely as you want to, when you talk with Negroes. For example, you don't talk sex to a homosexual; there's that kind of discretion. I can ignore whites if I feel like it. If I don't want to talk to a white when he comes up to me, I can just ignore him. But, if a Negro says, "Hello," I try to respond favorably. I have to make concessions.

PAULINE: When I first came here, I had to adjust somewhat because I came here from Amherst, Massachusetts, where there weren't any Negroes. It was a white upper middle class community. It was very literate and cultured. Negroes couldn't get a house there even if they wanted to. Course, there wasn't a working class as such in that community, so there weren't any working class people, white or black. I found it a little bit strange when I came here to Center City and found myself mixing with Negroes. But, I think I've adjusted to it.]

It is particularly noteworthy that, although these girls express profound interest and sympathy for the Negro, we do not get the impression of any real white-black equality as we listen to them. Instead, we feel the same sense of distance noted before—as though all the blacks were a faceless community, a "they" to be discussed and thought about somewhat patronizingly and in the third person. It appears that the young women think of the "plight of the black people" as a "cause." They think and feel about this cause self-consciously, and this self-consciousness, because of its implied virtue and condescension, lacks a feeling of genuine equality.

As these young women discuss the degradation in which Negroes find themselves, they wonder whether segregation is social and economic, rather than purely a racial, problem.

[ERIKA: I think my brother has summed up Center City aptly. He says it's a generally backwoods southern town.

BLANCHE: Another thing about Center City which makes you laugh is that they're always priding themselves in that they don't have a slum. What they mean is that they don't have the rat infested tenement slum houses. In Center City, there are individual houses instead of the tenements. Center Citians say we don't have any slums, but they're blind. As you go down into most parts of the community where these individual houses are falling down, with poor sewage, no toilet facilities and rats galore, then tell me that they don't have any slums.

PAULINE: Last summer I worked for operation Head Start in South Center City. It was really an eye-opener. Kids were dirty, and you'd find mothers with ten kids in a filthy shack; color TV and a big car outside. You ask them to clean up, and they say, "What have I got to clean up for?" This one family I'm thinking about is a white family, so it's not just Negroes.

ERIKA: I want the Negroes to have a separate state, to have self-respect. That's what I want them to have. The only way they're going to get that is to have a separate state and decide things for themselves instead of always being told.]

[QUESTION: Which kids get along better in school, girls or boys—interracially, that is?

AMY: Well, in school the boys get along better. I guess it's through sports. It doesn't last outside, though. The kids on the teams aren't always together when they aren't in school or not engaged in some sport activity, but they do have some contact. This is the Negro's main way to be accepted by whites. Once these kids receive this kind of acceptance and recognition, they're very reluctant to give it up. For example, there's no Negro cheerleader, so we tried to get the Negro basketball team not to play. The whole team is black; but, they wouldn't do it. They wouldn't give it up. They only say, "The problem around this school is partly a social class problem." You do see poor whites running around with the poor Negroes. They don't pay much attention to school work, and they're rough and tough. They're not going to finish school as a rule or do anything with their lives. Also, you see the rich Negroes with the rich whites. I think it's more than that, certainly. But a lot of it is probably due to social class.]

Where and when does prejudice start? To what extent is childhood the breeding time for attitudes which are then maintained into later life? Our young women seek to locate the beginning of "anti-attitudes" and to show how they themselves, as children, either accepted or rejected these.

[AMY: In general, I think the younger kids get along pretty well. It's amazing to me to walk home from school and walk through some of these areas and see some of these little Negroes and whites playing together, without really knowing that there's any difference.

ERIKA: Yeah, it starts in the homes.

PAULINE: Last summer when I worked with pre-schoolers, there was this little boy who liked to hurt people because people always hurt him. It was pitiful to watch him. He was only three or four. There was this teacher who really didn't care about doing the kind of job she was supposed to. She was a good Christian type. She hated it, but it was her duty. Kids'd make themselves throw up just to get attention. This one kid who was really bad, this four year old, one day was acting up. The teacher said to take him into the next room, and I had to take him into the next room. I didn't like to do that. That was her way of punishing these kids, isolating them. So I took him in. And he said, "Take your damned black hands off me." Imagine how pitiful that is! To have a child that young say that. He must have had that said to him a number of times—"Get your black hands off me"—so he said that to me.

BLANCHE: For me it started at school, not so much at home. My parents are white liberals. They weren't really prejudiced. With me it started in grade school with nigger jokes. I didn't know what a Pollack or nigger or moron was. To me they weren't real people. In school we heard jokes about Pollacks, niggers and morons.

PAULINE: Well, when I was three, I would've killed anyone who said "nigger." It even bothers me now to hear Negroes call each other nigger. They do this occasionally at school.

ERIKA: People just don't know what things are about.]

[QUESTION: Is there any violence in the schools?

PAULINE: Well, I was scared of physical education class. There're a lot of rough kids in that class. When I first went into that class, I was terrified. For one thing, they talked casually about knifings and things like that.

ERIKA: Well, I wasn't afraid in physical education class. The Negroes trusted me. I think if they trust you, it's different. Amy and I have met a lot of Black Power people. They tell us just about everything they're going to do—which places they're going to burn and everything. They take us into their confidence. One day the two of us were out talking to some Balck Power people in front of school. Adults going by in cars would make filthy remarks. You can imagine what they think about white women hanging around talking to Negroes. Well, they shout it right out as they drive by. These are the good, upper middle class people in our community, making all kinds of filthy remarks. These Negro boys occasionally would say something like, "Just don't stop your car." I think if any of them *had* stopped, they would've pulverized them.]

[QUESTION: How much integration is there in school activities?

BLANCHE: Of course, we don't attend any of the school activities ourselves. And for the most part, we don't have any Negro friends. First of all, they're not in our classes because they're in shop and the industrial courses. And they don't live in our neighborhoods. Part of this is the school as well. Our school has a beautiful knack for squelching intelligence. Our counselors discourage Negroes from going to school. They don't even tell them what tests are coming up if they want to go to college. The real smart kids suffer.

ERIKA: For example, I took the California tests in the ninth grade, and I did real well. I took it just recently and I dropped considerably. I went to an experimental lab school that teaches you how to think, until I came to Center City.

PAULINE: I was in a lab school as well. My knowledge has decreased, I'd say, since I got here, particularly my vocabulary and math really has gone down. I finally got interested in math through geometry. I used to have some interest in it. However, the teacher at Plains High was a retired football coach, so even my interest in geometry has disappeared. Biology is the same way. The biology teacher, on the first day, had us sit quietly and read the first chapter in class. Every third day we had a test. If you ask a question, you never get an answer. You know that they skipped the chapter on Darwin here? I asked him one day about evolution. He said, "You don't have to read that chapter, because we all know how the earth got here." I said that I didn't and asked him if he would tell me. He said, "God created it." I said that I thought man created God. Boy, you should've seen his look. He didn't talk to me for the rest of the semester. And he gave me a "C."

ERIKA: The only teacher up there who's any good is this Spanish teacher, Thaler. She's fantastic, but she's going to have to leave soon. She's the best teacher they've got there. She doesn't have long for this system.

AMY: In none of the textbooks, literature or otherwise, is there anything mentioned about Negroes. I think that's a shame, because they've helped the development of our country and nothing is said about them in our school. This is the kind of education we receive.

ERIKA: I know a Negro girl who was in my home room. She's going to this dinky college in Georgia because she received a scholarship there. She says, "I won't learn anything there. I'll just go and come back and become a teacher in a Negro school." I know counselors who've told Negro girls that they don't need college prep courses to go to college. I even had to tell this one Negro girl, who's really intelligent, about the college board exams that were coming up. Otherwise she'd have missed them. These are the kinds of things that the counselors do at school. I'll tell you something else. There was this Negro kid at our school who was a National Merit Scholarship finalist. He only got two small scholarships. Can you imagine that? A Merit Scholarship finalist only receiving two scholarships. A lot of times, they'll put smart Negro boys in a lower stream. One time they put this smart Negro boy in the lower stream and his white girlfriend in the higher stream. She went down and complained about it. She said, "If you don't put him up here, I'm going to go into the lower stream. He's as smart as I am." Well, they changed it. When you speak up that way, they'll change things, if you're white.

PAULINE: This is a poor school. I was put in lower stream English because it was the only hour available. I was in upper stream for everything else. English is one of my favorite subjects. It was horrible. The kids could hardly stay awake. Nobody brings a book. I tried to switch classes, but they wouldn't do it. The class was ordering *Reader's Digest*. That's the height of their reading ability.

ERIKA: Well, we're lucky because we come from homes where our parents make up for this lack, but the Negroes' don't. We can teach ourselves, and that's what we end up doing. We teach ourselves. The thing is reading extensively, and the Negroes just don't do it. There's this English teacher, Miss George. She thinks she's very literate; she thinks she knows all the correct symbolism. She tells us what's good and what's bad, what a symbol means and what it doesn't mean. We're never permitted to oppose her or to think for ourselves. She says, "Write down what I tell you or you won't pass."]

As was stated earlier, it is puzzling to learn that these young women do not have black friends. While one has the impression that a good deal of contact exists between them and black students, this contact apparently does not extend to friendship. Again, one seems to meet up with a de facto segregation which separates blacks and whites (even whites that declare their deep dissatisfaction with this situation), on the basis of future plans to attend college.

This group of women students is obviously deeply dissatisfied with the way the educational system is organized in their high school. They are dissatisfied with aspects which other students either do not mention at all or with which they declare their satisfaction. One wonders, however, how much of the dissatisfaction is at least partially a reflection of a more general unhappiness which these young women feel with their lot in life at this time. One has the feeling that they are not simply unhappy with the way the school is run, but that it would be difficult to organize things to their greater satisfaction. They express a general air of gloom, and the racial situation seems only a part of it.

[QUESTION: Where does the least amount of integration take place?

PAULINE: In cheerleading, some of the clubs, and particularly in the cafeteria. You find clusters of all Negroes or all whites. [It is difficult at this point to keep the young women on the topic. They have started to argue with each other and to tell each other stories about various things. When one is talking, the others are not content to listen, but want to talk as well. They are asked about violence at school again.]

PAULINE: Well, last year this Negro boy was after my brother; this Negro boy sang temporarily in the band until the regular singer came back. Then he was kicked out. He held my brother responsible for it. One day in the hallway, he said to my brother, "Shake hands." My brother put out his hand, and he hit him with his left. This kind of thing happens occasionally.

BLANCHE: This white boy and I were walking home and these Negroes were in this car nearby. They said, "Hey, you got a cigarette?" and he said, "No." They followed us. Five of them circled us and said, "Did you say 'hell no'? We detected a note of disrespect." Before we knew what happened, this boy was hit from behind. They only hit him a couple of times, and then they left. I was furious. I started yelling at them, but it did no good. This boy who generally appears to be liberal started yelling, "I hate those God damned niggers."

ERIKA: Negroes are like children and animals. They can sense who their friends are. They come up to me, and I never have any problem. They can spot me. They somehow know I'm their friend. I think that makes the difference. They never bother you, if they sense you're their friend.]

While Erika does not mean her explanation in a derogatory manner, it nevertheless sounds strange and condescending to hear her say that Negroes are "like children and animals." In the past, one has so often heard more or less prejudiced whites speak of Negroes as "children." Thus, even among such apparently pro-black persons, as in this group of students, implicit anti-black attitudes are evident.

[BLANCHE: Well, Negro girls are not friendly with me. But I'd say that I get along better with boys, anyway. I just don't seem to get along too well with girls.

PAULINE: When they're with me, I just don't act differently, so they don't. I think we get along pretty well.

ERIKA: A lot of it is sex. There's this sex jealousy between the races. Particularly the Negro girls are jealous of the white girls. This creates a lot of hostility between white girls and Negro girls.

AMY: There's this white girl from a very bigoted family. She's reacting against her family because she never goes out with white boys. She only goes out with Negro boys.]

[QUESTION: Does the white girl who dates Negro boys also date white boys?

PAULINE: If a white girl dates a Negro boy, white boys won't date her. A white girl also loses her friends when she's dated by a Negro. White boys say they won't take her out because she dates Negroes. I know this Negro boy who likes this white girl, and she likes him, too, but he won't attempt to date her because he knows what will happen to her. He's a senior and about to graduate. She's a junior and will be a senior next year. He said if he started dating her now, that next year when she's a senior, she won't get to go to any of the activities because they won't date her, and he doesn't want her to suffer that way. It wouldn't make any difference to me, because my friends wouldn't care if I date a Negro. But most of the kids do care. It makes a difference.

ERIKA: It's all part of the complex dating system. I think the big wheels in school are the most immoral of all. Yet, if a white girl dates a Negro, this is what they think of. They think that you're immoral. It's the big wheels that do the immoral things. If a white boy dates a Negro, it's okay, but if a white girl dates a Negro, they call her trash.]

The accusation of immorality, probably meaning "sexual immorality," is used as a weapon to maintain the status quo. Any young woman who seriously attempts to change the integration-segregation pattern, is accused of being "immoral"; it takes immense strength to deal with such a potential accusation. Adolescence is a time when "popularity" is of particular importance, so that an adolescent white female must be willing to undertake a major risk to her reputation if she is to date a black.

CHAPTER 6

The Peaceniks

While the Peaceniks say they fully accept the Negro as equal, it is obvious that Civil Rights is not their battle. They declare themselves against prejudice, yet they feel the battle against racial injustice is not nearly so important as the battle against war. The Peaceniks feel Civil Rights is secondary to peace in Vietnam, so that they appear to have an attitude of "live and let live"—nothing more active—toward blacks. The rejection of middle-class values also creates a dilemma for the Peaceniks, so that toward the end of their interview, they say, "Why help the Negro attain the very things [e.g. a car, a home in suburbia, good clothes] that we consider to be the trouble with American society?"

George was graduated recently from Plains High; Harry and Charlie still attend.

[QUESTION: What pressures do you feel from the fact that you attend a desegregated school?

GEORGE: Most of the pressures I felt were in the area of grades. Grades have always been a big thing with me. As far as race goes, I didn't really feel that much pressure. I think because I don't associate with that many black kids.

QUESTION: Why didn't you associate with black kids?

GEORGE: Well, mainly because they weren't in my crowd. I never got to know that many black kids. I don't think that we do many things in common. I guess there're some things that we've in common, but we've never done them together. I think when I was in junior high and elementary school, we did mix a little more. I think we had more in common. But when I got in high school, my interests changed, and there weren't many black kids with the same interests.

CHARLIE: Well, I haven't been paying too much attention to any changes from junior high to high school. I think I've gotten along with black people, those that I know; but, I haven't associated much with black people. I think some black people are easy to get along with and nice to socialize with. I get along with them, but I don't pay too much attention to the other kind of Negro.]

116

Comments such as "some black people are easy to get along with ... but I don't pay too much attention to the other kind of Negro" reflect the Peaceniks' lack of involvement in racial matters. The comment also reflects the easy dismissal of the entire question of race relations, and the lack of motivation to work for improvements in the area. Being a Peacenik is certainly not synonomous with actively working for equality between the races.

[QUESTION: Do you ever watch what you say in front of Negroes?

CHARLIE: I was never too worried about what I said. I've worked with Negroes at different jobs. On those jobs, I was friendly with Negroes. I never had trouble talking with them. But I found that they were reluctant to talk to me, particularly about race. I'd say that Negroes don't bother me too much.

HARRY: Well, I went to grade and junior high school in South Center City—there were always Negroes. I think I got along well with the Negroes in junior high and grade school, and I think I've gotten along well with them in high school. I think I became more aware of civil rights, though, in high school, and once I gained this awareness, I became more aware of what I said. I really wasn't inhibited in talking to Negroes, but I think I watched what I said more carefully so as not to offend anybody.

QUESTION: Do you discuss race in school?

GEORGE: Well, in Current Events class we talked about the race problem. There was one Mexican girl in there and one Negro boy. Sometimes the discussion would get carried over from class to the lunchroom, and we'd discuss race informally as well. I don't think, though, in all the times that I discussed race at school that I had to weigh my words. But there were times in the lunchroom, for example, when some race joke would be told, and before telling it, the boy would look over his shoulder and all around before saying the word "nigger." That's the only thing I can remember happening where people would be careful about what words they used.

HARRY: I know sometimes at school we'd rib the Negro boys about Black Power. Usually it's someone you know real well. There's this Negro boy who's a Black Power advocate that I know real well from class, and I'd tease him about Black Power.

GEORGE: Well, there's one kid I know who's really militant, and I think he'd probably blow up if you ever said anything about Black Power.]

When asked about Black Power, the current group of students did not respond as many of their fellow students have. They do not speak of Black Power as something to be feared. Perhaps this is because of their realistic understanding of Black Power as nothing more or less than economic and political power. In our interviews, we often found that Black Power was distorted into a wild picture of rioting and burning.

[QUESTION: What's your conception of Black Power?

HARRY: Well, let's see, the first time I heard it was in a discussion in Current Events. The way the speaker talked about it, it was economic power and not so much burning power, although he said it might get to that. If the Negro didn't obtain economic and political power in the community, he might just burn the communities. But, in general, I get the idea that Black Power is the same kind of power that white people have.

GEORGE: I'd agree with what Harry said. I think Black Power is just power in general—economic and political power—power to own your own home, get the kind of job you want and send your kids to school. It's not just militancy and burning.

CHARLIE: Well, I never really thought about Black Power myself. In fact, I hate to judge people as a group anyway. I try to judge people as individuals. I don't like to deal with people as groups, so I don't like to think of black people or white people. There're people I like and people I don't like.]

Next follows a good deal of serious soul-searching, and the discovery by these young men that their feelings are not always the ones of which the liberal community approves. Yet, this kind of introspection is more likely to bring about a profound and lasting change in the direction of serious improvement in race attitudes than is the easy and wholesale denial of all prejudice. We must be willing to look at an unpleasant issue if we are going to deal with it.

[HARRY: There's something that worries me about my own thoughts and feelings. For example, if you visited Plains High School, the first thing you'd notice is that it's very loud and the noise comes from the colored people. I know a lot of people say that they don't want to go to Plains High School because of all the Negroes. Well, I think that the colored people are loud and boisterous at Plains High School, and I'm worried about my own thoughts. I wonder, are all the colored people like this? Or is this just a teenage stage? This image I have of a group of loud, rude colored kids at Plains High School—I don't really want to think these thoughts about Negroes. That's what bothers me. I really hope deep down that it's just a few of them, and not something which is typical of Negroes.

GEORGE: Well, there's a lot of noise at Plains High, but it's white kids that make some of the noise, too. What Charlie said about groups comes into my mind. Because everytime I think of Negroes, I can't really think of individual Negroes. When I think of Negroes, this group image comes into my mind, of people who think alike and talk alike. I really think of Negroes as a group. I hate to admit that, but I do. Maybe they're just like us, though, with parents who disapprove of them like ours do. And maybe they're just like us in many other ways. But I find it hard to think of Negroes as individuals.

CHARLIE: Well, the more I think about it, as much as I hate to admit it, I do have some stereotyped ideas about Negroes. But usually these stereotyped notions fall away when I start to talk to an individual and get to know him.

GEORGE: I don't know that many Negroes. Something happened to me in my sophomore year which may have influenced me and which may explain why I haven't met that many Negroes. Three buddies and myself were jumped one afternoon, while going home, by five or six Negroes, and we were beaten up. I don't know whether that influenced me or not in my relationships with Negroes.

QUESTION: Were you jumped for any particular reason?

GEORGE: No. We were jumped because they wanted someone to beat up. I know I was a little bit afraid of them after that, and I really didn't care to go out and deliberately meet a Negro.]

Ironically, the Peaceniks reflect more of an atmosphere of violence than many other groups. It is difficult to know whether this phenomenon is the result of the Peaceniks' mixing with different fellow students, whether Peaceniks have less need to deny violence that is around them, or whether they are more sensitive to violence.

[QUESTION: Is there much violence of this sort at Plains High?

GEORGE: Well, I only know of one other case in which some whites were jumped by some Negroes. But this actually happened at a drive-in last summer. In fact, it was almost a race riot. The police were there to stop it. Whites were lined up at one part of the drive-in and Negroes at the other part, and they were going to fight each other.

HARRY: Well, I can assure you that if I was provoked into a fight by a Negro, I'd hesitate to hit a Negro kid because I know he has friends, and they stick together. I think that if I hit him, I'd also have to fight his other friends.

GEORGE: Well, I've heard this said often. If you fight one, you have to fight them all.

HARRY: I've this fear of a big mob of black kids who'd be after me. If I hit one, I'd be thinking of all the kids who'd be after me, and I'd have to fight them, too. But this is also true of the white kids, because they do this. They gang up on others. It's true of the trashy white kids, but when I think of this ganging up on others, I usually think of Negroes. I guess because they're easier to indentify.

CHARLIE: In answer to your question on violence, in study hall this year, I noticed a couple of Negro kids playing with switchblades. They'd take them out of their pockets and flick them open. They'd walk over and talk to certain kids, and they'd flip open their knives and act big. I know when I saw this, I wondered how many Negroes have them. Also during the last week of school, a group of colored kids were standing around in the hallway, and one called me over. So I went over there, and he grabbed me by the neck and threw me in the middle of the circle. He tried to knock me down. I suppose their intention was to knock me down, and then they'd play kickball with me. But he wasn't successful. I just smiled at him and said, "See you later, man" and walked away. I wasn't really angry with these Negro kids when they did that, though, because I thought it could've been white kids. There'd been a lot of talk around school, by the Negroes, about getting fights started in the last week. So I really didn't think of it as anything personal. I just happened to be around, so I happened to be the white guy who was picked on. In general, though, I wouldn't hold this against the Negroes. I know some nice Negroes, and I know some not-so-nice Negroes, the same as white people. I know quite a few Negroes who're responsible people—ministers and policemen—the same as white people. I think there're bad white people, and there're bad Negroes. Also, there're good white people and good Negroes. So I can't condemn the whole race of people, because of what a few may do.

QUESTION: What about the girls? Do they fight as well?

CHARLIE: There're more fights among girls than between boys, but mostly the fights are between Negro girls. You don't see too many fights between white girls or between a Negro and white girl. I think the white girls avoid fights, while the Negro girls tend to fight more. They get pretty wild when they fight. Some of the teachers are even afraid to break it up. Even if there're three or four teachers around, they hesitate to break it up because these girls are pretty wild. One reason is that when colored girls fight, there're a lot of colored kids standing around in a circle who're watching. If the teachers try to interfere, these kids might jump them.

QUESTION: Do you think the teachers generally are afraid at Plains High School?

CHARLIE: I wouldn't say that they're really afraid. I think they're a little more cautious. They're cautious because they think something could happen. I'm not sure whether this means that they're really afraid.

QUESTION: Do the teachers treat kids from the two races differently?

CHARLIE: Well, some teachers are harder on Negroes, and some are easier on Negroes, just because they're Negroes. There're some people who're so conscious about the Negro getting a fair shake that they're overly easy. I think this is true of a number of teachers. On the other hand, there're some teachers who discriminate against the Negro. On the whole, though, I'd say that I think the Negroes at Plains High get away with a lot more than the white people.

GEORGE: I really can't answer that question because I only had two classes with colored kids, and there weren't but two colored kids in these classes. They were from the upper class. They were real studious, and not cutups.

CHARLIE: This is true for me, too. Most of the colored kids I had experience with in class were responsible ones. They were interested in education, not just in fooling around. I never really got to know the kids who were interested in goofing off. The ones I've known were the most conscientious ones.]

These young men point out one dilemma which all teachers in a desegregated school may get themselves into. By leaning over backwards in order to appear nonracist, the teacher may inadvertantly engage in a sort of reverse discrimination, but a discrimination nonetheless. Other teachers, the Peaceniks point out, make discriminatory attitudes directly evident.

While George tends to dismiss the lack of Negroes in the college preparatory classes without much concern, Harry thinks there may be some cause other than simply a lack of black motivation to want to go farther in school. One does not know whether these young men have given the question of black people's education much thought until now (George says he never did), but in the interview all three students begin to recognize factors to which they had been blind until now.

[QUESTION: Do you think it's strange that so few Negroes have been in your college prep classes?

GEORGE: I never gave it too much thought. I think the reason why they're not in these classes, though, is because most of them just don't plan to go to college.

HARRY: I wonder about that. I wonder if it isn't just a lack of opportunity in this town. I wonder if the schools, for example the grade schools, are guilty of failing to prepare them to get into college prep courses when they're in high school. I wonder if they aren't inadvertently prepared, and this is why they're not in these courses. Or I wonder if it isn't because their parents don't have good jobs and so don't have the money to send them to college. I think some of these other things are involved. I don't think it's just because they don't want to go to college.

QUESTION: What about the counselors? Do they give the kids a fair shake?

GEORGE: Well, I'm not sure how they react towards Negroes, because I've never seen them. I've never really talked to any Negroes about this. But I know in my case, the counselors have been more than fair. In my senior year, I got away with altogether too much. Mr. Frank was my counselor, and he was too lenient. I flunked five classes out of eleven. I'd have about twenty absences per semester, just skipping out because I didn't care. I should've been thrown out of school according to the blue book. The rules said I should've been kicked out, but they never kicked me out. I overheard Mr. Benefield one time give this kid hell. He pulled out this kid's record and just read the riot act to him. So I know that they're not this lenient with all kids. I often wondered why I got away with so much.

CHARLIE: Well, I've wondered this, too. I did the same things as George, except I didn't flunk. But in my case, a lot of the teachers didn't say anything about my being late or being absent, or things like this, so it wasn't brought to the attention of the counselors. It made me feel kind of good that the teachers didn't do this, because I've sat there and seen some other kid walk in late, and the teacher would send him down to the office for an excuse slip. I'd come in late, and the teacher wouldn't say a thing.

GEORGE: I think one of the reasons why we get away with this is because we live in an apartment of our own, and the teachers know this. So they make excuses for us. You know, when you live in an apartment and the alarm clock rings, you just turn it off and go to sleep. You don't have a mother there to get you up. I even told my counselor once that one of the reasons why I was skipping so many classes was because I was bored. I also told him that I don't have a mother to push me out of the house when the alarm rings. A lot of times, I'd just go down to the counselor and shoot the bull with him. I got to know him real well. I also made some points by going down and shooting the bull with him. I played on his sympathy by telling him that I don't have a mother to kick me out of the house in the morning.

CHARLIE: Mr. Frank, the counselor, and I got to be good friends. I've even been over to his house, so I think this is one reason why they treat us differently.

HARRY: Well, I don't break too many rules, or I didn't break too many rules. I did skip out every day at lunchtime. I was a proctor for the French teacher. There was this door proctor who was supposed to be there to keep the kids in school during the lunch hour. He and I used to go out together. One day we got caught coming back. They were really mad, but they were more mad at him because he was the door proctor. They never called my parents to tell them that, when they were supposed to.

GEORGE: These are all examples of how easy they've been on us. I don't know what they'd be like with black kids, but I'd say on us they've been easy.]

As were the teachers, the counselors tend to be seen as benevolent, helpful and friendly by this group of Peaceniks. These students are more concerned about the counselors' attitudes toward them (toward their latenesses and toward their cutting of classes) than about the counselors' attitudes towards Negroes. In this respect, they are altogether different from the hippies of the previous chapter.

A discussion of discrimination fuses into a discussion of white and black dating. Discrimination, as these young men see it, applies primarily to their fellow students, rather than to adults. The Peaceniks see discrimination as a subtle phenomenon, involving a lack of "togetherness," rather than an active act of rejection. While these young men display considerable courage and depart considerably from the values and preoccupations of most students at Plains High School, interracial dating requires courage of such an extraordinary degree, particularly when dating involves a white male and a black female that they, too, have been reluctant to date black students. The kind of courage, which requires going against explicit and implicit values of friends and associates, is more than most students are able and willing to bring to the dating situation.

[QUESTION: Have you ever seen any acts of discrimination in school?

GEORGE: You mean on the part of the teachers, the students, or both?

INTERVIEWER; Yes.

GEORGE: Well, I've never seen any open discrimination. But I think it exists, because you never see much socializing between Negroes and whites. The only Negro I've ever seen socializing with white people—in fact, every time I've seen him he's been with white people—is Charles Baldwin. I think he's always been accepted by white people, but this isn't true with the rest of the Negroes. You don't see them mixing with the whites very much.

HARRY: You never see it much after school, either. Of course, I've never socialized much until this past year, until I got involved with the Peace Movement. I think I'd like to socialize with more Negroes, but the opportunity was never there.

CHARLIE: Well, I've worked with two Negroes after school, and I found it easy to get along with them. We'd go out together occasionally, play pool and have a beer. I never thought too much about it. One time when I was messing around with some colored friends, some friends of this colored friend came by and invited me to go to an all-Negro party. I didn't especially like that idea because I didn't know what the other guys would be like. So I told them I didn't want to go especially. And I told them why. We sat and talked for a while. They asked me what I thought about black people, and things like that. We talked freely. I think if you get to know certain Negroes, you can talk that way, and you can have intelligent discussions.

HARRY: Most of the socializing I've done in school is with this Negro girl. I'm in music, and we were in the operetta together this year. You know, between rehearsals, a lot of the times you're not on stage, so you sit around in the auditorium. I'd always sit with her and talk to her. I even considered dating her. I don't know why I never really asked her. I guess I'm all hung up on this idea of dating anyway. I'm afraid if I ask someone, I'll be refused. With a Negro, there're other hang ups. I wouldn't know where to ask her to go. So aside from fear of being rejected, I wouldn't know where to go, because people would stare at us and make us uncomfortable. I've kind of tested out the idea with my own brother. I was shocked by his reaction. He said, "If you're going to do that, I don't want to be your brother—if you're going to date a Negro girl." I know if I did this, that some members of my family would never speak to me again. If I ever married a Negro, my family would be very upset. I don't know how upset my parents would be, but I know my brother and grandmother would be upset.

CHARLIE: I think if you dated a Negro, what would happen is that you'd lose a lot of your so-called white friends, and probably gain some Negro friends. I also contemplated asking this Negro girl for a date, but I chickened out. I thought, where would I take her? The only place where I could take her—where people wouldn't stare at me—would be at a drive-in movie, and I don't have a car. If you went to a restaurant, you'd get dirty looks from people. I couldn't take her home and introduce her to my mom. She'd probably kill me. So I decided it wasn't worth it and chickened out.

GEORGE: Well, I think if I took out a Negro girl, I don't think my folks would give me too much trouble. But that's because my dad's decided that I'm just not worth it anyway. My mother is more liberal about my ideas concerning peace and school. I don't think she'd give me as much trouble.]

The Peaceniks feel that prejudice is directed against them, too. They feel, however, that Negroes, by and large, are less prejudiced toward them than whites are. Although the Peaceniks are negatively aroused by the school administration's views regarding interracial dating, one has the feeling they are warm, rather than hot, under the collar about the matter.

[QUESTION: Charlie, you said earlier that you think you'd lose some white friends and pick up some Negro friends if you dated a Negro. By this, do you mean that Negroes are more accepting of interracial dating?

CHARLIE: Definitely. I think that Negroes are definitely more accepting of interracial dating than white people. There're some Negroes who certainly don't like it, but, on the whole, I think that the Negroes are more accepting of integration. I also think that they think it's more important to further relations between whites and blacks, so they'd accept interracial dating more than whites. I think the majority of white people would think it disgusting.

GEORGE: I think the Negroes are more tolerant, even more tolerant than most of the friends I've met since I left home, such as the Hippies, Peaceniks and Radicals. I still think the Negroes seem more tolerant. At school, there's a different type of discrimination that you don't talk about often, discrimination against kids like ourselves. I've got the reputation of being a local Communist because of my feelings on Vietnam. In Current Events, the teacher, who's a gung-ho ex-army officer, discriminated against my point of view. One time in class when we were discussing Vietnam after Johnson said he wouldn't be a candidate, everybody tried to overwhelm me because they were against my point of view. Every time I said anything, I was overwhelmed. Near the end of class, I raised my hand one last time. I said,

"Mr. Reynolds, I'd like to make one more point." He said, "Well, you can say something, but you haven't made any points yet." Everybody laughed. Also, in that class, there were little jokes about drugs, Hippies and Peaceniks. And there's this kid who always calls me a Communist. I surprised him by calling him a Fascist. He just can't believe that anybody could feel that the war in Vietnam is wrong. He thinks because the government said it's good for us to be in Vietnam, that nobody should go against the government and if you do, you're a Communist.

QUESTION: Is there any interracial dating in high school?

HARRY: Well, there was this white girl who was in my home room, who was dating this colored boy. I heard she was called in by the administration and told to cool it. I'm not sure if this really happened, but that's what I heard. If it did happen, this really makes me mad.

CHARLIE: Well, I know of three or four colored fellows who're dating white girls. Personally, I never thought much about it. It's their business if they want to date each other. I can't think of one case where a white fellow I know has dated a Negro girl. I think that's because, in our society, it's the boy who asks the girl out, so if you're seen out, everybody would know that you instigated it. People would really look down on you.

HARRY: If I ever do decide to date this colored girl, I was telling you about, if people didn't like it, I'd say, "Damn you, it's none of your business. If I want to date someone, you have no right to interfere with my life."

QUESTION: How do the students act toward the couples who are interracially dating?

CHARLIE: Well, I don't know how many students are even aware of it. So I don't know how anybody else reacted toward it or what they said about it.]

[Authors' note: None of the other young men had had too much contact, either, with their fellow students, so they did not know how interracial dating was received as an issue among their peers.]

George indicates that "most Negroes seem to be more interested in Black Power and their own problems at school." He does not seem to sympathize with this position and, at the same time, he seems hardly aware of his own impatience with concerns other than those of discontinuing the war in Vietnam. He feels that blacks ought to be as interested as he is in ending the war, and he finds himself impatient with Negroes who focus their attention only on black issues.

[QUESTION: Just how integrated is Plains High School?

GEORGE: Well, it's integrated six hours a day in the classroom. But out of class, I'd say there's a split between the two groups. Negroes and whites don't mix much.

CHARLIE: Well, I haven't found it exactly like that. Because occasionally, for example, I'll stop and chat with a Negro I know or say "Hi." I've been to two or three different parties where there've been a couple of Negroes. They fit in real well at these parties. They act just like anyone else at the party, except, for the most part, the Negro kids at these white parties are a little more friendly than the other kids. Sometimes I think they get along with the white girls too well, and sometimes the white boys get pretty up tight about it. And there might be some fights.

HARRY: Well, I don't do much socializing with Negroes, or anyone else for that matter. I think that's because we don't have many common interests. Right now I'm taken up with the peace movement and working for McCarthy. They don't seem to have the same interests, so we don't meet. I'd like to meet some Negroes, but they're not interested in peace or McCarthy.

GEORGE: Most of the Negroes seem to be more interested in Black Power and their own problems at school. They don't have as much interest as we do in Vietnam. I don't know why there isn't as much interest on their part in Vietnam, because they have to face it as well. Also, the Negroes I've come into contact with aren't as interested in the candidates and in politics. They're more interested in militancy and riots. After Dr. King died, I was really surprised. I was at the grocery store, and these five-year-old kids came up to me and said, "We're going to get you and get your house, too."

CHARLIE: I always thought that Negroes would be more interested in the peace movement than the white man, because, as Martin Luther King said, "It's the white man's war. Black people should be more interested in ending the war." Martin Luther King said that black people should refuse to serve. If Negroes would stop and realize it's against their best interests to fight in Vietnam, maybe they'd join the peace movement. But their interest is in getting a new house and getting a new car and sharp clothes.

GEORGE: Well, the peace movement is not too compatible with Black Power. Black Power is militant. The peace movement is for peace. In fact, I've even heard some Black Power kids say that they want to go to Vietnam to get the experience to come back to this country so they can use it. I think it's the militancy in the black movement which is keeping them from getting involved and interested in the peace movement.

QUESTION: How did the students react when Dr. King was killed?

CHARLIE: Well, a lot of the militants really got up tight about King's death. A lot of the other Negroes who knew what King stood for were really shocked. I think, though, a lot of the militants thought this was an excuse to burn. They're not concerned with King as a person. But they were looking for some excuse to riot and burn. As far as I'm concerned, I don't care whether a person is white or black. I don't make divisions on whether people are white or black. Whether or not I like a person depends on whether or not he's tolerant of my beliefs.]

These Peaceniks divide white students into liberals and conservatives. This division, somewhat different from that of other students, is probably based on the Peaceniks' concern with their own political preferences. While Peaceniks are highly liberal in some respects, they are not so liberal in others. So, for instance, while there is a wish to think of individuals as individuals, rather than as members of groups, George finds himself thinking of all Negroes as belonging to a single group of the loud and boisterous. Being an individual, he feels, tends not to be so characteristic of the Negro.

[QUESTION: How many different classes of kids are there at school?

CHARLIE: I don't like to type kids into classes, but if I have to, I'd say there're the tolerant, liberal minded white kids, who come mainly from the middle class—the same environment I come from. Then there're the conservative kids. They're mostly white. They're in school offices, presidents of clubs, interested in football and sports, interested in where you buy your shirts, worried about whether they have a new GTO and things like that. I'd say there're two kinds of white kids, the liberals and the conservatives.

GEORGE: I hate to be too harsh on the conservatives because until my junior year, I was just like them. I worried about where I bought my clothes and cars and things like that.

QUESTION: Where do you find these liberal kids?

GEORGE: I can only think of one place in which I've met a lot of them, and that was in my Spanish class. The kids were more tolerant in Mrs. Thaler's class. We argued about a lot of things, but we never called each other names.

QUESTION: How many classes of Negroes are there?

GEORGE: I don't know, because when I think of Negroes, I think of a group. I think of all Negro kids as loud and boisterous.

CHARLIE: I think of two classes of blacks; one, the loud and boisterous type and, the other, the individuals. They may not think like I do, but they're quiet and studious. As far as whites, there're the liberals and conservatives as we said earlier. The conservatives are the Sing-Out types.

GEORGE: My Spanish teacher, Mrs. Thaler, has something to say about the Sing-Out types. She said they remind her of Hitler's Youth.

HARRY: I'm ashamed to say this, but up until last year, I used to say "Fight Communism in Vietnam, rather than in California." When I think of it now, I'm so embarrassed. I still dress straight, as you can see, and my hair isn't too long, but my parents last night, for example, were yelling at me to get a haircut.]

The Peacenik's discussion of the administration and teachers reflects their more differentiated, more thoughtful attitude. Things are neither all one way nor all the other. While they consider teachers as primarily conservative, they also mention three who are liberals, and one who seemed to be liberal but turned out not to be.

[QUESTION: What is the administration like?

HARRY: Well, I know the principal real well through Student Government. I know last year we tried to get a bill passed to enable that liberal doctor from one of the clinics to come speak to us. Mr. Ewing said it was all right for someone as radical as him to talk to a small number of students if they were interested, but not to the whole student body. He said, "Form a club and have him come speak to you." From that experience, you'd think he was ultraconservative. Sometimes I think he's ultraconservative, but sometimes I also think he's a liberal. I know we had a survey at school in which they wanted to know what percent of kids were in the different racial groups. In Mrs. DeWitt's class, we spoke out against this. I opposed it. I didn't think it was right. She told me Mr. Ewing had opposed it, too, but the Board of Education forced him to conduct this survey. She said that he didn't want to do it. He's a funny person. Sometimes he's so conservative and other times, he can be a liberal. At graduation, when we had Mrs. Winget talk to us, Mr. Ewing was impressed with her. I was in his office a couple of days after, and he talked to her over the telephone. He really enjoyed her talk. Some of the teachers and a lot of the kids didn't. To say nothing of the school board—they were very upset with her talk. But Mr. Ewing wasn't. Personally, when I read that Mrs. Winget was going to come talk to us on protests, I thought she was going to say things like "Be good," and "Obey your parents," and other platitudes. But she didn't. I was surprised at what she said. When I was talking to Mr. Ewing later, he said he thought it was a very good talk.

GEORGE: I kind of thought she was going to say those kinds of things, too, and not really talk about protests. She really surprised me in what she said. Dr. Willis, one of the assistant principals, made me mad after her talk, because he got up and said something like, "It's all right to get involved in protests, but watch out for those nuts and radicals." Then he gave a hippy definition. He said, "A hippy is like Tarzan, who has hair like Jane and smells like Cheeta." The whole audience laughed.

QUESTION: Where do most of the teachers fit politically?

GEORGE: Most of them are conservative. I can only think of three liberal teachers, Mrs. Thaler, Mrs. Dufree and Mrs. DeWitt. It's funny they're all women.

HARRY: We did have another liberal teacher, Mr. Evers, our French teacher. We discussed the draft a lot in French, and we discussed draft dodging, leaving the country, and things like that. He kind of went along with us in these discussions. Then it was a funny thing, he had a change of heart.

He was drafted. We asked him what he was going to do. He said that he was going to serve his country. This kind of changed our ideas about Mr. Evers.

QUESTION: Where do you find the most integration in school?

GEORGE: In sports.

QUESTION: What about clubs?

HARRY: Well, there aren't many Negroes in clubs. The Math Club has one Negro in it. In the Rush Club, there's one colored boy. There're a few Negroes in government, but not many.

QUESTION: How about the least integration?

GEORGE: In the cafeteria and in social contacts. You generally find the black people at one table, and the whites at another. This is also true of before school and after school. Whites hang around together; blacks hang around together. There're a few that hang around together in the halls, but not many.

CHARLIE: I think the Mexicans and Negroes get along quite well. You see them together more than you'd see Negroes and whites or Mexicans and whites. I don't think white kids especially want to get to know the Negroes or the Mexicans. They may say hello to one or two that they consider exceptional, but they have to meet their standards.

GEORGE: There's this one white guy I know who lives in a classy neighborhood in the Eastern part of town. He's pretty liberal in most of his ideas, and one day he was saying that he didn't want any niggers moving out into his part of town or his neighborhood. I was surprised because he was tolerant in other areas. I was really surprised. I think you'll find a lot of white kids who think the same way at school.]

[QUESTION: What's it like between the generations on this issue?

CHARLIE: Well, for the last two or three years when I was living at home, we've live in an integrated neighborhood. When some Negroes moved into our block, my mother wanted to sell our house. She got up tight about it when the first Negro moved into our block. Within a short time, five or six families moved into the neighborhood. She's gotten used to the idea now, but they're all conscientious types. They're ministers, two policemen and two families that work at the State institutions. They're these kinds of Negroes. I've never had any trouble with them. My mother didn't like the idea at first. I'd say she's less tolerant than I am in this area. Grandmother is even less tolerant.

HARRY: Well, this disturbs me. I used to think my parents were pretty liberal. We lived in Winton. After the tornado, we wanted to sell our house. There weren't any Negroes in our neighborhood. We lived in a white neighborhood. I remember when the real estate woman called up. She said she got a call from someone who "sounded like a nigger." She said, "Should I show them the house or tell them it's already taken?" My mother said, "Well,

I guess we shouldn't ask for any trouble. Let's just tell them it's already taken." This has bothered me ever since 'cause I always thought my parents were liberal. But they really aren't. They didn't want any trouble because the next door neighbor said, "If you sell to a nigger, I'm going to sell, too." My grandmother is even worse than my parents. One time I was staying over there, because my parents were out of town. She saw this picture in the paper of a white man who married a Negro. My grandmother carried on about this. She said, "It's shameful. It's disgusting." I think a lot of people feel this way. They think it's all right to associate with Negroes, but don't marry them. It's out of the question. You find this a lot in people who're the same age as my parents or my grandmother.

CHARLIE: My mother told me about a girl from her church, who was respected but went ahead and married a Negro. She was upset about this, and told me she never wanted me to have anything to do with Negroes. She said it's disgusting. That kind of burned me a bit, but I didn't want to argue with her, so I didn't say anything about it.

GEORGE: Well, as I said before, I don't think anything I'd do would please my father. As far as race goes, I've never heard either my mother or my father express any opinion. I know we live in a neighborhood which is sharply divided. There aren't any blacks where my parents live. They live in the blocks away from us. As far as the generation gap is concerned, though, I think there's a big gap between my parents and myself on issues such as Vietnam, drugs, homosexuality and the race issue, although we never talk about it. We never really talk to each other. Even my brother, who's ten years older than I am, is an entrenched conservative. He's a veteran, lives in an expensive apartment, drives a Cadillac and thinks that Washington knows all.]

This group of students tends to give the present day socially approved view of school integration, although they present the view in a rather low key. George poignantly presents the dilemma of the Peacenik: he thinks of himself as a radical and feels that the radical rejects some of the very things for which the Negro is striving (e.g., a house in suburbia and a big car). For that reason, he feels he cannot be of much help to the Negro.

[QUESTION: What do you think going to Plains High has taught you about race relations?

CHARLIE: Well, I'm glad I went to Plains High. I think it helps you to be tolerant of other people's race and other people's beliefs. If you fight it, you're not going to be tolerant. But if you'll allow it to go, being in contact with so many different people, you learn to be tolerant. You learn to get along with Negroes, whites and Mexicans. I think if I'd gone to some other high school like East Plains, I'd probably still have my sterotyped ideas.

GEORGE: I don't know. I think it still would've been the same if I'd gone to any other school. There just isn't that much mixing. I learned about tolerance when I moved out of the house and started associating with white radicals. But I really haven't learned that much about races because I haven't had much contact with blacks. I think the black people have legitimate reasons for rioting. I don't think riots are right, but I think their reasons are legitimate. I also don't think you can legislate civil rights. It has to be an attitude that has to be changed. I'd have to say, in all honesty, that I'd never go out and deliberately try to make a Negro friend.

HARRY: Well, if I'd gone to a segregated school, I wouldn't have been as aware of the problem. I can see why there's dissent and dissatisfaction in our society. I'm not sure about the riots, either. In fact, I'm disenchanted with a lot of the riots. You see pictures and you realize that most of the people rioting are just out for personal gain. They're not dedicated revolutionaries or out for social change.

GEORGE: As a radical, it's very difficult to help Negroes. Why should a radical help a Negro gain the things that the radical's rejecting? Why should he help him gain an income, or a house in suburbia, a big car and things like this? Seems kind of a paradox. I like to see Negroes accepted as people. But as far as helping them into suburbia, I'm not interested at all.

CHARLIE: Well, I just think Negroes are entitled to the same freedoms as I am, and I think we're both entitled to more. I think that if people discriminate against individuals because of their ideas, that's all right because there're people who discriminate against me because of my ideas. I don't find this offensive. But I think if people discriminate against other people on the basis of skin color, then it's wrong.

QUESTION: Did you see any discrimination against skin color in high school?

CHARLIE: Definitely. I think most of the discrimination was by Negroes against white kids. Like Negroes who're always pushing white kids around just because you're white. Like the story I was telling you when they ganged up on me, all because I'm white. There're some white kids, too, who discriminate against Negroes. But I don't think it's as bad in school as what you find in the community. I think there's more discrimination against blacks in the community than in high school.

Charlie's last comment takes one aback. It is undoubtedly true that black anger and consequent discrimination against whites is strong, and yet one does not expect a "radical" to stress it. We tend to think that radicals are equally radical in all respects, and we are therefore surprised to see that, while, for instance, they may be extremely liberal with regard to war, they are in some respects rather conservative when it comes to race relations. At best, their attitudes towards blacks can probably best be described as "live and let live."

CHAPTER 7

On Being Black and White

Part 1

Next we meet two white and two black groups of students. These groups were not selected because of their similarity to one another; on the contrary, the two differ from one another a great deal. What they have in common is that they have achieved what each race defines as appropriate success. Two of the three white young women in the first interview are cheerleaders, while one of the white young men in the interview that follows holds a high ranking school office. Two of the Negro young women are successful athletes, and one of the two Negro young men is popular among whites and blacks alike. This last student's recognition, however, is not for accomplishments such as those of the Negro "elites." Jackson does not deviate from the group's definition of a "respectable" grade-point average (i.e. between "C" and "D"), he has been dismissed from school a number of times, and he has a steady, white girl friend.

Negroes obviously tend to reject any system which denies them the right to hold a school office, to be a cheerleader, to belong to social clubs and to enter college preparatory classes; yet the Negro who does these things—the "elite" Negro—is rejected by other Negroes for doing the very thing demanded by them as their right. To do what "whitey" does is the Negro's right, but once the right becomes a reality, the black is "playing it white." Thus, the Negro who is at the frontiers of integration is doing what his race demands but is, simultaneously, rejected by many other Negroes. Jackson is not at the frontiers of integration. He is not running for a school office heretofore held by whites; he does not have the highest grade-point-average in an accelerated course; he is not integrating a previously all-white club. He does, however, date a white fellow student, which is a frontier of another kind. But dating whites does not generally cause a black person to be labeled an "Uncle Tom." (Paradoxically, the "Uncle Toms" in our sample do not date whites. Although their parents urge them to compete with the white man, "elite" parents want their children to stay with Negroes socially.)

The three white young women we will meet first are seniors at Plains High. Two of them, Donna and Betty, are cheerleaders, the other one, Lois, is popular but not a cheerleader.

[QUESTION: What are some of the pressures you feel from attending a desegregated school?

LOIS: You know how to watch what you say, because when you turn around there're different races standing around you. You find that you might be saying something you shouldn't be saying. So you usually try to watch what you say. If you happen to be talking about somebody, or just in general, you may find that what you've said will cause trouble, so this is why you watch what you say. I think this is true in almost every case, though. I think you'd have to watch what you say even in a nonintegrated school.

BETTY: I think that's only true when you identify the race of the person you're talking about.

DONNA: I was thinking about this the other night and I think that it may be better to go to an integrated school, because you have to watch what you say. I think it teaches you just that, and later in life you should watch what you say to certain people, anyway. So I think it's good training. I've never run into a situation where anyone's bothered me. I think that kind of thing happens mainly in junior high school. In junior high school, I was really afraid of the colored girls. They'd come up to you and say, "I'm going to meet you in the alley after school." I was really afraid, but this sort of thing doesn't happen at Plains High School.

LOIS: Well, I went to a segregated grammar school, so when I went to junior high, that was the first time we ran into colored people. I didn't know what to expect, so I was a little afraid, too.

DONNA: I know I was afraid of them.

BETTY: Well, I think a lot of the kids out at East High, who haven't associated with Negroes in school, are afraid to associate with Negroes. But I'm not, because I've always been around Negroes, and I'm comfortable with them.

LOIS: Well, they're still a few at school that I'm afraid of. They're the big colored guys with long hair, who wear earrings and are kind of dirty. I'm afraid of them.]

Fear of the Negro, before coming into contact with him, is reported frequently by the white students. Part of this fear can be attributed to the widespread community belief about the type of Negro who attends Plains High School—the belligerent, stupid, dirty in looks, mind, and word, crap-shooting, wine-drinking, sex-crazed black. This myth is exploded after going to Plains High for a short time. There are some isolated cases of belligerent Negroes, as Betty tells us, but the white students often learn that the Negroes are very similar to whites—even as far as their prejudices are concerned. Later in this interview, Donna tells us how surprised she was to find Negroes thinking about the same things as herself—whom are you dating, where do you go on a date, and other questions of the same sort.

[BETTY: Sometimes there're some isolated cases of a Negro girl out to get a white girl. Some of these Negro girls are belligerent toward the whites. But I think we found that a lot of the Negroes are just as prejudiced as the white people.

QUESTION: Can you give an example to explain what you mean by, "The Negro is as prejudiced as the white?"

DONNA: Well, there was this girl, she's our age. In fact, she's a friend of ours, who started dating this colored boy. At first it was a secret, but then everyone at school knew about it. He found that he lost some of his friends. The Negro boys wouldn't talk to him. If they talked to him, they'd tell him he was wrong, going out with this white girl.

BETTY: I know of another example. In American History class, there're two Negro girls who're quite intelligent, and a lot of the time we discuss contemporary problems. We often discuss the race problem. We'd carry on a very good conversation and ask these girls real open questions about the race problem. One thing that one of these girls brought up once was that one time a girl was visiting her from the south, and this Negro girl in the class was taking the girl around the school to show her what it was like at Plains High School. Down in the lunch room, she took the girl to meet some of her Negro girl friends. Then she wanted her to meet some of her white friends, and this girl said, "No, I'm afraid of them, I don't want anything to do with them." Then she said, "A lot of the Negroes from the south feel this way and actually are prejudiced toward white people."

DONNA: I'd like to say something about this white girl who dated the Negro boy. She's a good friend of mine, and, at first, I couldn't believe it. This girl would always do different things, so she'd stand out in school. She was involved in a lot of things, and she was in student government and very popular. At first, I thought it was a passing thing, but it wasn't. But I'll say one thing, I don't think she lost any of her true friends. She did lose friends, but these weren't her true friends.

BETTY: I think she really went through a lot, being talked about and cut down. It was very hard for her.

LOIS: I think the white boys were very hard on her, particularly. Before this happened she had a lot of dates with white boys. She was really popular and was one of the most dated kids in school, until this happened. Now she isn't going with this Negro anymore, and she doesn't have any dates, either. None of the white boys will date her. She isn't going with this Negro boy anymore because of the pressures put on her by her parents and the counselors at school. I think it's awful that none of the white boys will have anything to do with her just because she was dating this Negro boy.

QUESTION: Do the teachers and counselors always get involved in the personal life of the students?

DONNA: I proctored the first hour, and this boy was in that class. The girl he was going with was also a proctor. She'd come into the class and talk to him almost every day. At one point, this teacher asked me if she was dating him. I said that they were friends and that they saw each other. He said he wanted to know more about it, and he wanted to get involved. So he did. The counselor also called her in to talk to her and to tell her the problems she'd face if she got involved with a Negro, because of the way society feels. Other teachers also got involved.]

A number of students, both black and white, indicate that the involvement of teachers, counselors and school administrators in cases of interracial dating is selective. In telling about this, the Negro students are angry—not because the school interferes with interracial dating, but because by interfering selectively the white community seems to be saying to the blacks, "We won't let you drag down our important people." As one Negro says, "They don't care if a Negro dates someone who is white trash. . . . It's the important ones they want to save."

[DONNA: There're other kids who also date Negroes. I think that in this case, because both kids were so popular, we found that a lot of the teachers and counselors got involved and tried to break it up.

BETTY: I don't know whether the teachers actually discriminate. Some might. I think this is true of anywhere, though. You'll find that some people will discriminate and others won't. I guess I'd have to say that some of the teachers do discriminate. This one counselor said she tried to make her realize what it'd be like for her to date a Negro, because she wouldn't get any dates from white boys. I think the counselors realize this and tried to make her realize what would happen.

LOIS: I'm sure that the teachers wouldn't have gotten as involved with other kids, but they got involved with her because she's considered a school leader.

BETTY: Well, that's true of the colored boy, too. He's very well known, and he was an athlete.

QUESTION: How do the Negro girls react to interracial dating?

DONNA: Well, this white girl was in my Spanish class, and there were a couple of Negro girls in that class. She got to be real close to a couple of Negro girls during the year, when she hadn't been close to Negroes before. I think that was because she was dating a Negro boy. They seemed to accept her fairly well. These two girls in class did anyway. But as I think of it, I kind of remember her saying that the colored girls resented her for dating this Negro boy. Actually, I think most of the colored girls wouldn't like it.

QUESTION: If you wanted to date a Negro, who would put pressure on you not to?

BETTY: Well, I don't believe my best friends would react badly. I think that they'd accept it all right. I'd lose some friends, but not my best friends. I think my parents would try to understand because they always try to understand what I do. I think the white boys would be the ones who'd put the most pressure on me.

DONNA: I think my parents would be the worst ones. They wouldn't like it at all. They'll put an awful lot of pressure on me. My mother often talks to me about this; in fact, I can't stand to listen to her talking about it anymore. I get very upset when she talks about the race issue. I just tell her that I don't want to talk about it anymore. Then I think that the white boys would be the next ones. They'd put an awful lot of pressure on you.

LOIS: I think my parents would also be the worst. And then I think the white boys. Although I don't know really whether the white boys or my parents would be worse.

BETTY: Oh, I know definitely that it would be the white boys for me, because they wouldn't date me anymore, and this would be very hard. I think my parents would try to understand, because they always try to understand, so I wouldn't expect too much pressure from my parents.

DONNA: Well, my parents really upset me more than the white boys would. My parents are always bringing things up about this. For example, this year at the All School Party we elected a Negro King and Queen. My parents talked a little about this. But we disagree on several things; particularly my mother and me, we disagree a lot. I usually end up saying I don't want to talk to her about it anymore. I think I'm a lot more liberal than my mother, although she's told me that she's a lot more liberal now than she used to be. But she says, "I never want my kids to go with a Negro." Other times she says, "You'll probably have colored grandchildren." She makes me so upset that at one time I said, "You'll probably have colored grandchildren, too." I only said that to get back at her, but she didn't hear me anyway. I think I'm a lot more liberal than my parents. I think they're prejudiced.

LOIS: I also feel that I'm more liberal than my parents. I don't believe my parents are really prejudiced, but they're not really openminded either.]

Donna, Lois, and Betty are no exception in reporting a generation gap between themselves, their parents and their grandparents on the race issue. Most of the students we talked with agree that this generation is more liberal. Whether or not these young people will remain liberal is yet to be seen. Will they, as preceding generations, find their liberalism dissipated as they join the ranks of adult society? Another interesting question to ask is to what extent attendance at a desegregated school is responsible for the selfconception of a "liberal"? Some students at Plains High, for example, assume they are more liberal than their East Plains High counterparts. The latter lack contact with blacks since there are only four black students at East High. There is no evidence, however, to support the assumption that contact alone between whites and blacks fosters significant positive racial attitudes.

Discrimination and prejudice by the teachers is frequently mentioned by the black students. Betty's answer to the question, "Do the teachers treat all students at Plains High alike?" represents a mature point of view.

BETTY: Well, teachers are just human beings. They're just people who have different ideas. I'd say that some of them are prejudiced and some aren't. I think that you'll find the teachers are just like what you find in society. There're some people that are prejudiced and some aren't. I think the ones that are prejudiced don't try to help them, or they don't try to give them special attention or treat them like they do the white students. They don't try to include the Negroes much in their class activities. I think in some classes it's fairly obvious when the teacher is prejudiced. I think some of the counselors are prejudiced. They don't do as much for the Negro students as they do for the white students. Then there're some teachers who're really liberal. I know something about the counselors, because in Spanish class we talked about the counselors. We've this very liberal Spanish teacher, Mrs. Thaler. We talk about the Negro problem in her class. One time she asked the class, "Why do I have only one or two Negroes in all of my classes?" She asked us if we knew why this happened. We said, "Well, we don't think that Negroes usually take courses such as physiology, chemistry, or foreign languages." We also said, "We don't think the Negroes take the harder courses, or the college preparatory courses." She said that she thought it was the counselors who discouraged Negroes from taking college preparatory courses, and that the counselors encouraged the Negroes to take the duller and easier courses. Mrs. Thaler is a very intelligent woman, so she was probably right.

DONNA: I don't know because you usually make out your own schedule. All you go to a counselor for is to sign the schedule. I don't ever talk to a counselor. I don't think they've had much influence on the courses I take. I think the only time they do is when you have a conflict, where you need some kind of course to fill in your schedule, and you don't know what to take. So I really haven't had that much experience with counselors myself. I don't know whether you could really say that they discriminate against Negroes and help the whites more.

LOIS: There's a situation at school that I really don't understand. We have a Negro counselor, and I'm told that not many of the Negro students go to him. Whenever you see this Negro counselor, he's usually talking to white students. He'll be standing out in the hall talking to kids, and usually they're all white. I think these Negro students could go to this colored counselor if they wanted to, so if the white counselors discriminated against them, it seems to me, that if they went to Mr. Lewis he'd help them.

QUESTION: In which areas of school life do you find the most integration?

BETTY: Well, I sure wouldn't say it was basketball, because that's segregated the other way. Just about all the players on the basketball team are Negro. Track, I guess that's integrated a great deal, and football, but not swimming. Negroes usually don't swim. I think we've had only one Negro on the swim team in the past two years. I really don't know why. I think they don't learn to swim. I teach swimming during the summer. I've been doing it about five years now, and all the time I've taught swimming, we've only had a couple of Negro children come for swimming lessons. I think Negro parents don't learn to swim when they're young, and I think Negroes have a fear of the water. The couple that I've taught have a greater built-in fear of the water than the white kids. I think this is something which is just true of Negroes, so not as many of them learn to swim as young kids. They have this fear of the water.

QUESTION: Don't all students at Plains High have to take swimming?

DONNA: Yes, in Physical Ed class you have to swim. You should see the beginning classes—99% in the beginning classes are Negroes. They just don't know how to swim. I'd say that most of the sports are pretty well mixed, though. Did you happen to see the editorial in the paper about our basketball team a few months ago? Some of the quotes were very funny. I thought it was the greatest editorial that we've ever had in the paper. It was on the subject of integration, and how well the kids on the basketball team got along with each other. I know these things are true, because I don't think the person writing the story could've really made them up. There was this out of town game, and there was this one white boy on the team, and one of the Negro boys hurt his leg, so he bandaged his leg with white tape and came out on the court and yelled, "Hey, we have three white legs here." On the way home from a game one time, they were riding the bus, and they turned off the lights and the white boy said, "Hey, where did everybody go?" I thought it was really a great editorial. The editor said, "If everybody could get along in this way, we certainly wouldn't have any problems."

BETTY: Do you know anything about our basketball team?

INTERVIEWER: Yes, I heard you have a very good one.

BETTY: We do. We really had a great basketball team. We took second in the State. I think the whole team is Negro except for two whites. This kind of put the Negroes on a pedestal, because of how good the team was. Everybody loved this team. This is getting off the subject a little bit, but you know the one thing I really like about Plains High School is that we have Negroes. The funny thing about dances, for example, is that the Negroes know how to dance, and they teach the dances to the white kids. I think this is great. It's really cool. The Negroes have sayings you can't beat. And, you know, we kind of pick them up. I think this is really cool about Plains High School.

DONNA: Our coach had an assembly, and said that the team this year worked out so well together, and he was praising them. He said that it was one of the most courteous teams he's ever seen. This is true, I went to all the games, and the team never lost its temper. You were just proud to see them out there.

BETTY: I was really proud, because the general attitude of the people in Center City and the country is that the Negroes are hot tempered. I was at a lot of games where some of the white boys on the other team would come down the court elbowing and would get mad at our boys, but our boys didn't get mad at them or use foul language—they're really gentlemen.

QUESTION: Do you think they're overcompensating because they're Negroes?

DONNA: No, I think it's the coach. I think if you like him, you really like him, and if you don't, you don't. He sits there on the sidelines very cool-like and he always preaches, "Play it cool." He's very calm. I think he's really done a lot for them in this way. He just doesn't get excited himself. I think the players pick this up.

LOIS: I think one reason you see more colored basketball players than you do white is because I think the Negroes have a natural talent for jumping higher and running faster. I know I've attended all the games and whenever there's a jump for a ball, you always see this Negro arm a lot higher than all of the other arms. I really do think they have this natural talent, so they're much better players.

BETTY: This is evident in track, too. They're a lot faster than the white guys.]

The sterotype of the Negro as a superior athlete, because he has a natural ability to run fast and jump high, is a recurring theme in a number of our interviews. A Negro—identified by other Negroes as an "Uncle Tom"—told us, "Negroes have more rhythm than whites." Even he believes that blacks are "born with" this rhythm. Yet, in each of our informal trips to senior high, junior high, or elementary school playgrounds, on Sunday or any other day of the week, the students practicing their set-shots, dribbling, running, broad-jumping, hurdling, and so on, were black. Few of the students recognize that the black athlete practices his game constantly. The idea of a "built-in fear of the water" is another example of a grossly oversimplified stereotype.

[QUESTION: Are the clubs at school integrated?

BETTY: Well, the clubs aren't too well integrated. There is some integration, but mostly you'll find it's just white kids who belong to the clubs. Pep Club is integrated somewhat, but Honor Pep isn't. There isn't one Negro in Honor Pep.

QUESTION: What's the difference between Honor Pep and Pep Club?

BETTY: You have to earn points to belong to Honor Pep. You have to attend most of the games—not the out-of-town games, because that would cost money to ride the bus, and maybe some of the kids couldn't go because of the cost. Also, you have to make posters and work a little bit. You earn points, you aren't elected to it. You become a member of Honor Pep by earning points. I think they see to it that anyone could earn the points. There aren't any points gotten for things which would cost you money. I think they try very hard to exclude any discrimination in that respect, but you never see a Negro in Honor Pep.

LOIS: This year there weren't any Negro girls in Honor Pep. I think last year there was one. There was a lot of griping about this among the Negro girls. I don't know why they gripe, because anybody can earn the points and get into Honor Pep. You're not elected to it.]

Much of the tension at Plains High can be attributed to the cheerleader incident: the blacks wanted a Negro cheerleader, but a black cheerleader was not elected. Before talking with Donna, Lois, and Betty on this issue, we had already obtained the opinions of male and female whites, blacks, and Mexican-Americans. This, however, is the first time we hear from some cheerleaders in regard to how they judge the matter. The facts are presented differently this time.

[QUESTION: Why aren't there any Negro cheerleaders at Plains High School?

DONNA: Well, this year we changed the elections just for them. This year was the first time that cheerleaders were elected by an all-school election. At first, they were going to make it an election by kids who hold activity tickets, but then they decided that would be discrimination. Activity tickets cost money and some of the Negro kids don't have it. So they decided to make it an all-school election, and all you had to do was register to vote. Many of the Negro kids registered to vote, but they didn't show up in time to vote. I think the school really tried hard to get a Negro elected as a cheerleader. Two of the Negro girls made it past the primary election. The primary, you know, was held on the day of King's funeral. But both Negro girls made it through the primary election anyway. It was in the final election where they lost. We really felt that we should have a colored cheerleader, because the teams are almost all colored. In the final election, anyone that registered to vote could vote. The voting was from 7:45 to 8 in the morning. There weren't that many Negroes who showed up for the election. Mr. Ewing was very upset, because he was the one who actually talked us into having an open election. Before, the cheerleaders were selected by Boys Pep and Girls Pep and by the teams. Mr. Ewing thought it would be fairer if we had an open election. He just couldn't believe that a Negro girl wasn't elected. He had them recount the votes three or four times to make sure. Nobody could understand why they didn't get in. They lost only by a couple of votes. This one girl did anyway. She lost by two votes. Mr. Ewing kept asking them for recounts to make sure, but she still lost. It was the Negro kids who didn't get out to vote for her.

BETTY: I think Mr. Ewing tries hard. There was this lady who gave a speech in church and said Mr. Ewing was prejudiced and that the elections were rigged against the colored people at Plains High School, and that was why they couldn't get a colored cheerleader. I wanted very much to have a colored girl become cheerleader, if she was good. One thing I don't want is to make sure a colored girl gets to be cheerleader because she's Negro, or, I don't want a girl not to be elected a cheerleader because she's Negro. I think, personally, that the cheerleader elections couldn't have been fairer than they were this year. School starts at 8:25. You could've voted as late as a few minutes after eight. It was publicized in the bulletins every day that we were going to have an election. The kids just didn't come out to vote.

QUESTION: In the past, has the selection of cheerleaders been fair?

BETTY: You'll have to admit, in the past, the elections weren't fair. I think in the past there've been situations in which a Negro wasn't chosen as cheerleader because she was a Negro.

DONNA: There're things that go on at school in which you see discrimination. I don't know if the other girls here know about this. But I know of a situation, from a very good source, that certainly involved discrimination. Last year, we had a Negro king and and white queen at the All-School Party. When they found out that the boy elected was a Negro, and the girl was white they first called up the white girl to see if it was all right with her if he was king. If it wasn't, they'd take the next person in line. I know that's hard to believe, but they actually did that. If she'd said, "No," they actually would have selected someone else, even though he won. Fortunately, she turned around and said, "Well, if he won, he deserves it. So I've no objections."]

In what follows, we learn that the segregation between whites and blacks is so complete that the black students do no more than demonstrate dance steps for whites who are eager to learn them. The "teacher," however, never actually dances with his white pupil. Betty does not see this as indicating a lack of "integration" between whites and blacks. To her, the willingness of the Negroes to teach her the dance steps—and to leave it at that—is "cool."

[QUESTION: How well do the students mix at school varsities?

BETTY: Well, I think the Negroes are the coolest things at the varsity dances. They can really dance. But the dances are divided. The Negroes dance in a group, and the whites dance in kind of a line, at different ends of the gym. I know a lot of us try to dance like the Negroes, but we really can't. The Negro boys will tell you what you're doing wrong. But you don't see much dancing between colored and whites. Sometimes a Negro boy will come up and start dancing right next to you. He doesn't dance with you, but next to you to show you how to do the dance. I think the cool thing is that they'll teach you how to dance. The Negro boys will explain what you're doing wrong. I think that most of the whites really respect them in dancing, because they're real good.

QUESTION: What's so "cool" about the dances if you don't get to dance with the kids who know how?

BETTY: Well, I think the cool thing is that they're willing to come out and show you what you're doing wrong and help you. You know, we don't get to dance with them much, but we get to learn.

QUESTION: Why don't you dance with Negroes?

BETTY: Well, white boys don't like to see white girls date Negro boys. I think this is also true for dancing. I don't think the white boys would like to see white girls dancing with Negroes.

LOIS: There're some changes, though. I've a younger sister in junior high, and she said that this year at the varsity dance there was this Negro boy, who has a lot of white friends and is usually seen with white kids, who danced with the white girls and nobody thought anything about it.

BETTY: I've seen a Negro boy who runs around mostly with white boys in high school dance with white girls. This is not at varsity dances, though, but at other places in the community where dancing is allowed.

LOIS: Also, at the junior and senior prom this year, I noticed there were two mixed couples.]

Almost to a person, the students agree that the young men mix interracially more than the young women. The former also kid more about racial issues. The present students tell us that Negro and white young women share fewer experiences than their male counterparts, with the result that there is less congeniality between the women. Yet, there is little evidence that the "friendships" which white and Negro young men establish on the "playing field" continue off the field. Racial cleavage exists even at supposedly "integrated" social activities, as the graduation party sponsored by Plains High's black students exemplifies. Although there apparently was "a lot of mixing," separate tables were nevertheless maintained.

[QUESTION: Do the students mix socially at parties?

LOIS: When the boys have parties, they're mixed. I think the boys mix more than the girls, anyway. Boys have parties all the time, and they're mixed, but you never see this kind of mixing among girls.

DONNA: At graduation, the colored kids rented the Highway Motel, and they invited everyone to a party. There were about thirteen white couples there; about two tables were white, and the rest were black. I heard there was a lot of mixing, and everybody had a good time. Nobody thought about color at that party. I would've enjoyed going there myself. I have a friend who was there. She said it was different being in the minority, but that she enjoyed herself. I think, in high school in many cases, the boys do kid around with each other about race or about being Negro or white, but you can't kid around with the girls like that. The girls are more touchy, and you don't ever bring up the subject of their being Negro.

BETTY: I think the girls are more sensitive about race. I've even seen boys call themselves "nigger," and stuff like that. I think they're more friendly.]

When the students are asked about Mexican-Americans, the most frequent response is, "They're just there." Even some Mexican-Americans in a subsequent chapter, agree that Mexican-Americans are more isolated than Negroes, an isolation which to some extent is voluntary. The "nigger" equivalent for Mexican-American students is "greasers" or "taco-benders," but the reaction of Mexican students to such pejorative name-calling is more apt to be internal than overt.

[QUESTION: Where do the Mexican-Americans fit in at school?

BETTY: They're really kind of funny. I don't know where they fit in.

DONNA: I find that they really are by themselves. For example, in the morning, in the west part of the main hall, you'll find white kids. The colored kids are mainly in the front part of the main hall, and in the east part are the Mexicans. It's almost exactly like that all the time. Each group has their own waiting place.

LOIS: This is true in the cafeteria, too. The colored always sit in one section, the whites in another section and the Mexicans in another section. I don't think the Mexican kids mingle as much as either the whites or the Negroes.]

[QUESTION: Has your relationship with Negroes changed since you were in elementary and junior high school?

LOIS: I don't think I've changed too much from junior high to high school. I think, though, when you're in junior high school, and you can't drive, or anything like that, there isn't as much mixing. I think in high school you get around more, and there's more mixing.

DONNA: I'd say there's a change. When I was in junior high school, I was really afraid of them. I think, in the ninth grade things got better. In the ninth grade, I felt more relaxed and started to mix with the Negroes. They try to help you dance, and things like that, and I feel freer.

LOIS: In the seventh and eighth grades, everybody says, "Don't mess around with them, they'll get you." But when you get to know them, you're not afraid anymore.

DONNA: I think the first time not to be afraid of them was in gym class. There was this Negro girl who started talking to me and just asking me things any girl would ask. She'd ask me things like, who I was dating, and things like that; you know, where I was going on a date, and things like that.

LOIS: In the seventh grade, there were some real tough girls who'd day, "Watch out, or we'll get you." There was this one girl in gym class I said something to that sounded kind of funny, and ever since then she's really hated me. She threatened me, and I was afraid of all of them after that.

BETTY: I think if we were to combine East Plains High with Plains High School there'd be a lot more trouble. There'd be this feeling that they were out to get the East kids. I think that's because the East kids think they're better students, or that they're high class. I think the Negroes would kind of resent this. There might be some trouble. If you've always been around Negroes, I don't believe you've anything to be afraid of.

QUESTION: Do you think the students transferring from East next year will have trouble?

DONNA: I think if they said all the kids at East must go to Plains High School next year (you know, it's optional the first year), then I think there'd be some trouble.

LOIS: I think the white kids would get into trouble.

BETTY: The Negro guys would resent the fact that they didn't want to go to Plains High because of the Negroes. You know, everybody knows that that was the reason they didn't want to go to Plains High School. They made up a lot of funny excuses for not wanting to go. But everybody knows that it was just race.

QUESTION: Is it the students who feel this way or their parents?

DONNA: I don't think you think about parents at a time like that. You just associate what the parents think with the kids, so you think they're rich kids, and they thing they're better than we are. So there might be some trouble.

LOIS: There's this girl friend I know at East. She asked me about the violence at Plains High School. They've heard a lot of rumors. The kids out East just don't believe that we can get along so good at Plains High School. They're really surprised when they see us mixing with Negroes, and the atmosphere is free.]

The belief of widespread racial conflict is one of the most pervasive misconceptions about Plains High School. In reality, interracial conflict—leading to fighting—is almost nonexistent. While there is some fighting, it is generally among students from the same race. Between the races, conflict is expressed in such behavior as not voting for a qualified Negro cheerleader because of her color or in whites and blacks sitting at separate tables in the cafeteria.

[QUESTION: Are there any fights between white and black students?

BETTY: Oh, there're a lot of fights. It's usually between Negroes and Negroes and whites and whites. I haven't really seen fights which involve a Negro and a white person.

DONNA: Well, there was going to be a fight between a Negro and a white person once, because this white boy said something bad about this white girl that was dating a Negro. The Negro boy was going to get after him, but the white boy didn't show up.

BETTY: You know, I've never seen a fight, I always hear about it. I'll come up and somebody'll say, "Say, did you see the fight between classes?" Somehow or another, I always miss them. I don't think there're that many fights.

LOIS: I've seen a couple of fights, but most of the ones I've seen have been between white people. I wouldn't say the colored people get into more fights than whites, although they think this is true. A lot of people think that the colored people fight more. But I think it's the white people that fight more, except for girls. A lot of the colored girls will fight, but I don't ever see white girls fighting. In fact, a lot of girls fight at school, and this seems kind of strange.]

Unlike the white "racists" in an earlier chapter, these young women recognize at least two classes of Negroes. Their description of who belongs to the three white classes and the two Negro classes is interesting—inclusion or exclusion is not determined so much by the person's economic status as by his behavior. For example, lower class whites are easily identified because they usually are tough; middle class whites tend not to participate in school activities; and upper class whites participate in many activities and occupy positions of school leadership.

[QUESTION: How many different classes of kids are there are Plains High, starting with whites?

BETTY: There're the lower class whites. These are the whites that live in the poor sections, like in South Center City. They have it real rough in life. They're poor and they don't have many things. They want clothes, and they don't have them. These kids are usually tough. That's the first thing you think of when you think of these kids—they're tough. Then there're the medium class kids. These are just the average family kids. They don't hold offices, and they aren't in many activities. They're not very popular. They don't participate in a lot of stuff at school. A lot of times they have to work to help the family. They're nice kids, but they don't have time to participate in school activities. Then there're the high class kids. Kids in this class are the kids who do things at school. It's not always based on money because there're some kids without money who belong in this class. These are the kids who're the officers and are in a lot of the clubs and activities. Some aren't really rich. You don't have to be rich to be in this class. It's mainly the kids that are involved in the school.

QUESTION: How many classes of Negroes are there?

DONNA: There's the lower class. These kids are the kids that wear their hair slicked back and pierce their ears. They wear tight pants. The girls wear dresses up to here [she pointed to her hip.] They have a dirty appearance— hygiene-wise and morally. They look like their parents hate them. They don't get any love. They're always looking for excitement because that's the only way they can prove themselves. These are the agitators. And there's the medium class Negro. These are the ones that care about school and the activities. They don't have to be rich because a lot of them aren't very rich; but they're at least clean. Even if they're poor, they're interested in sports and the clubs.

QUESTION: Who mixes best?

DONNA: Well, the middle class Negroes mix most with the high class whites because they participate in the school activities.

BETTY: I think there's an equal percentage of prejudice, though, in the middle and high class whites as there is among any group. But the high class mix more with the Negroes. I think that's because they participate in school activities.

DONNA: I think out of school that the high class whites don't mix with the Negroes. I think the middle class kids do because they might work with them.]

For these students, as with so many others, interracial dating is associated with sex. The moral standards of young men and women who date interracially are considered lower than those of young men and women who date fellow students of the same race. Moral standards may not be questioned if dating takes place within the same race, but once the same young woman participates in mixed dating then her "reputation" is tarnished.

[QUESTION: Earlier you mentioned a white girl who dated a Negro. Are there any white boys who date Negro girls at school?

LOIS: I've never seen a white boy date a Negro girl.

DONNA: I've never seen that, either. I think it would depend on the couple. But when you think of mixed dating, you always think of a colored boy with a white girl. When you think of this, you always think it's the white girl who's low. If it was a white boy with a colored girl, then it'd be the white boy that was low. I don't know. It's kind of hard to think of that kind of situation.

QUESTION: What do you mean by "low"?

LOIS: The kids that don't associate with the girl, and who don't really know her, think that her morality is lower than other kids.

QUESTION: Does worrying about your reputation stop you from dating a Negro?

DONNA: Yes! But, also, you'd have no dates with white guys. I think we'd really suffer if we started dating Negroes, and things wouldn't change. You'd have to go away from here to where you weren't known and nobody knew that you'd dated a Negro.

LOIS: This white girl who dated this colored boy was teased by a lot of the kids. She'd actually kid about it. The couple also kidded about it, but they knew it was a serious problem.]

Again we find that race is not a topic for discussion in class. There are some exceptions; the Spanish instructor, for example, allows such discussions provided they are held in Spanish. In this way, the topic is not bootlegged, but is legitimate, since the instructor's primary object is to teach her students Spanish.

Lois tells of a temporary "closeness" between blacks and whites, precipitated by Dr. Martin Luther King's assassination. The students participating in this interview did not, however, enjoy the silence at school that day.

[QUESTION: Do you discuss race issues in school?

BETTY: We discuss race a lot in two classes, in Spanish and History. But I think, in general, it depends on the teacher. A lot of teachers don't like to discuss the race issue.

DONNA: In Speech, the teacher wouldn't let us discuss race at all. The teacher thought it was too hot an issue and didn't want us to talk about it. I think a lot of the teachers feel the same way, so you don't really see that much discussion on race in class.

LOIS: When King died they had a prayer—everybody stood up for a silent prayer, and then we were all asked to leave the school silently, and we did. That was one time when whites and Negroes stood together. It was really nice. After King died, it was really quiet at school, too. A lot of the Negroes stayed home and a lot of the whites used this as an excuse to stay home.

QUESTION: Did you like school on that day?

DONNA, BETTY, LOIS: No!

DONNA: It was too quiet, it was more like East High or more like college. There wasn't any excitement. I like it when everybody's there.]

The present group of students reflect on what attending an integrated school has meant. For one thing, it has meant learning what the world is "really" like. Unlike some of the conservative students in Chapter 4, Betty would go so far as to pay the tuition at Plains High School for her children, were she to move outside the Plains High School boundaries; then her children could also go there. Attending an integrated school allows more than simply learning about blacks and whites, however. Donna, for example, has "learned to accept all kinds of people. Material things don't mean as much to me anymore."

[QUESTION: What has your experience at Plains High taught you about race relations?

BETTY: I wouldn't trade going to a integrated school for anything. You learn to live like you're going to have to live in life. There's no course you could take that would teach you more at Plains High School as you get from the experience of going to an integrated school. I think I've matured a lot. I think some of my viewpoints have changed. I've come to realize what the world is really like. We had some conflicts—whites and Negroes—and I think we've seen things in miniature at Plains High School that you'll see in the world—such as the cheerleader election. There were a lot of conflicts between Negroes and whites—we had them, but we talk about them. I think it teaches you to cope with these problems. After going to an integrated school, I think you're better equipped to cope with the problems of the world because the race problem does exist.

DONNA: I've learned to accept all kinds of people. Material things don't mean as much to me anymore. I've learned to mix with different classes of people and different races. I think that I can explain what I mean by a situation that happened. There was this white girl from East High who was an exchange student at Plains High. She was in my Spanish class. I asked her if she saw a difference between schools. She said she did, and the thing that she really noticed was that the people at Plains High looked at her to see what she was like as a person. At East High, they looked at her to see what she was wearing and judged her on that.

LOIS: I agree. I went to Seaburg High School as an exchange student—it was all white and it was boring. I think by going to an integrated school you learn to get along with everybody, and when you go to college you know what to expect. I think it's great, I wouldn't trade it for anything.

QUESTION: When you have children, will you send them to integrated schools?

BETTY: Even if I lived in East Center City I'd pay the tuition to send my kids to Plains High.

DONNA: I think you could compare an all-white school to what it would be like at an all-boy school, or an all-girl school. I think it would be the same way. You don't really know how to act with boys if you went to an all-girl school, or vice versa. I think integrated schools teach you an awful lot about life.]

On Being Black and White

Part 2

The three students in our next interview—David, Karl and Mitchell—do not feel that they know Negroes. Although they have attended "integrated" schools since, at least, junior high school, they have not been in situations where they could easily mix with blacks. Each of them is in the college preparatory curriculum, in which there are very few Negroes. None of them are athletes, so that they do not meet the Negro as a teammate. While one of the young men is active in student government, Plains High School does not have many Negroes in elected school offices.

In general, these students are knowledgeable about the problems of the society in which they live. However, they do not think that the Negro at Plains High has it "bad" Mitchell says that the opportunities are available, and it is now up to the Negro to act. This kind of reasoning presents a chronic dilemma for the Negro: whites in most communities tend to believe that racial problems exist elsewhere—not in their own communities.

One of the students, David, thinks there is some discrimination, because few Negroes are in the college preparatory program. He charges that the school is systematically keeping Negroes and Mexican-Americans in the "dumber" classes. His charge is a serious one for, if true, the school has substituted one system of segregation for another. In the final analysis, if minority students are denied the quality of education necessary for them to take their place in society on a par with whites, then whether such a denial exists within structurally segregated or integrated schools is of little importance. Of importance is that blacks are denied equality of education.

[QUESTION: What are some of the pressures you feel from attending a desegregated school?

KARL: When I first went to Plains High School, I had this idea in my head about what to expect because there were Negroes there. A lot of these ideas were untrue. I thought that there was a line right down the middle, separating the white students and the black students. I thought people referred to each other as, "He's white" or, "He's black," when they talked about each other. But it turned out that these things aren't true. I think there's pressure not to mention certain words. I think there's some small pressure to be careful of

150

what you say. I think I seem to watch my conduct more in a Negro group than I would in an all-white group. I tend to watch my words carefully, so as not to select the wrong word and offend someone. When Mr. King died, I wasn't so blatant about expressing my feelings about the Negroes, in a Negro situation. I tended to keep my feelings to myself.

DAVID: When I think of pressures, I think in terms of physical pressures, in terms of, you're going to get beat up. That's what I thought, anyway, before I went to Plains High School. I thought, if a colored boy asked you for a dime and you didn't give it to him, you'd get beat up. But it turned out that this isn't true. For one thing, we don't come into contact with Negroes. If you're a little bit above average, there aren't many Negroes in your class. The ones that are in your class, usually it's just one or two, aren't particularly proud of being colored. I think they feel a little bit above their race, so there isn't much tension between whites and blacks in this group. The second floor is where the lower class kids hang out—it's almost 100% colored. But you don't find many Negroes on the third and first floors, where we have our classes.

MITCHELL: Every school is supposed to have its back halls and great pressures. But I find that at Plains High School all of the stories about the back halls, and things that were going on in the back halls, aren't true. I attended Franklin Elementary School. There was one colored person there, when I attended. Then I moved up to Plains Junior High, which is by no means predominantly colored, but there're a lot more colored people. There seemed to be more pressure in junior high because you have to learn to mix with colored prople, and that was my first real experience. At Plains High School, though, I'm so used to it now, I don't feel the pressure any more.

QUESTION: When you left junior high to go to high school, were you afraid because of the stories you heard about Plains High?

MITCHELL: No. I had older brothers and sisters who'd been there before. They told me what I could expect and told me about it. I think if I didn't have older brothers and sisters, who had experienced it, I'd probably have been more afraid. They warned me, so I knew what to expect. I didn't feel uneasy at all. I think once you're around colored people, you become familiar with their ways and some of their habits, so you're not as afraid of them.

KARL: Well, I was at McKinley Junior High and before that I came from Webster Elementary School, which was all white. I'd never really come into contact with any Negroes, except maybe once or twice at a movie or a swimming pool, but even then our contacts were limited. I think I found the situation at Plains High School a little bit different. For one thing, at McKinley, we did have a couple of Negroes, but they weren't popular colored students, so we tended to think of them differently. But at Plains High School some of the colored students are up there—they're popular and respected. I found, when I got to Plains High School, that so many white students respected some of the Negro students. It was strange to find some Negroes who were more popular than some white students.

DAVID: I went to Pierce before going to McKinley and there weren't any Negroes there. When I was going over to McKinley, a lot of the other kids said "Watch out for the Negroes—they'll beat you up." But now that I think back, you know I can't remember any Negroes at McKinley, so I guess they really didn't leave that much of an impression on me. As far as Plains High School, I don't really get the feeling that it was a big jump for me from McKinley because the classes are set up so you aren't with them much. I really don't know that many Negroes.]

Mitchell attempts to explain why white and black students are segregated at Plains High School. He pays little attention to David's suggestion that the way in which the classes have been administratively arranged may be part of the trouble. Instead, Mitchell suggests the segregation is voluntary and a carry-over from patterns established in the neighborhood. He only speaks of Negroes forming groups and, in this way, segregating themselves in the cafeteria. He does not mention how white students behave in the same way. His statement that Negroes mingle more with the white these days implies that blacks are responsible for segregating themselves at Plains High, and that black students have to make the first move to change.

[MITCHELL: I think there's some segregation at Plains High School. I think the colored people kinda keep to themselves—particularly at lunch time. In the lunch room, I notice this a great deal. This year it's not as bad as it has been in the past. But I don't see this as a problem. I think it's because the Negroes come from the same neighborhood, and they form small groups. I think, however, that more and more they're mingling with whites, and you even see less of this.

KARL: I think you notice Negroes more at school, even though they don't make up that large a percentage of the student body. For one thing, in the halls you notice a Negro group is louder. I think they let their feelings be known more than white people do, but I wouldn't say you're afraid to walk down the areas in which they hang out. I think most people just feel free to walk wherever they like.

MITCHELL: Well, there's been some racial tension in small groups. When I was a sophomore, there were some colored boys who were setting up a Black Power thing in school. I think they were doing that because it was the in-thing to do, not because they really felt there was any prejudice toward the Negroes. This year, for example, the senior class president is colored. I'm in the student council, and one of the student counselors is a colored girl. I think when tensions exist at Plains High, it's the people from the outside who come in and cause it. Or they'll point out to some of the Negroes that there's prejudice at Plains High School. There's always a lot of talk about a colored cheerleader. I think it'd be great to have a colored cheerleader, but I don't think it'd be good if one *had* to be a colored girl. It would be great if she were elected like any other girl in school. But to set up a situation like they have in some other cities, in which they said one cheerleader must be colored, I think this is wrong. This year there were two colored kids in the primaries. They didn't make it, but I think that's because the Negroes didn't get out there and vote. If they'd stick together, you know, they could vote as a power block. But they didn't do this. I don't think the kids at school really see this as prejudice. I think when this is pointed out to them as an example of prejudice, by outsiders, then they feel some resentment.]

The cheerleader issue comes up everywhere. It has assumed enormous importance to the question of race relations at Plains High. The question is, of course, whether more central issues are overlooked in all the excitement. Still, cheerleaders are a here-and-now event; as such, the importance to the issue at stake is considerable. With the cheerleader issue, basic questions related to race relations are simply played out in a smaller arena.

[KARL: Well, previously there might have been some prejudice in the election of a cheerleader because you had to have a six-dollar activity ticket to vote. I'm a homeroom representative and I can tell you that there weren't many Negroes in my homeroom who had tickets. A lot of Negroes go to the games, but somehow or other they can't seem to scrape up six dollars at any one time to buy an activity ticket. It's a lot easier to pay a dollar and twenty-five cents to attend one of the games. I think the way they have it this year, though, that it was very fair. They had primaries, and two Negro girls made it past the primaries, but they weren't elected in a general election. Anybody could've voted in the general election, provided he'd registered to vote.

MITCHELL: I agree with Karl. I didn't think it was very fair that the Negroes had to have an activity ticket in the past to vote for the cheerleaders. Also, it wasn't very fair because the cheerleaders were nominated by other cheerleaders and the pep clubs. But with the general election, anybody can vote as long as you register. But this year, again, even though it was a fair election, there was an uproar because a Negro girl didn't get elected. I think if the Negroes had taken a real interest in it, that they could've elected a Negro girl. In fact, I think anytime that the Negroes want to elect someone, if they'd stick together, they could do it.

DAVID: Well I hate to disagree, but I never knew, myself, that there was an election. I didn't vote. I don't think it was too well publicized, and it wasn't clear that there was going to be an election of cheerleaders on the day that they held it. I didn't know exactly when it was going to be held, or how it was going to be held. I think we discussed it *after* the election was held, about how it was going to be changed, and so on. But it wasn't clear beforehand that it was going to be held that way.

MITCHELL: Well, as I recall, we discussed it before, because it took an amendment to the school constitution to change the way in which cheerleaders are elected. I was on the commission, so I certainly knew that there was going to be an election. But I'm not sure that it was that well publicized, either. I knew because I was on the commission. Maybe if you didn't get to school on time, or didn't pay any attention, you might not have heard the morning bulletins. I know it was in the morning bulletins. It's true that you could perhaps not have known that we were going to have an election.]

[QUESTION: Do the teachers treat all students alike?

DAVID: I really can't answer whether the teachers treat Negroes and whites differently. I've only had one colored girl in my classes. It was an English class. I've thought about that, why there're so few Negroes in our classes. Maybe they do treat them differently. They don't seem to have the same breaks as the white students.

MITCHELL: Last year there was this Negro in one of my classes, and I felt that the teacher was going out of her way to be especially pleasant to this colored girl. I don't really think the teachers discriminate.

KARL: Well, in all of my college prep classes I've only had one Negro, so it's very hard for me to know whether they do, or they don't.

DAVID: I think it's kind of strange that there're so few Negro and Mexican kids in our college prep classes. I know some Negroes who're real smart, and I've heard some people say they go out of their way to put real smart Mexican and Negro kids in the slower classes, even when they're smart and could do well in these smarter classes. I think there're a lot of kids who're Mexicans and Negroes, who should be in our classes. I don't know. Maybe they want to give these kids to teachers who're used to having Negroes and Mexicans, but it doesn't seem fair to me.

KARL: Well, you know, that might be a carry-over from junior high school, because in junior high school the teachers make recommendations as to what kinds of classes the kids should be placed in. They seem to follow these recommendations at Plains High School. I think you get some weird recommendations from junior high. For the most part, I don't think the teachers in junior high are recommending Negroes for college prep courses.

There're very few Negroes who go to college, and maybe this is one reason why they don't.

QUESTION: Do you think the counselors encourage Negroes to go to college?

MITCHELL: I think the counselors, as I know them, are pretty fair. I can't see that they discriminate. Some discrimination might be worked into the system, like, for example, maybe some of the teachers in junior high don't recommend Negroes as often as they do white students for college prep classes. But that's part of the system. I wouldn't say the counselors would deliberately discriminate. I think there might be something in the system, though, which causes discrimination. In fact, I'd say I know it happens, because there just aren't that many colored students in preparatory classes, so it must happen.

DAVID: The problem is so deep, it's not really just Plains High School. For example, it's a fact that many of the Negroes are from poorer homes, where they're not exposed to books and things like that. So maybe they couldn't compete as well in some of the college prep classes. Getting back to counselors, I don't think the counselors impress me much. I don't think they really help any students that much.

KARL: I can remember one incident where the counselors called some twenty students out of this study hall to tell us about the Merit Scholarship examinations that were going to be held. There were a lot of people in that study hall, and about fifty percent were Negro. As I recall, they didn't call one Negro out with us. They told us we were the best in our class, with the best grades, and that we should take this examination because a lot of the colleges were looking at the scores on this Merit Scholarship exam and were basing their acceptance or rejection of students on the basis of these scores. As far as seeing colored students, it's only in study hall and physical education classes. They're about the only places where college prep persons would meet Negroes. There were four Negroes in this public speaking class that I took. But that's the only class I've ever had, other than physical education, where there were that many Negroes. I learned an awful lot in that class about how Negroes feel, because we discussed civil rights a great deal. I think I learned more from these discussions than anywhere else. I learned about their ideas on rioting, and so on. These four boys really were quite different. One was militant, one was conservative and the other two were somewhere in between. In fact, one of the Negro boy's family supported Barry Goldwater in the last election. The other boys there called him an "Uncle Tom."]

When we ask David, Karl and Mitchell for a definition of an "Uncle Tom," they repeat previous explanations. Although the example used to illustrate what an "Uncle Tom" is is not always the same, the behavior of the individuals who are labeled this way has one thing in common—they do relatively well in the white man's world. Thus, the president of the senior class is called an "Uncle Tom" because he *is* president. Or a wealthier Negro is called an "Uncle Tom" because his wealth makes him stand out. While these are standards of achievement which no Negro should be denied because of his "Negroness," blacks feel that other blacks should not work to achieve standards established by the white community.

[QUESTION: How would you describe someone who's an "Uncle Tom"?

DAVID: Well, there's this kid, Fred, who's the president of our senior class. He might be called an "Uncle Tom."

KARL: There was this boy in our junior high school class. His father worked at the VA Hospital, and they were fairly wealthy and well-to-do. I think this had something to do with it. He seemed to be discriminated against by the other Negroes. I think that they'd call him an "Uncle Tom." Maybe because he's wealthier and stood out more from the other Negroes.]

Mitchell says that he would date a white girl who has dated a Negro, because he is "not prejudiced." At the same time, he has accepted some popular stereotypes of the black, a position which reflects prejudice of another sort. So, for instance, he thinks that the most integration takes place in sports and music—not simply because these fields are easily accessible to the black person, but because the Negro (naturally) excels in them.

[QUESTION: In which areas do you find the most integration?

MITCHELL: Sports are integrated most. I think that's because black persons can really excel in that field. If they aren't as smart as the other people, they can really excel in sports. So you find an awful lot of Negroes in sports. I think the other field, in which you'd find integration most, would be in music. But very few Negroes go into the clubs. I don't think that's because there's discrimination, but they don't try out for these clubs.

DAVID: At Plains High School, I'd say that the colored persons are definitely lethargic. They don't really care about their situation. But if someone comes into the school from the outside to agitate, then they can be aroused. But to get up on their own—they don't do that. [One of the boys asks, "What about Tim Howard?"]

DAVID: Well, when they had the ceremony downtown when Dr. King died, Tim Howard was out there. He had a sign with a couple of other Negroes that said, "You Killed the Only Friend You Ever Had." But I don't know whether he's really that outspoken.

MITCHELL: I know Tim Howard very well. I've known him from junior high school. I think he's the kind of guy who'd do it for the sake of raising a little bit of hell. I don't think he really harbors any hate against the white person. I think he does it because it's the in-thing to do.

KARL: During this time, I heard this one man speak on TV, and he said he wouldn't riot again. He'd been in a riot, but he said he wouldn't riot again, because he had a job. I think if more of them had jobs, they wouldn't think of rioting. It's really kind of messed up. I know this one guy whose father has a real good job, and they have plenty of money. In fact, I know a lot of Negroes whose fathers have good jobs. They seem to work and have good money, and all that. Yet, this one friend that I know said he's been discriminated against, not in jobs but when they wanted to buy a house. But he, himself, doesn't approve of open housing. I don't know! He said, "People should have the right to sell a house to whomever they want." Yet he disapproved of it when they weren't sold a house because they're black.

QUESTION: In which areas do you find the least integration?

KARL: Well, Debate, for one thing. There's only one Negro in Debate. I think more Negroes could get on the Debate team, if they wanted to. But there's a sort of feeling that they shouldn't try out, because other Negroes haven't been on the debate teams in the past. We've debated other Negroes from other schools, and I think the Negroes make good debaters. I know a couple of guys who'd be very good. But they don't try out. I think this is worse than discrimination. There really isn't that much discrimination in school. I think the worst thing is that the Negroes, as a rule, don't try out for these things, and they all know it. I think the worst thing is that they're apathetic.

MITCHELL: In this respect, I'd say it's the colored people who're going to have to make the move. When my mom went to Plains High School, things were really different then. They had separate parties, separate teams, they even had separate wash rooms, which is hard to believe. But that's the way things were at that time. Now I think things've improved a great deal. There may be some hidden barriers yet. But, for the most part, things have improved, so I think it's up to the colored people to make the move to try to get into these things.]

Mitchell thinks that Plains High would be more integrated if the Negroes were less apathetic. Other students, both white and black, however, say that the Negroes have tried to penetrate white activities in the past, but have failed. The knowledge that others have tried and failed may partly act to keep some black students from also trying. Whatever the reasons, and while one may blame black "apathy," it is certainly an oversimplification to say that, "It's up to the colored people to make a move."

[QUESTION: How do the students mix socially?

DAVID: Well, there're a couple of instances, I know, where white girls have dated colored guys. There's this one girl, in particular, that we know—we all know her—who started dating this colored guy. I don't know whether she's really serious about it, because she's always trying to prove things. A lot of kids asked, "What's she trying to prove?" when she started dating this colored guy.

MITCHELL: At dances, or something like that, even at parties, if there're Negroes and whites, the Negroes take their place at one part of the room and the whites in another. They stay pretty much separate all evening. I think one thing is, that the colored people are so much better dancers. I think everybody was pretty skeptical of this white girl who dated a Negro boy. But I think this, too, is even becoming a lot more relaxed, like the movie, "Guess Who's Coming to Dinner?" I think there'll be more of this next year and in the years to come.

KARL: I've heard some Negroes say that the Negroes who fit in best with white people are the light-skinned Negroes. There was one boy last year—he was quite light, he was a senior—I know a lot of the other Negro boys hated this guy, 'cause he fit in real well with the white people. The other Negroes thought that this Negro had betrayed their plans to walk out of an assembly. I've also heard stories that the counselors had threatened this white girl and Negro boy who were dating. They gave them a lot of trouble about dating and tried to break up the relationship. I think a lot of Negroes were upset about this and about the cheerleader incident. Some of them started making signs, or writing on the boards, that the student council is going to give us a Negro cheerleader, or else.

QUESTION: If a white girl dates a Negro, is she dated by white boys also?

KARL: I think this girl is definitely off-limits until it's known that she's not seeing this Negro boy anymore.

MITCHELL: No, I don't think she'd be dated by white guys. It's just not acceptable yet. Oh, there're some prominent people who have intermarried, like Dean Rusk's daughter and some of the people in Hollywood, but it's not acceptable yet.

KARL: You'd feel you were intruding into someting that's too different. It's too hot to handle. These two kids are in the limelight and well known. I just wouldn't want to intrude. I wouldn't want to get involved.

DAVID: I've heard a lot of kids say that this colored boy and white girl didn't really mix because they liked each other, but they did it to prove they could. She walked around and bragged about it a great deal. I think she was doing it just for the sake of doing it. I know this girl. She was in my history class. She's always speaking out about things. She's always yelling about the wrongs done to the Indians, when we were taking up the American Indians in our class. One thing about this situation is that this guy is really a nice guy—everybody likes him. She started at the top, that's for sure.

MITCHELL: Well, we all know this girl, and it seems to me that she just wants to spit in the eye of society.

QUESTION: What's the white girl's reputation like after she's dated a Negro?

MITCHELL: The white girl's reputation is tarnished if she dates a Negro guy. I can't explain why this happens. Maybe it's because it's so different. If it was a girl I liked myself, I don't know how I'd feel.

DAVID: There was this girl that I had a date with once. I heard she dated Charles Baldwin a couple of times. He's a Negro. This didn't really cool me out with her. I only dated her once, though, and I learned about this after I dated her. I guess it would depend on the girl. I don't think it would bother me. I think I'd just go ahead and date the girl if I wanted to. But I don't think of myself as being prejudiced, while some people are.

KARL: You know, the Negroes feel the same say. I had some definite ideas about what the Negroes thought, until I talked to Negroes in some of my classes—like in my Speech class. They were all the way from pro-Goldwater to people who'd say they'd join the riots. So there're many opinions among Negroes on this issue, too.

QUESTION: Are there cases at school in which white boys date Negro girls?

DAVID: We couldn't do that. I'd just be chastised if I ever took out a black girl. There was this guy at work who asked me about this. He said, "Do any white guys take out Negro girls at school?" I said, "No!" He said, "If I ever saw that, I'd shoot the white guy."]

The three white young women in Part 1 of this chapter did not like school on the day of Dr. King's funeral because things were too quiet. A number of other students, however, enjoyed school that day for that very reason. Both black and white students questioned the motives of some of their fellows who stayed home, ostensibly to watch the funeral. They doubted that these students stayed home because of respect for Dr. King.

[QUESTION: What was school like when Martin Luther King was killed?

MITCHELL: Well, I thought the school handled Dr. King's death really well. They really couldn't call an assembly because they didn't do that even for President Kennedy. They had a special bulletin sent around school with some words from one of his speeches. I don't remember which one it was exactly—it wasn't the "I Have a Dream" speech, but it was something like that—which was read by the teachers. Then we had some silent meditation, and you could leave the school when you wanted to. I thought it was real tastefully done. There was a lot of tension in school at that time, and something needed to be done. I thought the school handled it real well. The school was really quiet the day of the funeral. There weren't too many Negroes, and a lot of the whites also stayed home from school.

DAVID: I don't know how true it is—funny thing was, though, that I heard that the reason why there were riots in some cities was because the schools weren't let out for the day of King's funeral. I've heard that's why they rioted. But I know here in Center City a lot of the colored kids just took the day off to play around. I thought this was disrespectful. They really didn't go to mourn King's death.

KARL: It seems more disrespectful for Negroes and whites to do this than to have gone to school. I know a lot of them came back to school at 3:20, when school was let out. They were out there to meet all the guys. I didn't like that too much.

QUESTION: Did you like school the day of Dr. King's funeral?

KARL: It was really quiet. I liked it a lot. I don't know, maybe the Negroes are more boisterous than the white people and that's why it was so quiet. I enjoyed the quiet and the lack of confusion. But I think that it's going to be quiet and less confusing whenever seven hundred and fifty kids are absent from school anyway. Sometimes I feel like all the walls are going to close all around you with the noise, when everybody is there. I enjoyed it on that day.

MITCHELL: I'm amazed because people expect so much from Plains High School. For example, there was supposed to have been a bomb threat to blow up the school tower after King's death. I think this is what people always think from outside of Plains High. That it's so bad, and all kinds of things are going to happen. I think the atmosphere is relaxed there. I think the problem is that the people from the outside expect things to happen.

KARL: It's the same way at East High. They always expect these things to really happen at Plains High School. When King died, this white student I know out East called me up and asked me what it was like at school. He wanted to know if there were any riots or anything. They seem to expect these things to happen there. That whole incident with the East people, that was something else, too. They listed a number of reasons why they didn't want their children to go to Plains High School. They were picking out many defects that the school had which weren't true. It's amazing how many of them could talk on the subject and still not know anything about it.

MITCHELL: I was talking to Mr. Ewing, and he told me that a handful of businessmen from there came to look at Plains High School. They were the only ones who came to look. The rest of them just assumed that all of these things they were saying were true. Mr. Ewing said that these people were really amazed because one of the things they said was that Plains High School had no space. Mr. Ewing showed them empty classrooms. There're always empty classrooms.

KARL: I was at that second meeting they had. There weren't as many racial overtones at that meeting as there were at the first meeting they had. But that was an open meeting, so all of these people more or less sat in the back of the room and didn't say much. When they did, their arguments were really foolish. But they didn't want to appear to be racist. I know definitely that at their first meeting one person said he didn't want his kids to go to Plains High School because of the racial situation. At the second meeting, they had a lawyer there, and nobody discussed race.

MITCHELL: I enjoy going to school with colored people. In gym class some of the pranks that they pull really keep you rolling in the aisles. I think the kids at East, when they come to Plains High School, will have to learn to adjust to being with Negroes. But they won't have any trouble. I got a big kick out of that meeting because the wife of a prominent physician got up there and said she wanted her kids to go to Plains High School to get in on the hard knocks of life. She thought she was being so egalitarian, and she's really prejudiced, because I don't know what hard knocks exist at Plains High School that don't exist elsewhere. She thought she was being nice, but I thought she was very tactless. It made me laugh.]

Unlike his two friends, David expresses surprise that there is not more conflict at Plains High School. He finds it hard to believe that the Negroes do not complain about being placed in "dumb" classes. It is obvious, from his preoccupation with this, that he sees education as the Negro's way out of the ghetto. Blacks see academic competition with "Whitey" as "Uncle Tomism," however, so that whenever blacks do strive for grades, they are contemptuously disparaged by the other Negroes. For this reason, it is not too surprising when black students fail to protest when they are not included in the same classes as whites.

[QUESTION: Is there much violence at Plains High School?

KARL: Well, occasionally there are fights, but I've never seen an interracial fight. If people fight, they fight because they're mad at each other. But it's not interracial.

MITCHELL: A lot of the kids out at East High and other people, hear about the violence, and they just assume it exists. I think if the people would take the time to look in at Plains High School, they'd be surprised. They expect things to happen, but things don't happen.

DAVID: The thing that amazes me, the question I'd like to ask, is why there isn't more of a problem at Plains High School? Why is it so calm? I've never heard any of the Negroes beef about being put into the dumb classes. I've heard them beef about other things, but not about that, and that's a legitimate beef. It seems to me that things are quiet, and I often wonder why they are as quiet as they are.

MITCHELL: I think it's because, for the most part, the Negroes do get a fair shake at Plains High School. As far as the clubs are concerned, it's up to the Negro to get into them if they want to.

DAVID: Well, I think they segregate the kids by putting them into these dumb classes. That's some form of segregation, as far as I'm concerned. For example, on second floor they have a course called physical science. It's a course for the dumb kids. Also, there's this one class on the third floor. I hear it's a dumb math class, and all the Negroes are in that. I think they have some segregation by putting all dumb kids together.

KARL: I'd have to go along there because I'm just in regular college preparatory classes. There aren't many accelerated classes at Plains High School, anyway, and these college prep classes should be open to everybody. But there aren't many Negroes in them.

DAVID: They definitely are open to everyone, because there're some real duds in our so-called college prep classes. I don't see why some of the Negroes couldn't be in there.

MITCHELL: I never realized this problem existed until you talk about it now. I'd like to hear what the administration has to say about this. I'm not sure about how they go about assigning kids to their classes. I know just some smart colored kids who're in the college prep classes, but there're only a few. Now that you raise the issue, it seems odd to me that there aren't more Negroes in these classes.

DAVID: When we took our college entrance examinations there weren't many Negroes in there at all. Maybe most of them don't plan to go to college, but then maybe they're not told about them.]

We have just been witnesses to an interesting process. Mitchell, who heretofore did not perceive any discrimination at Plains High, now acknowledges that the class placement of Negroes may be discriminatory. Although David repeatedly suggests that the absence of blacks in college preparatory classes is an example of prejudice at Plains High, this fact is too new an evaluation for Mitchell to accept the situation. But Karl concedes there might be some discrimination because even though he is *not* in accelerated courses, there is nevertheless a conspicuous absence of Negroes in his classes. Mitchell agrees that some discrimination exists at Plains High when two of his friends point out that it does. It seems probable, however, that in Mitchell's case his awareness will be short-lived and that, once he leaves the interview situation, he will return to thinking, "The Negroes get a fair shake at Plains High School." (Two months after this interview, however, Mitchell got in touch with his interviewer (F. P.) to discuss some implications of this study. The change in attitudes which started to unfold during this first interview was actually more complete at the second meeting.)

[QUESTION: Which sex mixes better interracially?

MITCHELL: I think the boys mix better. It's because of sports, mainly.

KARL: I agree. I think the Negroes feel more at ease in sports. There're so many good Negro boy athletes, they can gain respect this way. The white kids always support all Negro teams, too. We're right behind them. Everybody attends the games.

MITCHELL: There were some parents who were horrified by the fact that we had five Negroes on our starting basketball team. I know for a fact that some of the parents didn't like it this year when both the King and Queen were Negro.[Mitchell shows what can happen to a person when his once firm attitudes have been shaken] I see two alternatives: either the colored people are being discriminated against in these college preparatory classes, or the Negroes just don't match up to the white people in this respect. I don't know, I don't like to make hasty conclusions and say that there's discrimination. There might be, but I'd like to look into it more. As I sit here, I find it kind of hard to think of a colored boy that would fit into some of these college preparatory classes.

DAVID: Well, if a kid is between an average class and a better class, it seems to me that it'd be better to put him into the higher class, so it'd give him something to push for. I think a lot of times they just automatically assign a Negro to a lower class, even if he's marginal. Can we mention names? Mrs. Thaler says she thinks the Negroes are discriminated against a little because when they are borderline, they're always put into the lower classes. I think it'd be better to put them into the higher classes first.

MITCHELL: I think a Negro person who's above average could go to college, because the colleges are going out of their way to get Negroes. I know, where my brother went to school they tried to get some Negroes, but they couldn't get any. I think it might be hard for some Negroes to go to school because of the economic situation. I think it's possible, though, to go to school because the schools are making more of an effort to pave the Negro's way.

DAVID: A lot of the Negroes don't know about scholarships. In my home room, there was this Negro boy I was talking to. I asked him if he was going to take the scholarship tests, and he said, "No." I asked him why not. He told me, even if he made it, it'd still be an uphill fight all the way. He's going to go down to the railroad, just like his father. On this issue of who gets along better with whom, I'd say, the girls. I think the girls are a little bit more liberal than the boys. I don't know, I see as many girls, I think, as I do boys hanging around with each other. I think girls are more liberal.

MITCHELL: I think both sexes seem to mix fairly well.

[At this point Karl leaves to go to work, and the interview was continued with only David and Mitchell.]

DAVID: In the cafeteria, there's this one big table with all Negro girls. So I don't know, I really haven't made up my mind on this issue. I think, in general, there're some Negroes who mix well, and others who could care less.

MITCHELL: Well, I think the atmosphere is really relaxed. If a colored boy sits down to eat lunch with us, nobody thinks anything about it.

DAVID: Well, that's true, but only if we knew him. If we didn't, we might get a funny feeling.

MITCHELL: I think the parents at East High are the ones looking for the racial trouble. We kinda accept the mixing of the races now because we've been going to mixed schools for awhile. We accept it. I went to an exchange school. There were only five Negroes in that school. It was in a very rich section. When I came back, I was talking to the assistant principal from Plains High School. We talked about the atmosphere in this rich school. It was kind of fanciful. He said he liked it better in an integrated school. He also told me that he lives in the East High district, but when his kids are old enough to go to high school, he's going to send them to Plains High School. I like it better in an integrated school, also.]

Mitchell, as many of his fellow students, maintains that his generation is more liberal than that of his parents. Part of this, he attributes to the fact that Plains High is no longer structurally segregated. When his mother attended school at Plains High, Negroes had separate washrooms, teams, dances and parties. Since this kind of formal segregation no longer exists there, Mitchell thinks the school has made considerable progress toward "integrating". However, we actually found little evidence of genuine "integration" beyond the fact that Plains High is attended both by blacks and whites. One could have characterized the school in almost the same way when Mitchell's mother was a student there.

[QUESTION: Do you think your contemporaries are more liberal than either your parents or grandparents?

MITCHELL: I definitely think that my contemporaries are more liberal than my parents or my grandparents. When Mom went to school, things were different. They even had separate bathrooms and different parties. Since then, I think Plains High School has gone a long way. They've made many advances. I think kids, nowadays, are less prejudiced than their parents. But I still think we'll have to make a lot of economic progress before racism can be eliminated.

DAVID: I don't know. I don't see too much difference between my parents and myself, particularly my dad. I think my dad is liberal. Most of their friends are, too.

MITCHELL: Well, I know a couple of my parents' very good friends were really up in arms when they learned that a colored boy was elected king and a colored girl elected queen this year. I was surprised at the way they reacted. I was really happy, myself, because I see this as the Negroes' making progress, because they're standing behind their race, and they're also getting out there and voting to see that their kids make out as well as the white kids. I know a lot of people who're also skeptical about our basketball team because it was mainly Negro. But I think it's great. After a while, a lot of the people just fell in line and didn't mind so much, and they did come to the games.

DAVID: Yeah, that's because they were winning all the time.

MITCHELL: As far as my grandparents are concerned, I think they're a little bit exceptional, because my grandfather is a preacher in a mixed church—so they're quite liberal.]

[QUESTION: Where do the Mexican students fit in at school?

DAVID: You know, you see very few Mexicans. I think they keep to themselves. I don't know, they seem to think they might get knifed or something. They're just a small group, and they tend to hang around each other. They don't mix with the other kids.

MITCHELL: They're a very small group, and they really seem to be clannish. I really can't think of any Mexican kids. You just don't see them around much. When you see them, they're always together.]

David closes the interview by explaining that attending a desegregated school teaches you how to act around Negroes. More important, he suggests that contact between the races removes some of the irrational fears whites have of blacks. Although such attitudes alone may or may not lead to "integration," removal of fear is at least a step in the right direction.

[QUESTION: What has your experience at Plains High taught you about race relations?

DAVID: I'd say that Plains High has taught me that mixing between the races is possible, that it can happen. I think it also teaches you to be conscious in what you say. There're some kinds of things that are no-nos. You don't talk about them. If you know the guy real well, you know what he's going to say and then it's okay. I know this one kid who's a militant. He doesn't really do anything in school, but he tells me how he beats up white guys after school, and all that. I don't know how true it is.

MITCHELL: We have a maid who comes every other week. She's a Negro. She tells me that the Black Power groups are growing in the southern part of town. But I don't see that the Negroes here have it so bad. There's a Youth Center at our church. It was built for the kids, and it's really nice. But the white kids won't use it. They sit outside and they smoke. Now the colored kids are really starting to use the place. My dad, who's kind of responsible for it, says that the Boy Scouts tear up the church more than this group. He said this group of Negro kids is real nice. The neighbors are up in arms around there, though. They don't like it.

DAVID: Well, that shows that Center City isn't that great.

MITCHELL: I'd go to an integrated school if I had it to do all over again, if I had a choice. After going to a segregated school for a week, I found that I didn't like it. I think one thing about going to Plains High is that it's taught me how to get along with colored people. You're going to have to mix with them in your life. I think it's a good experience to start mixing when you're younger. I'd certainly want my kids to go to an integrated school. I think you're more apt to be prejudiced if you don't go to an integrated school, or if you don't associate with Negroes.

DAVID: I'd agree with that. I wouldn't like to go to a segregated school for the same reasons. I was out at a drive-in out East one time, and this colored guy came in. He had his hair bleached. A lot of the East High kids out there were nervous, they wanted this guy to leave. They don't know how to act around Negroes. None of the Plains High School kids that I went with thought anything about it.

On Being Black and White

Part 3

The two young men in this interview are both Negroes. Jackson is a junior at Plains High. His experience there has been so unpleasant that he intends to finish school elsewhere. Walter is out of school and works as an IBM operator for one of the public utilities. At one time he dated a white girl, and Jackson still does. Both young men believe that, because of their relationship with white young women, the counselors and teachers at times actively made life in school unpleasant for them. Walter is more articulate than Jackson. Were he not black, he would probably be attending college, rather than operating a countersorter.

[QUESTION: What pressures do you feel from attending a desegregated school?

WALTER: The main thing is, I felt I was expected to do more. I was expected to be above average, or do more than the average white person. This was true both in my grades and in sports. I was expected to do more in football bacause I'm a Negro. I was expected to do more than the other guy, and to play better than he played, because they expect Negroes to be good in athletics. The same was true for grades. They expect Negroes to do a lot more than white kids if they're going to be recognized. I felt this constant pressure from the teachers. This teacher came right out once and said, "I think you're more well groomed and I think you're a nicer person and a smarter person than some of your friends." By "some of your friends," she meant Negroes. She also said, "You should do more. Your father is well known. He's a nicer Negro than most Negroes." I think it was because of this that they also expected me to be a "nicer Negro" than most Negroes. In class, when there were five or six loud Negroes, and I managed to be quiet, the teacher would always call me out and ask me to talk to the noisy Negroes. She said that I should set an example because I was more intelligent. I told her I appreciated how she felt about me and that this was a compliment, but I also told her that it was not up to me to tell the students to be quiet. I was there to learn, and that it was up to the teacher to take care of the discipline in the class. I just came right out and told her, "It's your responsibility and not mine!"

QUESTION: Did the other kids know you were being singled out this way, and how did they react?

WALTER: No, the kids didn't really realize that I was being picked out by the teachers. I presume, if they had, they'd have felt bitter toward the teacher and not me. It's very hard for me to express what I want to say, but I think that it was this constant pressure to excel and to do better in school because I'm a Negro that I felt while I was at Plains High School.

QUESTION: Who expected you to do better in sports?

WALTER: It wasn't just the coaches. This was true even in gym class. They expect Negroes to do better in gym because Negroes are supposed to excel in sports, all kinds of sports. And even in gym class, if some kids were cutting up, the gym teacher would ask me to go tell my friends to get back in line. I think perhaps they asked me to do this because the teachers found it harder to communicate with these kids. They felt I could communicate easier with them, because I'm a Negro. They'd listen to me better than they'd listen to the teacher who's white. At other times, I felt they were using me as a scapegoat and I've thought, why did they do it? Why did they pick me out? I really haven't come up with an answer. I even think about it sometimes now—why was I picked out and always told that I should do better, that I was a nice Negro and well-groomed Negro? And why was I picked out to keep the others in line? Maybe it's because if I had, it would've been easier for the teachers, but I really don't know.

JACKSON: I think that my pressures are basically the same as what Walter has been talking about. But, in school I'm known as a trouble maker. I'm loud, and I've been thrown out of a lot of classes and gotten into a lot of trouble. I've been kind of a leader in the classes; I'm in a lot of trouble. They're always calling me in to talk to me to try to straighten me out. There's one counselor I really like. Can I mention names? I really like Mr. Gage. He's more understanding than the other counselors. I feel more secure when he's behind me, or when I'm talking to him than I do when I'm talking to some of the other counselors. The others don't listen to ya, and they don't really give a damn. This whole past year I felt like the counselors and a lot of the teachers have been picking on me. Maybe they even have a right to, because of my past record. I've been in a lot of trouble at school. But I really like it when I go to Mr. Gage. He's not like the others. He'll bring me in, and he'll talk to me, and he'll let me talk to him. He listens, and tries to help me work out my problem. This year I had a lot of trouble. I was suspended from most of my classes. Most of it was for petty things—things that other kids wouldn't be suspended for. I think a lot of it's because I'm dating this white girl, and we've been open about it in the hallways. I felt it was because of this. The counselors and the teachers don't like it if you're going with a white girl. In the halls, I'm seen with this white girl. So, for every little thing that ever came up I was sent to the counselors' office and kicked out. I just haven't felt, particularly this year, that I've been treated justifiably by the counselors. I'll give you an example of what I mean. We usually have five-minute breaks between classes. I'll go to this class with this white girl friend of mine, and we'll stand outside and talk about five minutes until the bell rings. Then she goes into class, and I'll go to mine. Well, the teacher told her that she wasn't supposed to talk in the hallways, and that when she comes to class she's supposed to come right in. She wasn't supposed to talk to me between classes. That's not true for the other kids—everyone talks between classes. As long as you're not late for class, you can stand outside and talk to each other. If I was talking to another white boy or another Negro, they wouldn't say anything. They wouldn't have told the girl or the other boys that they had to come right into class.]

Similar feelings of being exploited have been expressed by the "elite" Negroes, who tell of academic exploitation and of being paraded before visitors to give the latter the impression that the "elite" black represents the Negro at Plains High. Now Walter says that Negroes are also exploited by the athletic department in that, in physical education classes, more is expected of blacks. Walter and Jackson believe that the teachers have accepted the "super-athlete" stereotype of the Negro. [This interview was conducted two months before articles appeared in *Sports Illustrated* and *Newsweek* on black exploitation in athletics.]

In some of the preceding chapters, we have been told how poorly interracial dating is tolerated at Plains High School. Many students say that teachers and counselors more or less openly punish students who violate the unofficial rule against dating between black and white. Jackson agrees from first hand experience that there is an intolerant view of such activity. Walter tells of a similar reaction from the counselors and teachers when he dated a white girl in junior high school.

[WALTER: I've felt some small things, too. I was involved with a white girl in junior high school for three years. I met a young lady through another friend at school. We developed a small, platonic relationship—it wasn't too much. I won't go into all of it, but I'll try to remember some of the discrimination I felt. I was called down to this woman counselor's office. She's really forward, and I dislike her very much. She started off asking me a lot of questions about the young lady. She asked me if I knew her, and for how long. Finally, one day she asked me if I was going with her. I said, "No!" She said, "Society doesn't approve of this." She came right out with it, that Negroes weren't supposed to go out with white ladies. She kept saying, "Society feels that it's not right." I was very young then. I didn't know how to answer her. Since then I really have thought about it, and I sure wish that I knew then what I know now. I sure wish that I was as verbal then as I am now. But I really wasn't able to answer her. I was too young. We broke up for a while, because the principal also called me down and told me he didn't want me to see her again. As I said, I was young and foolish then, so I agreed, which I would never do now. But then, during the summer, if I must say so myself, this young lady was more of the aggressor in the relationship. She kept calling me, and then I'd call her back, and we started seeing each other again. We'd go to a park, over here near my home. In September, when we got back to school, the principal called me back in again, and he told me he knew I'd been seeing this girl in the park, and he didn't want me to see her any more. I was really dumbfounded. I asked how the heck he knew. But, anyway, I agreed not to see her. I wouldn't do that now. After a while, these teachers and counselors didn't even talk to me in a roundabout way. They'd come right out and tell me that they resented the fact that I, as a Negro, was seeing this white girl. That part of my life really sticks with me, because I couldn't express myself then as I do now. I felt inferior, and it's bothered me ever since. I think this inferiority is just a carryover from everyday life. I tend to feel less of it now than I did then, but you know the average Negro just feels inferior to white people. I'm sure I don't feel that way any more. I also felt, when I was in school, that every time I was called down for something, it was because I was a Negro. Now that I'm a little bit older and think back on it, I think perhaps some of the times that I was called down race didn't have anything to do with it. But I used to think that it was always race. I do know of a couple of incidents, though, in which I'm sure it was race. Once I was kicked out of school for fighting. I was fighting this other gentleman. He hit me first, and I hit him several times. The principal kicked me out of school. I was also made to believe that he [the other student] had been kicked out of school, but he wasn't. He was a white boy. Well, my father took me back to school. I told the principal that I was led to believe that the other student was also ejected from school. The principal said, "Well, he wasn't." He said that I was the aggressor in the fight and I should be punished more than the other kid. He said, "Why do you Negroes always feel that, when we talk to you, it's discrimination?" I was a little more intelligent 'cause I was older, so I told him. I said, "Perhaps it's not always discrimination. But you must remember that we've been held down for so long by the white man, that it's a normal reaction on our part because we're black. We have a lot of things to remember—generations of discrimination and generations of making us feel like we're black and dirty and worthless. It's hard for us not to think of discrimination when something happens to us." Getting back to your original question, I'd say, most of the racial pressures come on the social level. One day, for example, I was going to the YMCA. This was about four years ago. I was going there with this other kid. We were going to shoot some pool. The man said, "There aren't any more pool tables." I said, "Well, there's an empty one right there." He said, "Someone else has it taken." I also have this friend who wanted to buy a house out East. He said that he looked around, and the realtors didn't want to sell him a home 'cause he was a Negro. It's a little more subtle. This Negro fella said that they just put such a high price on the house that he couldn't afford it. I went to the NAACP about the YMCA incident. The president said that he'd look into it. I went down there about a week later. There was another man at the desk, and I did manage to play pool this time. I don't know what would've happened if that first guy had been there.

These two young men think that while the Negro is accepted in sports (as long as he is eligible), he does not stand much of a chance in student government. Nor, do they feel, are Negro young women accepted in a traditionally all white activity such as cheerleading. The few Negroes who are in student government are dismissed by Jackson as "Uncle Toms." This is the same dilemma pointed out earlier. Jackson is angry because he feels "A Negro isn't allowed to participate in . . . student government or (to be a) cheerleader." At the same time, however, he rejects those blacks who have been elected to student government as "Uncle Toms."

[QUESTION: In which activities do you find the most integration?
JACKSON: In sports like football and basketball. But there isn't very much mixing in student government, except maybe for the upper class Negroes. I'm gonna be a little bit blunt. These are the kids who're Uncle Toms. Most Negroes are average and can't participate in student government. The way they keep you out is they've a set of regulations which the average Negro can't meet. I'm not saying he's too stupid to meet these requirements, but I don't think he really cares to meet them. For example, you have to pass a test on the school constitution and you have to have a certain grade-point average. Another area in which there's very little integration is with the cheerleaders. We've been trying for years to get a Negro cheerleader at Plains High School. The day King died, they held an election at 7:30 in the morning when most of the Negroes were excused from school. [But in that primary election, two Negro candidates were nevertheless nominated.] I feel that a Negro isn't allowed to participate in this sort of activity, either student government or cheerleader, or something like that. The cheerleaders that we wanted told us that they only lost by a couple of votes. I don't understand why the school didn't hold off on the elections until later that week. We didn't have anything planned. I'm sure they could've held the elections later. We went to them, and we asked 'em about this. The principal said that we

wouldn't have time to schedule it in later. We circulated a petition, but that didn't do any good. Then we were thinking of boycotting the sports, but that didn't work, either. A couple of the Negroes who're in sports agreed to boycott, but the rest said that they couldn't afford to, that they wanted to go to college, so they didn't agree to boycott. We've never had any luck in getting some of our wishes at school anyway.

WALTER: Let me tell you about another case. There was this young lady, a colored girl, who wanted to run for student representative. She was a junior, and she'd entered the race to run. She took out a petition, and entered her name. The following week, she was telling me that the principal said she couldn't run. This young lady was really upset. She was crying when she was telling me. He didn't tell her why she couldn't run, so I decided to go to Mr. Gibson. He's in charge of the elections. I asked him why this girl couldn't run. He gave me the silliest excuse I've ever heard in my life. He said that it was because of her age. She was a junior, and she wanted to run as secretary for the junior class. He said that the constitution says that no student may run for office if they didn't turn seventeen by April. This girl was going to turn seventeen on May thirteenth, I remember that because I thought it was so stupid. I told him, "Now, Mr. Gibson, that's ridiculous. Do you honestly expect me to believe this is your reason? This is absolutely ridiculous." He said this was the reason; that it was in the constitution. Well, I don't believe that one bit—I didn't then and I don't now. I talked to a lot of students about this. We got a petition up, but nothing ever happened. I feel that this is one of the reasons why a lot of Negro students don't take part in things. They just don't feel like fighting the situation. We don't feel that we have a chance. In order for the Negro to benefit, we'd have to have a good number of Negroes participating in student government. I think it'd be very rewarding and stimulating. But if only a few participate, it wouldn't do much good. The few couldn't set up proposals that would benefit the Negro.

JACKSON: I'd like to go back to the constitution bit. I think they rely too much on the constitution. Most of the Negroes don't even know what's in the constitution. During the end of the year, we got together with a psychologist from one of the clinics in town because we wanted to discuss the possibilities of having an open lunch hour. The psychologist and this teacher told us that the constitution said that we first had to take this idea before the principal. We circulated a petition to see how many kids were for an open lunch hour, and then we wanted to have an election. We went to the principal. The principal said the School Code wouldn't allow this. The average Negro doesn't know too much about the constitution or the School Code. I felt they just don't want to give us a chance. I think the only thing that they're willing for us to do is to participate in athletics, because they like to exploit the Negroes in athletics. It's all right for a Negro to represent his school in the field, 'cause he's good, but he isn't permitted to do these other things.

WALTER: I agree with that. I think that the Negro is exploited in athletics.]

As has been indicated before, the Negro who participates in traditionally white activities is labeled an "Uncle Tom" by other blacks. Even the liberal "Hippies" disapprove of the Negro who succeeds too well or too often in white activities. One definition of an "Uncle Tom" is that he participates in white activities and that he is more supportive of whites than of blacks. Jackson is more blunt in his definition, but, at the same time, he is self-critical. He is worried that perhaps he finds faults in the "elite" Negroes because they are doing better than he is. Walter prefers to be careful about labeling someone an "Uncle Tom."

[QUESTION: Can you describe an "Uncle Tom"?

JACKSON: Please excuse my English but that's a Negro that kisses the white man's ass. The white man says, "Leap," and the Negro says, "How high?" There're just a few of these Uncle Toms at school, these are the goody-goody guys. Maybe I say this, though, because they're doing a little bit better than I am. And maybe I'm a little bit ashamed of myself because I'm not doing as good as they are in school, and I'm jealous. Maybe that's why I think of them as Uncle Toms.

WALTER: Before I accuse a Negro of being an Uncle Tom, I think about it for quite a while. I don't want to accuse a man of forgetting his own race so quickly. I'll try to explain what an Uncle Tom is. You know, when you see Negroes, you usually see them together. But I guess that's true of all races, 'cause you see the white kids together, too. I hope you'll understand what I'm trying to say. I think it all boils down to, when you see an Uncle Tom, it's a Negro that you only see with white people; you never see him with other Negroes. He likes white people better than he does Negroes. Now maybe this isn't true. Maybe these guys like Negroes, too. But they don't seem to show it. But I really do think that we, as Negroes, are obligated to hesitate before calling another Negro an Uncle Tom. In general, though I'd say that when a Negro constantly associates with white people only, and not with other Negroes, he's an Uncle Tom. A lot of Negroes feel that a Negro who associates with white poeple is superior, so he feels lucky to associate with them.

JACKSON: I wouldn't say that. I run around with a lot of white people. I don't find them different than Negroes. They like to party, they like to drink, and they like to have fun, just like Negroes. I don't feel I'm lucky because I associate with white people. I don't feel I'm lucky if I associate with Negroes, either. I think they're the same as we are. The only difference I can see is skin color.

WALTER: Well, Jackson has a point. You know Jackson runs around with a lot of white kids, but he runs around with a lot of Negroes, too. We wouldn't call him an Uncle Tom. Now, I know some Negroes who do call you an Uncle Tom, Jackson. But I wouldn't call him an Uncle Tom, 'cause he's different. You know, I'm really for integration, and I hope that some day we can all live together without stares and live relaxed when we're together. I want people not to especially notice it when you see a white and Negro together. I hope this comes about some day.

JACKSON: There's this kid, Jeff; he's an Uncle Tom. I feel he's a real good example of this. When we see him in the halls in school, he's always with white people. I say "Hi" to him; he won't talk to me. He turns the other way. I go to both Negro and white parties. I see him at the white parties, but I've never seen him at a Negro party. He never associates with people from his own race. He's one of these goody-goody guys. He was elected to the Student Congress and other things. I think he has a very high grade-point average. I guess that's why he was elected. Sometimes I worry about my feelings Sometimes I feel sorry. Maybe I feel that I don't like Jeff because he's doing better than I am in school. You know, you don't like it when people are doing better than you are.

WALTER: Well, I think there's more to it with Jeff. I don't ever remember seeing him with a Negro. You know, I think that kind of person is more of a detriment to the Negro than an asset. I don't believe any Negro should ever abandon his own race completely.

JACKSON: Maybe his parents have something to do with it. Maybe they want him to learn to conduct himself as a gentleman.

WALTER: Well, I disagree with that. I believe you can learn to conduct yourself as a gentleman around Negroes, too. You know there're as many Negroes as white people who're gentlemen.

JACKSON: Well, that's true.

WALTER: The Negroes just don't like this when a person is always with white people. Maybe Jeff doesn't dislike Negroes, but in the average Negro's eyes, he doesn't show it. He's abandoned them; feels he's better then they are. One feels that he's put himself on a pedestal and has abandoned his race.]

These two young men, as many other young people with whom we have talked, blame much of the segregation on older people—not just older white people, but older blacks as well. A little later in this interview, Walter says that the older Negro is more "deplorable than the white man," because he resists "integration" as much as many whites. One should not assume, however, that older blacks prefer segregation for its own sake. To some extent, this "preference" is undoubtedly a defense against the past hurts and possible future rejections from the white community.

[QUESTION: Is there any mixing between the races at school?

JACKSON: Well, a lot of the kids mix between class. There's some difference, though. Most of the Negroes have their own meeting place on the second floor. But I think this past year there's been a lot more mixing than we've had in the past. Negroes and whites have been mixing more.

WALTER: When I was there, I felt there was a good deal of association between the races, and I think this was good. I think that a lot of the pressure not to associate was from the old cronies, the older generation—the principal and some of the teachers.

JACKSON: I think this generation doesn't really think of the races as different. I think we think more of each other as equal. The older generation doesn't want us to associate.

WALTER: I really don't think that my generation has as much of a racial problem as people think. All of my Negro friends seem to get along real well with white people. It's the older generation who's always talking about some friction between the races. I think their parents have a lot to do with it. With white girls, I think a lot of their parents tell 'em that the Negro boys are only out for one thing. They tell them that the Negro class is dirty. A lot of the white boys, I think, feel this, too. There's one thing that I can't understand. I don't understand why, after a white girl goes with a Negro boy, that white boys won't take her out. This has always bothered me. I just don't know what to make of it.]

White girls, we hear, are labeled "immoral" by the white community if they are merely seen talking in public with a black young man; if they date him, the social punishment is that much more severe. A label of "immoral"—referring to sexual immorality—may partly be attributed to the cultural myth of the black person's hypersexuality. In part, too, such name-calling may salve the wounded pride, particularly of white young men who have been displaced as the result of interracial dating. At any rate, the certainty of being judged "immoral" may very well prevent many a white young woman from dating a Negro.

[WALTER: One time I was walking down the stairs outside Plains High School. I was standing with this white girl, and we were talking. About six white kids drove by in a car. They yelled, "White trash—you're nothing but white trash." I guess, because she was white and I'm black, and she was talking to *me* that she was dirty. There're still a few that feel this way, although for the most part I'd say that the races are getting along better. This girl turned to me and said, "You know, some people are just very ignorant."

JACKSON: I'd say that maybe one out of every ten white kids don't want to associate with the other races, and that's probably true of Negroes, too. In my home, we're permitted to associate with anyone. My mom doesn't think anything about it. Anyone is free to come to my home—white or black. My girl can feel at home in my house. I think both my mom and dad are pretty understanding about it, particularly my mom. When I get a telephone call or something at home, and I'm not home, she takes the message. This happened just the other night. Some girl called me, and I called this girl back. She never met my mother, and she said, "You know, I carried on a conversation with your mother, and she's really nice." I think most kids can feel free at my house no matter what their color is. Course, you know, they're not permitted to destroy anything. But they can feel free. As for my girl friend's parents, her dad is more understanding than her mom. We were going together for a while before they knew anything about it. One day, I was dropping her off from school, and her mom was standing out there, and I thought, well, this is as good a time as any to go up to her and introduce myself. She saw us out in the car anyway. I thought it was time to do this. We went into her house, and we talked for a little bit, and then I left. Then this girl told me that her mom told her, after I left, to stop seeing me or that she would send her away. But her dad told her, if she felt it was right, that she should do it and not pay any attention to her mother. I kinda felt that her mother was two-faced about the whole thing, because she was very nice while I was there. Then she went ahead and said this thing. She doesn't like me as much as her dad does. We're still going together.]

Walter and Jackson have a serious discussion, precipitated by Walter's wondering, "Why does a white man hate us; what has the Negro done?" Jackson challenges the legitimacy of this hate—it is the Negro, he claims, who has the legitimate right to hate the white man.

[WALTER: I think the Negroes want to associate more with the white person than the white person wants to associate with Negroes. I often ask myself, why does a white man hate us; what has the Negro done? It may not help at all to think about this, but I think about it. Why does the white man hate me? I haven't done a thing.

JACKSON: It seems to me that the Negro should hate the white person. It was the white person who tricked the Negroes, and who sold them into slavery, and who told him that he'd be an indentured servant for a while, and then he'd gain his freedom, and he didn't give it to him. I think it's the white man who caused the Negro misery. We've a right to hate them.

WALTER: I disagree. I don't think we should hate anybody. It wouldn't help, anyway, if we did.

JACKSON: Well, I guess you're right. I don't mean that we should hate them. But I just don't see why the white man should hate us more than the Negro should hate the white man. I think the Negro has more cause.

WALTER: We talk about this a lot in my home. My mom and dad are always asking me how I feel about the race situation. I tell my parents all the time that I don't hate white people. I dislike the older generation, but I don't hate younger people. They've done nothing to me. When I see the older generation, I think of all the injustices that they've done to my race. It's so hard for me not to hate them. I think the main thing is trust. I know a lot of Negroes feel that you can't trust the white person, or the Negroes think that the white person is the biggest liar and the best liar in the world. In my job, I talk to a lot of white people every day, but I can't say that I trust one of them. Course, I've only been there a few months, but I don't know if I can trust them, because the white man has always promised things, and he never fulfills them.

JACKSON: Well, I trust people on my job. There're only 2 Negroes and 14 white people. I've been there for about nine months. We do a lot of kidding around together. I can call this white boy, Nigger, and things like that. This white boy one time, said, "You know, I'm a half-breed." I said, "You're not a half-breed. You're a liar, 'cause both your parents were Negroes." We all laughed; he's a white guy. We can say things like this because we're kinda friends. But you don't say things like this to someone you don't know.

QUESTION: Who does the most mixing, boys or girls?

JACKSON: Boys mix most of the time. To a certain extent, some of the girls do, too, but I think that white girls are afraid of Negro girls, so they don't do as much mixing. The Negro girls are rough. The white girls think they're rough. You know, white boys think that Negro boys are rough, too. Maybe they're a bit rougher, but there's not really that much difference.

WALTER: You know, I detect this fear all the time. I guess the Negroes have been typed as being the best fighters, so I always detect this fear among white people of the Negro, whether it's boys or girls. Not too long ago, there was this party that I was going to. It was a Negro party. Across the street there's this little bar, and these two white boys saw me, and they said, "Hey Walt, I want to join your party, but you better come with us or your friends might knock our heads in." It's this kind of attitude all the time. Now those kids wouldn't have knocked their heads in at all. They wouldn't have thought of saying that if the party had been a white party.

QUESTION: Suppose you were going to an all white party, would you feel the same way?

JACKSON: I don't feel any fear at all. I'd go to a party all by myself. I just feel free to go.

WALTER: I feel the same way. I don't believe a Negro fears being harmed as much by the white person. But these young white people think that they're going to get their heads knocked in by Negroes.]

In the next interview (Part 4) one of the black young women explains that Negroes are afraid to date white young men even if asked, because of the reaction of Negro young men. While Walter agrees with this explanation, Jackson does not. On this dating issue Jackson seems to identify more with the white than with the black community. He thinks Negro young women would consider it a privilege if a white person asked them out. He feels that if Negro young women are "good enough" to get a white date, they should go out with him. Jackson's point of view may partly be determined by the fact that he, himself, dates a white fellow student.

[QUESTION: Do white boys date Negro girls at Plains High?

JACKSON: I know of one case where a white boy wanted to date a Negro girl. He came up to me, and he was talking to me about this Negro girl that he'd like to date. I said, "Well, who is she?" He said "Jeannie Miller." I said, "That's my cousin. I'll fix it up for you." So I talked to her, and she said she'd like to go out with him. I told him, but I'm not sure whether they ever got together or not. I really can't say. But it's not many. You don't see many white boys dating Negroes. That's the only case I know of.

QUESTION: How do the Negro girls react to interracial dating between Negroes and white girls?

WALTER: I think the girls resent this. They don't like it very much. They don't put pressure on the boys not to do it, because it's kinda hard for them to do that. I think they're jealous. I think they feel that the Negro boy should be with her, or date her, rather than date a white girl.

JACKSON: I don't think most white boys would ask Negro girls out. Maybe I shouldn't say this, but I think any Negro girl would consider it a privilege to have a white boy ask her out.

WALTER: You know, I think that Negro boys would detest having a Negro girl go out with a white boy. They don't want Negro girls to date white boys. They don't like it. Now I, myself, feel that way and I think I'm a hypocrite because, you know, I've been out with a white girl. I don't like it if a Negro girl is gonna go out with a white boy. If I see a colored girl with a white boy, I think why didn't she date me, or another Negro. What's he got that I ain't got? Particularly, if it's a colored girl that I've been trying to get a date with, I'd really wonder about that. On the other hand, I think if the Negro boys felt that they could date any white girl they wanted to, if they felt that they were free to date white girls, then they wouldn't resent it if a Negro girl went out with a white boy.

JACKSON: Well, I don't feel this way at all. I feel if a colored girl is good enough to get a white boy, and if he's good enough for her, then they should go out with each other.

WALTER: Now that you've got me talking about this, I think I'd say that the colored girls don't like it when colored boys go out with white girls, and I think the colored boys wouldn't like it if colored girls went out with white boys.

QUESTION: Do Negroes and whites mix at dances?

JACKSON: I'm sure glad you brought that up. I was wondering if you would. At a dance, all the Negroes are in one corner; all the whites are in another corner. I think maybe part of this is because the white kids feel that the Negroes dance better, so they set themselves off in one part of the gym, and the Negro kids do, too. Very few mingle with each other at these dances. They don't even dance together.

WALTER: Well, I think a lot of the Negro boys hesitate to go up and ask a white girl to dance. For example, I'd be at a party, and I know these Negro guys will talk and wish—they'd like to dance with a white girl. But they feel inferior. They've been refused before, and they're afraid they'll be refused again. So he says, "No, I won't ask her." That's because it's happened so many other times, so they just stand there and wish. You're very reluctant to go up, because you're afraid that you'll be turned down.

JACKSON: Well, I don't feel that way. Course, I just don't go up to strangers, either. If I'm at a dance, and a white friend is there with his girl friend, and I don't have a date, I might go up to him and say, "May I dance with your girl?" Usually he says, "Well, it's all right with me, if it's all right with her." But usually we're friends. I don't go up to any white girl, because a lot of them will sneer at you. Some of them will say, "What do you want, boy?" So you just don't go up to anybody.

WALTER: In my opinion, there isn't as much trouble in my age generation as people say. I know I've said that before, but I want to make a point clear. There isn't much violence. At a party, either kids mix or they stay apart, but there isn't any trouble. I really do feel that each side wants to integrate. Take me and this colored girl that I know. If I felt it was easy for me to date a white girl, I wouldn't mind her going out with white boys at all. I'd be happy. I feel this is what we need to do. We need to feel free with each other.]

One cannot help noticing the contrast between these two young men and the black "militants," of Chapter 3, on the question of discrimination by their teachers. While both groups of students point to discrimination at Plains High, the militant feels he is left to deal with it on his own, without support from his parents. How different such a situation is from Jackson's, who senses a lot of support from his family, particularly from his mother: "She'll really go to bat for me." In this respect, Jackson's parents behave more like those of the "hippies" who support their children in confrontations with the school administration.

[QUESTION: Do the teachers treat the Negro and white kids alike?

WALTER: No! It's happened to me a number of times, and in junior high school, too. I remember this woman counselor at Plains Junior High. I was at this dance. I was dancing with this white girl. This counselor is something else. She came right up and told me she didn't want to see me dancing with this white girl again. At that time, I was afraid and I was very young, so I didn't say anything. I was afraid to tell my parents. I felt so inferior. I didn't want to cause any trouble.

JACKSON: I never had any trouble until I was in high school. But in high school, I felt all sorts of discrimination. My parents are real good about it, though. I feel that I can talk out any problem with my mom. I usually talk to my mom, because she's the boss in the family. I'm the only child, and she's very interested in what happens to me. She really will go to bat for me.]

Walter speaks of Mexican-American segregation in terms that are familiar to any concerned white person who has spoken to his white neighbors about the Negro in American society. Very often such a neighbor maintains that the Negro wants to be by himself, but this explanation is more an excuse than a point of view such as that of the black separatist. Walter, although he obviously has been the object of prejudice, uses the same excuse in reference to Mexican-Americans and in doing so, does not show much empathy.

[QUESTION: Where do the Mexicans fit in at school?

WALTER: In my opinion, the Mexicans set themselves off from the rest of the school. They're happy this way. There's a minimum of mixing among the Mexicans. They neither mix with whites nor the Negroes. They stay to themselves. They never express anything about race issues. They just go about their business. This is the way they want it. If you talk to them, they'll talk to you. They're very nice, but they don't want to get involved.]

[QUESTION: Do the students discuss race issues at school?

JACKSON: Well, we talked about race a little bit in History this year. But usually we don't talk about it in class. The only reason we talked about it in History was that it was in World History, and we were discussing Ralph Bunche and the U.N. We really didn't discuss race. The teacher just gave us the notes on Ralph Bunche. Some of the kids joke about race. But the joking only takes place between people who know each other. I wouldn't feel free to call someone a name or joke unless I knew that person. If a Mexican kid was walking down the street and I didn't know him, I wouldn't call him a taco bender, and I'm sure he wouldn't call me a nigger. But if you know each other, this kind of joking takes place.

WALTER: When I was in school, there was very little communication on race. When I was in school, I always felt, somehow or other, that the white leaders in the school must have been carrying on conversations about race. But I'm not sure that they did, because they never wanted us to hear anything, so we were never in on it. But I wondered, what do these white kids talk about when they get together? Do they talk about race? Sometimes in History, or World Geography, only if there was a part in the book in which we were dealing with the Negro, we would talk about race. But I can't remember too many open discussions about the race issue.

JACKSON: Right now in summer school I'm taking this class in Negro History, and it brings it all out. We're dealing with the Negro from slavery until now. I'd sure like to see more of this at school. I have this Negro teacher in this course. He presents the material in such a way that you just want to learn more and more.]

The blacks and whites who have been interviewed in this book have pointed to the generation gap as one cause of racial friction at Plains High School. In this respect, it is important to recognize that teachers, just as parents and grandparents, are at least one generation removed from their students. Much has been said by the students about individual white differences in liberalism and they strongly feel that liberalism is associated with age. They assume that older persons are less liberal and tolerant of others than are the young. In what follows, the symbolic weight which older Negroes place on the backs of younger ones is described with a great deal of exasperation.

[QUESTION: Is there a gap between the generations on the race question?
WALTER: In my opinion, the older generation Negro in town doesn't give a damn about the younger generation and what we're doing. We're always being criticized by the older generation Negroes. For example, these parents of a friend of mine are always getting after me about the "Movement." They're always trying to tear us down or criticize us for sit-ins, for pickets. They'll say it's just not right. I don't listen to 'em though. I tell 'em, "You're more deplorable than the white man." Most of these Negroes are satisfied with going to the railroad shops or to the tire plant, as long as they have food in their icebox, a roof over their head, and they can come home after their seven to three or three to eleven shift and watch TV. They're always tearing us down. You know, my father's always saying, "You just don't know the value of a dollar." This friend of mine, his father got him a new car. Then

one day he said, "Why don't you get off you lazy so-and-so and walk to school?" He's just a hypocrite. First, he gets the kid a car, and then he wants to know why he's driving it all the time, and why he doesn't walk. They always say things like, "I had to work for 25¢ an hour. You've never known times like that. I had to walk three miles to school," and so on. I always tell 'em, "Well, you know, why should we? You've made it possible for us so that we don't have to work for a dollar an hour." They're always saying "Why don't you mind your business and get an education? Why are you always bringing up this race stuff?" I think we battle the old Negro just as much as we battle the white man. In fact, I think they're worse.

JACKSON: Don't you think you'll be the same?

WALTER: No!

JACKSON: Well, maybe you'll say to your kids, "You don't know the value of five dollars," instead of a dollar.

WALTER: Well, I can't say what I'll say at this particular time, but I don't think I will.]

[QUESTION: Is the Negro encouraged as much as the white person to further his education?

JACKSON and WALTER: No!

WALTER: The Negroes are excluded in school. They're not encouraged to go on. The counselors don't encourage them, nor do the teachers. When I was in school, what I got I got on my own. I was never helped. When I was in high school, all of my white friends would tell me how they were always being called down to the counselors, and the counselors would discuss college with them, scholarships, or plan their programs with them so that they had the right prerequisites to go to college. I was never called down to the office. I was never asked about my future plans. This was never done to me nor my Negro friends.

JACKSON: I've received a lot of help from the counselors, but most of the Negroes I know haven't. I think, maybe why they trouble with me is that I've been in so much trouble at school, because of my attitude. My counselor does call me in, and he tries to help me plan my program, too. Course that might be because my mother has taken a lot of interest. If I'm ever in trouble, she calls up my counselor right away and discusses it with him.

WALTER: In my opinion, I think most of the counselors at Plains High School just think of the Negro as lazy. They see him as a shabby person. They say that he never wants to be anything anyway, so why bother with him? But most of the Negroes do want to be something. I had trouble in math, and I asked this teacher to help me because I didn't understand it. He never made attempts to help me. He never paid any attention to me. He didn't ask me to come in early in the morning, or stay after school, or anything like that—he just put it off. I've never received any assistance in all the time I was in school—not from the counselors and not from the teachers. I think they do treat Negroes and whites differently.

QUESTION: How does the administration treat Negroes?

JACKSON: The principal sucks!

WALTER: He's a white racist dog.

JACKSON: He only wants the Negro to excel in sports for his own glory. If you don't participate in sports, he doesn't give a damn about you. I know these two colored boys who were in a fight. The principal allowed one of them to play basketball on that Friday night, because it was a big game. He wouldn't even allow the other Negro boy to get into the gym to see the game.

WALTER: He told me, "We have more trouble from you Negroes than anybody else in school." One time my homeroom teacher found a hall pass with my name on it in the hallway. He called me down there and accused me of stealing a pass from his office so that I could walk around in the halls. He didn't even know this. He didn't even bother to find out. He's just a racist.

JACKSON: I never saw a person as open about being a racist as Mr. Ewing. The school would be a lot better off if he weren't there.

WALTER: Before I accuse anybody of anything I like to have facts, and it's so hard for me to remember all the things that Mr. Ewing did to me and that he's done to other people from my race. You'll have to take my word for it. I'm not exaggerating. He's the most prejudiced human being I've ever met in my life. I wonder if you'll allow me to come back again. I know tomorrow morning, when I wake up, I'm going to think of all these things that I wish I'd said to you. Could I come back and help you more and tell you more about what's going on? [The interviewer gave Walter his phone number and told him to call whenever he wished. Walter did not call back, however.]

The black students in the present sample consider that their attendance at Plains High School has, at times, been beneficial while at other times, it has been an assault on their sense of worth. Most seem glad to have the opportunity to interact with whites on an equal basis. For some Negroes, such an experience has resulted in the discovery that *all* whites are not necessarily more intelligent than *all* Negroes. But for Jackson the head-on confrontation with prejudice has overshadowed whatever positive effects he may have gained from attending a desegregated school. Walter, although less intense also feels, "I can't say it was a good experience."

[QUESTION: Has your experience at Plains High taught you anything about race relations?

JACKSON: In some ways, it helped me, but in some ways, I don't believe it has. I think I've encountered prejudice at Plains High School, and I think

I've been treated unjustifiably. Next year I intend to go to Catholic High School, because I want to try somewhere else. I don't think I could take it any more at Plains High School. They're against me, as I told you earlier, and I think it's because of my relationship to white people.

WALTER: I feel it was a stimulating experience. It enlightened me on different opinions. I got to meet different people and make many friends. It wasn't a bad experience, but, on the other hand, I can't say it was a good experience. I think I've felt as much prejudice at Plains High School as I would've felt anywhere else. It may be done in a more roundabout manner, but it's there.

On Being Black and White

Part 4

The three black young women who appear next are unlike the "elite" Negroes of Chapter 2. Velma and Joy excel in sports, rather than in classroom work. Lucille is relatively unfamiliar with algebra, French, and English Literature. She has specialized in cooking, sewing, and dressmaking and feels that college is a place for others to attend after they have been graduated from high school. For these young women, an early marriage is particularly in the cards—Velma, for instance, is already engaged.

At times, these students' behavior has been a good deal less than a model for others to follow, and they have had occasion to see the inside of the principal's office for disciplinary reasons. Now that they fight the academic structure less, however, they seem to enjoy school more. The rejection of former "bad" behavior is exemplified by Lucille's saying she does not like to be seen with Negroes who cause trouble because then "you get in trouble yourself."

Although the social world for these young women is different from that of the "elite" Negro, both groups of students share a number of dislikes about Plains High School. Their perception of the racial situation is, at times, strikingly similar.

[QUESTION: What pressures do you feel from attending a desegregated school?

VELMA: There was much more pressure at an all-Negro school. For one thing, you don't learn to get along with other people in an all-Negro school. The attitude is much more, "Don't mix." Everybody has the same ideas, and everybody's prejudiced. I think it's easier in an integrated school.

JOY: When the races are mixed, you act more like yourself. In a Negro school, they're stricter in discipline, although the scholastic demands aren't as high—but the athletic demands are higher. At Plains High School, you have to keep up with your grades, if you're going out for athletics. I think this is a special demand on us by going to an integrated school. They expect more academically. I think that Negro school teachers, in an all Negro school, act more like parents do. In Plains High School, if you don't care, they don't care either. It's pretty much up to yourself to see that you're in class and that you

185

do your homework, and things like that. In a Negro school, if your attitude is, "I don't care," they apply the belt to you. They use more physical discipline.

VELMA: I was in an all-Negro school once. It really was bad. There were police on every floor. The kids were rowdy. In sports, the boys had to protect the cheerleaders. It was really frightening. Then I went to an Air Force high school, which was better because there were people from all over. The Air Force was more accepting and less prejudiced. For example, on prom night I went to the prom with a Negro boy, and we went out to dinner afterwards. We were with a bunch of white kids. They were from the school, and they accepted us, but the man didn't want us to eat at his place.

QUESTION: What was the prom like at Plains High School?

VELMA: The races didn't mix at the prom here. They stayed in separate groups. In fact, they stayed in separate groups even at the prom. There isn't much of that kind of mixing at Plains High School.

LUCILLE: You don't get to meet as many people in a Negro school. I think the thing I like about an integrated school is that you learn to meet people in different social classes, and you get to know what the other person is thinking, or how he feels. You can't do this in an all-Negro school.]

Although the contacts between whites and blacks are limited, the desegregated school is preferred over a segregated one. The Negro students being interviewed here feel that at Plains High discipline is not as harsh, the athletic demands are not as great, and there is more emphasis on "book learning." The desegregated school, these young women feel, also offers the opportunity to meet people with different backgrounds. Velma, Joy, and Lucille think that such experiences lead to increased tolerance for others. They suggest that the segregated school—black or white—is a breeding ground for segregationist attitudes.

Most students agree that the student must be careful how he expresses himself at Plains High School; certain comments may be misinterpreted. But if two people are friends, and the otherwise offensive comments are made into a joke, then disapproval tends to evaporate.

[QUESTION: Do you have to be careful in what you say in front of other kids?

VELMA: Well, we joke about race. The boys are always joking about race. Negro girls and white girls do some joking, but it's mostly the boys. They call each other "nigger" or "whitey." You don't really have to watch what you say, providing the person knows you're joking. If they thought you really meant it, then it'd cause trouble. Some boys who come from segregated schools have a very bad attitude about this, and with them you have to be a little bit careful because they don't really understand it as a joke. I think the kids that go to segregated schools have a norrower race attitude. They think in terms of *all* black or *all* white and the teachers in a Negro school are stricter.]

[QUESTION: Have you had any experience with teachers who discriminate?

JOY: Well, there're two teachers who discriminate. They want to discriminate. I think if they weren't afraid of causing some bad conflict, they'd be more open about their discrimination. One is an English teacher, and the other is a Physical Ed teacher. Our English teacher read this article about the hundred Negro students who barricaded themselves in one of the college buildings, and the university decided not to prosecute them. Our teacher read this and told us that she thought they should be punished.

VELMA: You know at Plains High School, there're a lot of Negro students who cause trouble, and this is the real bad part of that school. For example, they want a Negro cheerleader whether she's qualified or not. If a Negro girl doesn't make cheerleader, they're always claiming that's discrimination, and that's not true because some of them aren't as good as the white girls. That's why they don't make it. I think the problem with the teachers at school is that they're not strict enough. They allow this sort of attitude to continue, instead of stomping down on it. Right after King died, a lot of the kids here just made hay with that. But they weren't really followers of King. King didn't mean much to these people here. He was a leader of the people in the South but not up here. The teachers didn't try to do anything to stop the trouble. They just let them go too far, as far as I'm concerned.

JOY: At the time of King's death, most of the kids stayed home, and they had a cheerleader election that day. Most of the Negro kids were absent, and they still had the election. Well, a Negro girl came within two points of making it. There was a lot of trouble about that, because they said it was unfair that the election was held on the day when most of the Negro kids were excused from school. Personally, I think they should've canceled the election until the next morning. One of the Negro girls that I know sent around a petition stating that it was unfair, and listing why it was unfair to hold the election on that day. But nothing ever came out of it. Tim Howard, who's a radical, said he wanted a special assembly to discuss the problem. But Mr. Ewing declined to discuss it and refused to have an assembly.

VELMA: Well, they did boycott the cafeteria for a while, and they were really rowdy down there. It was a mess. I think a lot of it is Mr. Ewing's fault—he's really prejudiced. He was my mother's principal, too, and when she talks about Mr. Ewing, she talks about how prejudiced he was. I don't think he's changed. He just doesn't like Negroes. He tries to do a few things, such as Tim Howard and a couple of other radical Negroes meet with him and talk about the kinds of things we're talking about right now—although I don't know what really comes out of those talks. Ewing isn't like the rest of the teachers or even the counselors. He acts like he doesn't want to associate with you. He doesn't have any warmth or feeling for you. I think he really dislikes Negroes. The Physical Ed teacher is really prejudiced. She expects all Negroes to be athletic. If they aren't, she's really angry with them and puts them in the back of the room and doesn't pay any attention to them. She just thinks, if you're a Negro you're supposed to be a top athlete.

LUCILLE: But you know, she's that way with white girls, too. If they're not very good, she really discriminates against them. I think she just hates everybody. She's always picking on kids. She's really vicious. She's always picking on a fat girl in our class, who weighs about 200 pounds. She just can't do anything, and it's awful the way she picks on her. She forces most of the Negro girls to swim. Negro girls don't like to swim because it plays hell with their hair. She's really outrageous, as far as a teacher is concerned.

QUESTION: Is swimming required?

JOY: Yes, everyone has to take swimming as part of their sophomore physical ed program.

QUESTION: Is swim class held toward the end of the day when it wouldn't matter as much if your hair was messed up?

VELMA: No, swim classes are at different times of the day, and even if they're late in the afternoon, a lot of those girls go right to work after school and don't have time to go home. Besides, the way we straighten out our hair damages our hair and it can hurt. You don't want to do it too much. It burns your hair. Another thing about this teacher, she doesn't really care about anyone. For example, a girl got hit in the eye with a tennis racket the other day, and she didn't even come down until the ambulance took the girl away. Then she came down and started screaming, "Watch out for those rackets, before someone gets hurt." There's a teacher there by the name of Mr. Thomas, he's a substitute teacher, but he's really great. All the kids like him. He takes his own time out to do things with the kids. He took me and a couple of other kids to the track meet at the university last week. He's always doing things like that. He's a real great guy. He's a substitute, but he's up at the high school every day because there's always somebody who's out sick.]

Aside from his teaching duties, the Negro teacher in an integrated school can serve as a positive model for the Negro student. The Negro teacher represents middle class society, and because of his own and his students' shared blackness, he offers the Negro student someone with whom to identify. Unless the Negro teacher, in turn, identifies himself with his black student, however, it is doubtful that he can serve as a very effective model.

[QUESTION: How well are the Negro teachers at Plains High School accepted by the Negro students?

VELMA: One of the women Negro teachers is prejudiced. Her attitude with the Negro kids is awful. She talks with white boys all the time, but she won't talk with Negroes. In fact, she flirts with the white boys all the time. She has a beautiful figure and a wild walk. You ought to see her. Man, is she something! But she's really very prejudiced. If we had more teachers like her, I think it'd do more harm than good, because the Negro kids can't stand her. One of the men Negro teachers is okay. He jokes around a lot, and he helps all the kids. He's not prejudiced.

QUESTION: Would it help to have more Negro teachers?

VELMA: Well, not if there were more like that Negro woman teacher. Her attitude is more outrageous than the white teachers' attitudes. The kids think they can run over the people now, and they just do the wildest things. In fact, the kids are really awful. More Negro teachers would make it more like a Negro school, with strict discipline. Negro schools use very harsh methods. They wash your mouth with soap, and they'll beat you. Lots of those kids need their mouths washed with soap because of the language they use. I think Negro teachers understand Negro kids more than white teachers do. Negro kids try to see what they can get away with, but really want to be stopped. Negro teachers understand this, but the white teachers are afraid, or they don't understand it. They don't do anything. When Negro kids act up, they really want discipline. They respect the teacher that makes them behave and makes them toe the line. I used to cut up when I was in junior high school. I was really bad. I got in an awful lot of trouble when I was in junior high school, but now that I've stopped cutting up, I enjoy school more. Now that I go along with the school and the teachers—I really enjoy myself. I'm kind of sorry that this is my last year, and I have to leave.

JOY: A lot of white guys also act terrible in school. There's this one white guy in our class who won't shave or cut his hair. He's always doing the damndest things. Like there's this one teacher who's always drinking coffee. Well, she got up to leave the room, and he went up and spit in her coffee. Or, when she turns her back, he'll throw some of her things out the window—like flowers, and other things that she has around. He's always doing things like this. She drank the coffee. She didn't know anybody had spit in it. He's really terrible!

LUCILLE: I know that teacher. She picks on kids all the time. It got so bad at one time, that the rest of the kids had to protect this one kid and tell the principal that he really wasn't doing anything. It took the principal to straighten it out. She's just so prejudiced and grouchy. She was picking on this Mexican guy in class, and it was terrible, because he wasn't doing anything. I think she deserves what she gets. Although I don't like the guy who does crazy things like spitting in her coffee. But she really deserves it, so I don't mind *that* much. She's always making fun of these two Mexican guys in that class, too, and if one is absent and the other one is in, she'll say things out loud in front of the rest of the class. She'll say something like, "You skipped class yesterday," or "Where is your other friend?" How does she know what the problem is with these kids? She doesn't take any trouble to find out what the problem is. She's just prejudiced and a loud mouth and deserves a lot of things that are done to her. I dislike teachers who try to second guess the kids, or try to tell you what your business is or what you've been doing, when they really don't know. I think she gets herself in trouble. She accused one boy of talking to another boy because his head was turned when there was noise in the back of the class. She tried to punish him. He kept telling her he didn't do it, but she didn't listen at all. She gave him a seventh hour slip, which is a punishment hour after school. He took it but kept saying that he didn't do it, and he didn't do it. He wasn't the one that was talking. A lot of the teachers are like that. They just don't give a damn. Another problem with a lot of the teachers is that they try to act like teenagers—to get the kids to tell them things, and then they tattle on them. They're always running to the counselors and telling the counselors secret things that the kids told them, thinking they'd never turn around and tell someone else.]

The students have accused the counselors of failing to provide them with adequate information about college requirements and of failing to help them plan good school programs. While the students who make such accusations expect to be helped with these problems, Velma, Joy, and Lucille have other expectations—they want the counselors' help when they are in trouble. They assume that counselors will help with the planning of a school program or entering college, but the three young women consider counselors to be of little actual help with personal problems. In fact, the counselors seem to meet few, if any, expectations. According to the students who have been interviewed, most counselors neither meet the expectations of those students who plan to enter college, by providing college information, nor do they often enough help "problem" students with their difficulties.

[VELMA: The counselors don't help at all. The counselors are about the worst group at that school.

JOY: The counselors don't really try to help you. If you ever get in trouble, and you're feeling all mixed up, all they ever do is tell you you'll get kicked out of school, or tell you the things you've been doing wrong. You already know that. You know what you've done that's wrong. You don't need someone to tell you what's wrong. You need someone to kind of help you and straighten you out. They're supposed to help you with problems. They just give you the same answers. The older ones are a little bit better—the young ones are really terrible. I've never seen a counselor that could help you solve your problems. They just aren't problem solvers. They'll help you get into a particular class, if you're interested in taking that class, and some of them will even help you write letters to college, if you're interested in going to college. But when it comes to real serious problems and the kind of things that trouble kids, they just don't help you at all.]

[QUESTION: In which activities do you find the most mixing between the races?

VELMA: Sports, except for golf and swimming and gymnastics. Most of the Negroes, particularly the girls, haven't had these things when they were young, so they aren't very good at them. They're a lot of Negro girls in track, so this is integrated. We don't have any trouble in track. In fact, we're always going out of town for meets, and we meet Negro and white girls from other cities. There's always a very good attitude. We never have any trouble at all.

JOY: There seem to be more Negro kids in the clubs this year than there were last year. There're more Negroes in Pep Club and Business Club. Also, you find more Negroes in political positions at school now. There're a couple of representatives and there's a Negro secretary-treasurer. There's even a Negro president. Kids this year seem to have more ambition and try to run for office.

VELMA: When I was a sophomore, you didn't run for things. The Negro kids didn't do anything, but the sophomore class this year isn't holding back at all. They're more outgoing, and they try to get in these things at school.

JOY: For example, we had a competition between sophomores, juniors, and seniors in Pep Club. We're supposed to look up to the seniors because they're supposed to be *it*. This is their last year, and they act more like just letting things flow by. The sophomore class is the most criticized class. They're criticized just because they're sophomores, but they try to do more and are doing more. Maybe part of it is because they're so criticized.

QUESTION: Do you think the younger Negro's attitudes have changed from those of older Negroes, in a way which might help explain the difference between sophomores and seniors?

JOY: Yes, I think the attitudes have changed some. Everybody tries to converse more and mix more now. When I was in junior high school, we stayed in little groups. In high school, we've the attitude that we want to branch out and get to know more people and get to do things. I think part of it is the fact that Negroes are expected to do these things, now. Maybe a few years ago they weren't.

QUESTION: When you meet new kids in high school, do you try to meet Negro kids you didn't know before, or do you try to meet white kids?

VELMA: Well, I know most of the Negro kids, so I try to meet white kids. I'd like to know what the white kids are like and try to understand them and hope they can understand me. It's hard, sometimes. I date Lincoln. He isn't well liked in that particular school. If you date somebody they don't like, they don't like you. Kids are real funny that way. The Negro kids don't like him because they say he thinks he's white and thinks he's better than most kids. Because of this, I have a hard time, too. They reject me. They're always saying that where he went to school before the kids think they're better than we are. They say he thinks he's better than most Negroes, because he went there. It's the same way with a lot of kids. I know a white girl who dates a Negro boy. She's afraid of what her white friends say. She's rejected even by her own family. She's rejected by these white kids. She has a hard time.

LUCILLE: You know, I like the white kids better, because the Negro kids really cut up bad. When they get in trouble, and if you're around, you get in trouble with them. At lunch time, they do just about anything they can get away with. They cut up real bad. When you're with white friends, they start rumors about you. I really hate those kids. I don't want to be with them, because if I'm with them, they think I'm bad, too.

JOY: For example, my sister won Student of the Year Award, and this boy said, "She must think she's really above everybody else." If you try to do something or better yourself, they think you're trying to snub them. They want to do things themselves, but they don't know how, so they don't want anybody else to do anything.

LUCILLE: For an example, my boyfriend used to run around with white boys all the time, and the Negro boys would reject him. They dislike him, because they think he thinks he's better than the other kids. The trouble is that they know he's better than most of them. That's their problem.

VELMA: My best girl friend is a Mexican girl. Every time I go up on the second floor where the Negroes hang out and I'm with this girl, they're always saying things like, "Hey girl, you're out of your place with her." Well, I don't listen to them at all. She's my best girl friend, and that's the way it is. Some of these Negro kids are really bad. In Physical Education class, they'll steal you blind. You just don't want to be in a group like that. It's not very good, because you get in trouble all the time. Most of the Negro kids are cut-ups. What you do is change groups to get away from them.

QUESTION: Are the cut-ups boys or girls?

LUCILLE: The girls are bigger cut-ups than the boys. Most of the fights are between girls. They're jealous of one another. These girls are so bad that they can't even get the boys to date them. The boys don't like them at all. Because of that, they act even worse. Most of these girls are big, and they're tough, and they look older. They go with guys outside of school, like airmen and older guys. They always find somebody else, but they're angry because the boys at school won't pay any attention to them. I don't blame the boys, because these gals are really bad.

VELMA: Those girls in that group are always doing what their friends want them to do. I know a girl who's in that group, who says that she doesn't like to date airmen, but she dates one, because if she doesn't date an airman, her friends will get after her. They're like that. I don't really call that being friendly. They criticize Negro boys who date white girls. You should see how mad the Negro girls get when a Negro boy rejects them. At one time it was really bad, but it's getting better now. A couple of years ago, the Negro boys wouldn't have anything to do with the Negro girls. They were just dating the white girls, or going after white girls. The Negro girls were really upset. There was a lot of trouble. They'd take boys and they'd beat up on them. I've seen some of those girls beat up on some boys really bad. But now it's better. The Negro boys are dating more of the Negro girls, but not those real bad ones. Another reason I think the Negro boys may be coming back now is because the Negro girls can go out with other guys. Now that the boys realize that, they're a little bit jealous, so they come back to the girls.]

The students in this study give various reasons why they would not date a white young man: some think their parents would disapprove, while others are worried about their reputations, or that white young men would be interested in them for sexual gratification only. Velma talks about the probability that Negro young men would not like her having a date with a white person. Walter's comments in Part 3 of this chapter give legitimate basis to her fear.

[QUESTION: Are there any Negro girls who date white boys?

VELMA: No. No Negro girls that I know of have ever been dated by a white guy. There're some that wish they could. As a matter of fact, I know some white guys, myself, that I wouldn't mind going out with, but the Negro girls are mostly afraid. Even If a white guy asked them, they wouldn't go out with them.

QUESTION: Who are the girls afraid of?

VELMA: The Negro boys don't like for the Negro girls to date white boys. Sometimes I see white guys that look nice, and I stop and talk to them, and the Negro boys get mad. They're real screwy. They can date white girls, but we can't date white guys. There're a lot of Negro girls that don't want you to date white guys, either. It's hard to stay an individual. If you do, you'll be hated. They think you're stuck up. Even if you're a quiet type and don't really want to be with a lot of people, or cut up, they say you're stuck up. They just have a negative attitude up there.

JOY: When I went to Plains High School, the kids didn't like me at all. I came from McKinley Junior High. There were only two Negroes there. I was the only Negro girl. Without even knowing me, just because I was from the East side and went to McKinley, all of the South Center City Negroes rejected me. I got along real well with the teachers at McKinley. I also got along real well with the kids. It was a shock to go to Plains High School and to be rejected. But now I'm getting along better. I found some kids who aren't that way at all. Usually these are the kids who can do things and are not the troublemakers.

LUCILLE: For an example, I go with a quiet guy who doesn't cut-up like the other boys, and he doesn't like parties and things like that. He's just quiet. He likes to do different things, but all the boys are against him. They discriminate against him. The crowd is always trying to influence you to do what they do. I get real mad because they're always talking bad about him. He's not bad. He's just that way. He's quiet.

VELMA: Well, the boys are jealous of quiet, polite boys. You know, most of the girls like quiet, polite boys. So whenever there's a quiet one a lot of the girls like him, and the other boys really act up. They try to break you up, and they try to say bad things about him, because they're jealous. Another thing I don't like about the situation at school is, if you go out with a boy twice, he thinks he owns you. "She's mine," he says, and nobody else can speak to you. I don't like that kind of attitude, they're real bossy and pushy. I'll tell you another thing about how nuts these kids are. My boyfriend and I are engaged, and I've an engagement ring. Something happened to it, and we had to take it back to the jewelry store and have it fixed. They're always looking at your finger at school. They saw the ring was gone, and this boy was telling me, in front of my boyfriend, that we weren't really engaged. We kept saying, "What do you mean we're not?" He said, "No, you're not. No, you're not." We said, "Sure we are." He kept saying we weren't. That's what I mean—they're always trying to tell you your business.]

The black "troublemakers," these young women say, are few in number. While each "troublemaker" has a following, in his absence the followers are usually not belligerent, or at least their belligerence is attenuated. In the presence of their leader, it seems the "belligerents" are pushed into being antagonists, but in his absence they become more congenial vis-à-vis their fellow students.

[QUESTION: Is there much violence at Plains High School?

VELMA: There's this big Negro girl in my gym class. She's a very good athlete. She pushed me around a little bit, but I told her off. Since then she's been all right. She's really murder. She could kill you, but I think once you tell her off, that's what she wants, and she doesn't push you any more. A lot of these girls are tying to cause trouble. They always talk about you and say bad things. But if their friends aren't around, things really slow up, and the rest of the girls will talk to you and act nice when their friends aren't there. The girls are afraid when the ringleaders are around. Because these girls are tough and will stomp on them. These real gossipy types frighten the kids, because, you know, they'll just turn around and make up some incredible lie about you and spread it around, and that's bad. You should see these girls. I wish you could come to school. They're like men—they're huge. I've seen a couple of them in action. They've whipped boys bad. They're the girls that put pressure on the kids. There're about twenty of them like this, and they just about run the school. Boy, was it nice when King died. All of these radicals and nuts were gone. It was great up there. Things were quiet. These tough girls do a lot of stealing. They're the ones that'll steal you blind in Gym class. They even break into lockers. It's just terrible.

LUCILLE: There's this one girl, they've ten kids in their family, and she comes to school with new clothes every day. Her mother and father are divorced. Her mother doesn't work, and her father just works at a lousy job. Can you imagine that—coming to school with new clothes every day when there're ten kids in the family? This girl steals everything. She was caught today, stealing in Gym class. She was the only one down there. She has to report to the office every day. Can you imagine that—that's all they said to her, "Report to the office every day." They just encourage these kids. Some other girl was caught stealing, and they suspended her from class for three days. Now what kind of punishment is that? I think the teachers are wrong; they aren't strict enough.

QUESTION: Did you attend school the day of Dr. King's funeral?

VELMA: Yeah, I went to school. It was really nice. I enjoyed it very much.

QUESTION: Did you receive any pressure from the kids who didn't go to school?

VELMA: Yeah, they were doing a lot of talking and a lot of loud mouthing about who in the hell did we think we were, going to school when Dr. King was killed, and all that. But he didn't mean anything to me. They just wanted a day off, because he didn't mean anything to them, and they really didn't watch the funeral. It was just an excuse to jet around town and cause trouble. The white kids acted surprised to see us there. They'd say, "What are you doing in school today?"

QUESTION: Did this attitude of the white kids make you angry?

JOY: A little bit, because they group you, kind of, by asking you what you're doing here today, as if we weren't supposed to go to school.

VELMA: The white kids accept you more as an individual than the Negro kids do, so I like the white kids better.

JOY: When I was in Junior High school, I got along real well with the kids. There were a couple of Negro kids in school, and whenever they got into trouble, the Gym teacher would call me to talk to them. Sometimes she'd ask me if I felt strange with all the white girls, but I said, "No." I pick friends on how they treat me—I don't care whether they're white or black. I just want to feel like a person. She didn't want me to tell her things that the kids said to me that would hurt them; she just wanted me to talk to them and kind of smooth things over.]

Racial mixing often depends on where the whites and blacks are in the school's and community's status systems. Negroes and whites generally agree that it is easiest for middle class whites and blacks, with the exception of the black "hoods," to mix. The students' definition of "middle class," however, does not necessarily agree with the adult definition. For example, the students place any Negro who is not a "hood" or an "Uncle Tom" into the middle class. There is concensus, too, that whites who occupy high status school positions and whose parents are upper class, rarely mix with Negroes. Perhaps there is some feeling among the latter that mixing with people of a lower status may, in turn, help to lower their own status.

[QUESTION: How many classes of white kids are there?

LUCILLE: Well, some of the kids are harder to get along with. These are the very rich and the so-called important people. They're very hard to make friends with. These are white kids. It's easier to make friends with middle class kids. Of course, there're certain things you can't do, even with these kids, or you'll lose their friendship. You're not supposed to date white guys. You can go to their parties and things like that, but they look down on you if you date white guys. It's mostly the girls that will do the looking down on you. Negro boys have white boyfriends, and these are guys that date white girls, so that's all right with them. It's the white girls that reject Negro girls if they date white guys. Of course, the Negro guys don't like it.

JOY: I went to some parties at the university. They're real nice. Everybody danced together—Negroes, Mexicans, Indians and white people. They don't cuss or talk loud. They just talk quietly. If a Negro guy goes up and asks a white girl to dance, she accepts and doesn't look over her shoulder to see who's looking. It's the same way with a white guy who asks a Negro girl. I sure like it in college. They accept you. It's really different. They're not loud and showing off all the time. They say, if you're my friend, what I do shouldn't bother you, and that's their attitude.

[Because the preceding question was not fully answered, it was repeated.] How many classes of white kids are there?

VELMA: There's the upper class whites—they don't mix with anybody but themselves. There're the middle class whites—these are most of the people, and they mix with Negroes. Then there're the poor whites—they don't associate with Negroes. They've their own crowd. They dislike Negroes.

QUESTION: How many classes of Negroes are there?

LUCILLE: There're the sedits. They date college boys. You're an outcast at parties unless you date college boys. They just sit and look at each other and don't do anything except drink. Then they get wild about two a.m. That's the time to split from those guy's parties. Then there're the middle class. Actually, there're two kinds of middle class Negroes. Individuals like ourselves who won't go along with the group, and then there're the rowdy kind. They're the majority.]

Although there is a tendency for whites and blacks to congregate in separate sections of the school, leading to the identification of certain hallways and floors with one race or another, most of the students feel free to wander in each other's "territory," notwithstanding the widespread community belief that it is dangerous to do so. These are not "territories" in the sense that they need to be protected from intrusion, but they become defined simply as spaces used primarily by whites or blacks.

[VELMA: The second floor and the main hall are where most of the Negro kids hang out. The third floor, at the end, is where the white kids hang out. The groups just have their own places to go. They aren't really restricted. Anybody can go there and not be bothered.

JOY: In fact, before I went to Plains High School, I used to hear all kinds of stories about riots, things in the back hall, and teachers being beat up and that kind of stuff. When I went there, I was really afraid. I used to run through the halls. But there really isn't anything like that. It's mostly talk.]

While it is expected that contact between whites and blacks in the desegregated school will improve *white* attitudes toward Negroes, few people think of improved *black* attitudes toward whites as the other possibility of desegregation. Generally the Negro's prejudice toward whites is ignored. The young women in this interview are aware of Negro prejudices. They feel that attending Plains High is better than going to a segregated, all-Negro school, because prejudice toward the white man is more intense there.

[QUESTION: What has your experience at Plains High School taught you about race relations?

VELMA: It teaches the students how to get along with other people and how to handle certain situations. In a Negro school, you've a negative attitude about whites. You get this from kids and from the teachers. I think you've more discrimination in an all-Negro school. In a mixed school, you have to learn to get along with other people.

JOY: It gives everyone an opportunity to understand each other. The Negro History program that's coming out is good, because it gives the background that most people don't know about. It also teaches you to shy away from violent conflict and how to avoid trouble.

LUCILLE: You learn how to meet people. You learn about their problems, and they learn about yours. You learn to accept people more. That's one thing that going to Plains High School has taught me. I think it's a good experience.]

[QUESTION: Do you see any difference between yourselves, your parents, and your grandparents on the race issue?

VELMA: Well, our parents don't want us to mix with the other races like we do. In fact, I used to go to a southern school because my father is in the Air Force. It was in Georgia. It's not the kids that want to be separate. It's the parents. It's the parents who influence the kids. The kids don't really know anything about race. Here it's the same way. The kids in school accept one another, but our parents just don't think as positive as we do. Our grandparents, they're worse yet.

JOY: My grandparents never mixed. They lived in the country. They never had much opportunity. I'll have to say my parents have never shown any prejudice, but I don't believe they're as outgoing as I am about mixing with white people.

LUCILLE: I think the younger the person is, the more apt they are to accept each other. My grandparents don't like whites at all. My parents like them a little bit, but they're not about to mix with them. I really don't see that much difference. I think it'll be better for my children.

QUESTION: Are there times when you think of yourself as black?

VELMA: Well, sometimes you have to think of yourself as a Negro. You can't really forget that you are. For example, there was a time when I was the only Negro on the team. Everybody'd look at me. You can't forget that you're a Negro then. Or we'd go out for dinner after a big game. Everybody is having a great time, and you don't think you're a Negro. But when you're with the team and you go into a restaurant and everybody gawks at you, then you know you're a Negro. On the track team, you can be a person. In a restaurant, it's hard to be just a person. They make you remember. In school, it's a little bit better. But even then, it depends on what you're doing. If I go swimming, I remember real quick that I'm a Negro. You know about our hair problem, don't you? Well, when we swim, it goes back like the boys. The teachers don't seem to realize this, or they don't care, so they force you to swim anyway.]

Teachers, counselors, and the principal seem most actively to interfere with "integration" when boy-girl relationships are involved. Where the dating issue is concerned, perhaps they over-react to what they feel to be community sentiment. Whatever the motives of the teachers, counselors, and principal are, however, there seems little doubt that, at times at least, they interfere with the integration process.

[QUESTION: Is interracial mixing discouraged by the school?

JOY: I'll tell you, the principal doesn't like it. He really interferes all the time if there's any interracial mixing between boys and girls.

LUCILLE: Sometimes it's hard because a lot of the Negro boys that date white girls are athletes. If they really put too much pressure on them, they might quit the team, and that would be the end of the team. For an example, it was the Negro basketball player who was named King, and the white girl that was named Queen. The principal didn't want their picture taken together. But this Negro boy insisted that they take it together, or else he was going to quit the team. The principal knew that this would cause trouble, so they had their pictures taken together.

VELMA: You should've seen our principal the other day. We had this senior assembly. He was real mad because the seniors always invite the class that graduated 50 years ago to this assembly and he kept saying, "You better not have all that soul music, because they won't like it." Well, he's just prejudiced because these old people really enjoyed it. We went ahead and had all that soul music and pop music, and our skits were real funny. The principal almost died when this white girl came out on the stage with her arm in a Negro's arm. She looked up and said, "Guess who's coming to dinner?" The old people enjoyed it. The principal's going to be sick next year. We used to have music in the cafeteria, and they used to play all this lousy music. So the kids started bringing in their own records. Then he put a stop to the whole bit. Well, our senior graduating class left the school a stereo to be used in the cafeteria, by the kids, as they want it. So next year there'll be plenty of soul music.

CHAPTER 8

The Mexican-Americans

Part 1

In this chapter, some members of another minority group at Plains High, Mexican-Americans, present their points of view regarding race relations. In many respects, they feel similar to the Negro groups; they speak about the fact that other Mexicans feel "superior" to them, when those others seem to have "made it" in the social hierarchy of the school. What is evident, particularly among the Spanish-American young women, is a kind of hopelessness and expectancy of nonacceptance by other groups, both of which contribute to a situation in which Mexican-Americans find themselves out of so many things at Plains High. In a sense, we are dealing with another self-fulfilling prophesy: The Mexican students do not think they will be accepted, so they do not try out for various posts and activities and, in turn, one does not find Mexicans in the main stream of school life. We find, too, that some Spanish-American students resent the fact that such great attention is paid to the black person as a minority group member, while other minority groups, such as Mexican-Americans, are neglected or ignored entirely.

In this chapter, two groups of Mexican-Americans are interviewed. The first group consists of three young women, all of whom have recently been graduated from high school. The group in Part 2 of the chapter consists of three male high school juniors, two of them Mexican-Americans, and one an "Anglo."

[QUESTION: What pressures do you feel from attending a desegregated school?

JOSEPHINE: The only one I can think of is that you feel kind of funny. The Mexican kids stay together, the Negro kids stay together, and the whites stay together. If you want to be a little daring and socialize with others from a different group, the members of your own group put pressure on you not to. They say, "You think you're better than we are," if you try to go out and meet friends who're whites or Negroes.]

Josephine suggests segregation, at least from her point of view, is a matter of the whites, Negroes and Mexican-Americans *wanting* to stay by themselves,

200

rather than being *made* to do so. Implicit in her answer is the assumption that segregation would be eliminated if the various groups stopped wanting to be exclusively with each other. While it may be true that the dominant white group does not want to mix with Negroes or Mexicans, it probably would not matter too much if the latter two groups wanted to mix with whites. The majority of whites would not accept them unselfconsciously at this time. It is not, in other words, just a matter of wanting to mix; it is certainly also a matter of being permitted to mix. Negroes and Mexicans perhaps keep to themselves defensively, so that they will not be hurt by the nonacceptance and rejection of whites. When whites accuse Mexicans, for example, of keeping to themselves, they conveniently forget that they have helped to push them into such a position.

[QUESTION: Who puts the pressure on them, boys or girls?
JOSEPHINE: I think it's mainly the girls. It seems like it's the girls more than the boys. The girls want to stay with their own group. The Mexican boys don't stay in one group like the Mexican girls; they mix more.
THERESA: Boys at school mix more. But this year, which was my last year in school, I also did more things than I've ever done before. I decided I was going to get out and mix more and meet other kids. I felt better when I did, too. I felt relieved. I'm proud of myself because in my last year, at last, I've really done something. We even went out for the senior class play. Some of the other kids looked at us and thought we were trying to be big shots. They thought we were trying to be better than they are, but we weren't. We just wanted to do some things.
JOSEPHINE: I was in the senior class play, too. There were three Mexican kids who tried out. We were in it. We were selected to be in the play. The students [other Mexican-Americans] thought that we thought we were better than them.]

Josephine found out how much of her lack of participation was self-imposed. It was a real discovery to learn that doors which she had thought to be closed were in reality open. Such an experience does not happen frequently to a member of a minority group. Usually it takes active outside effort from the majority group to persuade minority group members they really are welcome (if indeed they are). It is not enough to announce, "They can join if they want to," for their belief that they will be rejected often prevents them from trying out for activities in which they are convinced they are not wanted.

Josephine and Anna present, in greater detail, the reasons that Mexican-Americans remain outside the general stream of student affairs. Anna explains that the problem is not one of discrimination: "I think we just don't try out for things. I think we do this to ourselves. We don't want to mix; we stick together among Mexicans." The problem is not that simple, of course. A highly significant factor is that others of the dominant (in this case, "Anglo") group do not help the minority group to overcome their reluctance and fear.

[QUESTION: Is there a lot of discrimination against Mexican kids, and is this why they tend to stick together and not try out for things?

ANNA: I don't believe the Mexicans think it's because of discrimination. I think we just don't try out for things. I think we do this to ourselves. We don't want to mix, we stick together among Mexicans. This year I tried out for the Model U.N., which is held every year in Center City. Ever since I was in the ninth grade I wanted to try out for the Model U.N., but I never did. You feel like you're inferior. You're afraid to try. You feel you just don't have a chance because you're Mexican. It's just a feeling you have yourself. But I tried out this year, and I made it. I was the only Mexican kid out of about 300 kids. At Plains High School, there're so many kids, and the teachers don't have the time to encourage all the kids to get into things. They don't really exclude you. They may not tell you about it, but they don't really exclude you from these things. But usually the activities include the same kids. These are the kids who're in all the activities. They go out for many things. The feeling is that these kids can't be beat because they're in everything, and I think this is why a lot of the kids don't go into some of the things. It's hard to explain. Even one of the teachers asked one time, "Why do the Mexican and black kids sit and let the white kids answer the questions all the time? Why don't they also try to give the answers in class and try to do things?" I don't know, it's hard to explain. I think that we exclude ourselves, and that it's our fault. Well, the Mexicans feel that what they have to offer is not as good as what other people have to offer. In junior high school, there were a lot of Mexican kids where I went to school, and I think the kids tried more. In Plains High School there aren't as many, and you feel inferior. When I first went to Plains High School, I took out a petition to run for office. I really wanted to be the secretary bad. I was in office in junior high school. But once I started taking out the petition, all of a sudden, I gave up, and I didn't try because I didn't think I'd win. Another thing that's a problem is that at Plains High School the whites stick together and the Negroes stick together, too, but the Mexicans don't stick together. They don't try to support each other, so it's very hard for a Mexican to win an office or something like that.

THERESA: If you try to go out for an office, they snob you and look down on you because they think that you think you're better than they are. The Mexican kids don't stick together. If one of us tries to do something, or to become something, they look down on us. They think that we're forgetting our race, or trying to be better than our race.

QUESTION: Do you feel culturally inferior or is it an economic factor?

JOSEPHINE: Well, it's probably culture, but I don't think it's really economics. For example, I'm on the Human Relations Youth Council. Some of the kids there are real rich; in fact, the city attorney's daughter is on that council, too. They're all kinds of kids, and we all talk. We talk about racial discrimination, and we talk about social problems. Who's richer doesn't matter then. We talk free, nobody worries or thinks about how much money you have. I think with the Mexicans it's a feeling they've in their head that they're inferior.

ANNA: I don't believe there's that much discrimination, particularly at Catholic High School, so I'm not sure why the Mexican feels that way, either.]

"You think you're better than we are" echoes once again; the "elite" Negro speaks of a similar reaction among fellow Negroes. Both of these reactions should be carefully noted for they represent prejudice toward a minority group by members of that same minority. Generally, we only think of the forces of prejudice as something which exists in the host community and as something which is directed toward a minority group by members of the majority group.

Next, these young Mexican-American students talk about the discrimination they feel from their fellow *white* students. They deeply resent the fact that white students "use" them and speak to them only when they want or need something, a resentment which may partly explain an apparent "sour grapes" reaction. ("The white girls are always tearing each other down.")

[QUESTION: Is there any discrimination at Plains High School that you can think of?

THERESA: Well, Josephine and I had a dancing teacher. She was white. The white girls in this dancing class would try out for things, and they usually got them. Mexican girls and the Negro girls didn't make it. The Mexicans and the Negroes have to be at their best all the time or they're never selected. Mexicans and Negroes don't make the performances. But this teacher is really mean. Most of the girls realize that she's mean, and she's that way against Mexicans and Negroes. Even the white girls say that she's mean. She yells at you if you make a little mistake. I didn't like her at all. I think she discriminates.

JOSEPHINE: In baking class, you feel prejudice in there. I think the teacher is prejudiced. When the Negroes and Mexicans talk, she makes us shut up. But all the girls talk in there. White girls do, too, but she never tells the white girls to shut up. The Negro girls can't stand her at all. They said she was so prejudiced. In baking class, there's usually a white baking table, a Negro baking table, and a Mexican baking table. They're all separate. I don't like to brag, but the Mexican table usually makes the best pastries. But she always tries to find fault with it, even though it's the best. She doesn't allow the Mexican and Negro kids many privileges. As part of the class, we have a lot of teas. Some men from the State University come down sometimes, and our class would make cookies and serve tea. She never allows a Mexican or a Negro to serve, or to meet the people at the door. I think this is discrimination. I finally told her how I felt. She was really surprised. She tried to improve a little bit after I told her, but not that much. I'll tell you how separate the kids are, too. In that baking class, as I told you, there's a white table, a Mexican table, and a Negro table. I cook with a Negro, because I cooked with her last year. So this year, I wanted to cook with her again. I felt funny because the people in the class kept looking at me and made me feel funny. They were saying, "There's a Mexican bakery. Why don't you bake in a Mexican bakery?" But this girl was my friend, so I stuck with her—I didn't care what they said.

THERESA: There're a lot of white girls at school who think they're better than everyone else, too. In this one class that I have, there was this group of white girls who wouldn't talk to anybody. They didn't want to talk to us at all. There were some other white girls we talked to, and these white girls who excluded themselves wouldn't even talk to these white girls we talked with. The white girls who excluded themselves were prettier, but I don't see why it should be that way just because they're prettier. One of the white girls who used to talk with us, she was real smart and maybe these other white girls didn't consider her a friend because she was real smart. But I liked her. The only time they talk to us is when they need something. If they want a piece of gum, or if they need your help with something else. But they never come to you or talk to you when they don't need your help.

ANNA: There're a lot of students who'll never talk to you, and a lot of the kids'll only talk to you when they need something, like paper or a pencil or some gum; then they come up to you. But they never come up to you just to be sociable or for fun. And you're never included in their activities when they're having fun.

JOSEPHINE: This is true, and particularly among the white rich kids. But I don't think I'd like to be with them, anyway, because they're always talking about each other when they're together. They're always tearing down each other's clothes, and things like this. I don't like those kids because they only come to you when they need something. In the halls, they always act like they're too good to speak to you. If they speak to you at all, you always have to speak to them first. Otherwise they'll never talk to you. If you're downtown, they don't speak to you either, except maybe to say "hi." But there's never any conversation. It's like they don't want to recognize you.]

These students present a fairly similar picture of "violence" at Plains High as do the other students who were interviewed. They stress the unfairness with which various destructive rumors, particularly those concerning violent behavior, have tagged Plains High. They have found that almost none of the rumors are true. Perhaps the rumors were started in the first place as a reaction to the racial composition at Plains High.

[QUESTION: Is there much violence at Plains High School?

JOSEPHINE: There's an awful lot of talk about violence at Plains High School, but in all my time there I didn't see so much violence in the halls, like most of the people expect. A lot of people I know come up to me and say, "How can you stand it at Plains High School?" But you know, there isn't that much trouble. If I don't bother them, they won't bother me. I think a lot of the things they say about the Negroes are unfair, too. In our Composition class, this girl made a survey about the knives and guns and things like this that were found on kids, and she reported this in class. The school authorities have these figures. It was part of a class project that our Composition teacher had us do. They found more knives and other weapons on white kids, not the Negroes. You know, this really bothers me, that they say it's a bad school. I really liked it at Plains High School. I didn't think it was bad at all.

JOSEPHINE: When there're fights, it's usually kids of the same race. Once in a while it's mixed, but usually it's two kids of the same race who're doing the fighting.

QUESTION: How do the girls get along?

THERESA: Well, the girls are tough, but even girl fights are always between two Negroes or two white girls. Every now and then there's a girl fight between the races. When two Negro girls fight, I think a lot of times they're fighting over a boy. Most of the white girls, though, are afraid of the Negro girls. The Negro girls think they're always toughest, and they are. If they think you've said something against them, they'll breathe down your back. I'm always careful about what I say. I don't want to say anything about them. I'd rather have them as friends anyway.

JOSEPHINE: I think it's getting better, though. Before you were afraid to say anything, for fear they'd be offended. This year, in dietetics class, we weren't so afraid to say anything. We were a little bit freer.]

At times Mexican-American students seem to identify themselves with white students, and at other times with Negro students. However, even when Negro friendships are described, one cannot overcome a faint feeling of "theyness." It may be that the present interview situation encourages a "theyness" toward Negroes. Still, Negroes tend to be made into somewhat distant objects, even among persons who apparently have little prejudice toward them.

[QUESTION: Do you speak about race relations openly in school?

ANNA: Well, after Dr. King died, just in this one class, Social Problems, we discussed violence, and the different kids gave their opinions about how violence begins and what's the cause of it. But there really wasn't what you could call a discussion about it. Most of what was said was very personal. The white kids in class were kind of prejudiced, and many of them were putting the Negroes down. The whites kept saying that they were watching the riots on T.V. every day, and they couldn't see how Negroes could do that. They didn't understand that the Negroes felt hurt.

JOSEPHINE: In Composition class, this teacher is really great. We can discuss anything we want. When Dr. King was dead, we talked about it in that class, and some of the kids felt that with King's death nonviolence also died. Some of the Negro kids said, "Now that they've killed him, violence is the only answer. Now that King is no longer alive, we've got to turn to people like Stokely Carmichael or Rap Brown." I always find it easier to talk to Negro people about problems, so whenever I talk race or social problems, I usually talk to Negroes and not to the white people. With the white kids, I get the feeling it goes in one ear and out the other.

THERESA: In my first hour class, there's this Negro girl who sat behind me. She's the best friend I had as a Negro. She said what she thought in class. The teacher encouraged her and the rest of us to say what we thought. She and I talked like real good friends. We'd say anything to each other, but I don't feel this free with white kids.]

[QUESTION: In which activities do you find the most integration?

JOSEPHINE: Mainly in sports. Usually in football, basketball, and track, but not so much in tennis or golf or swimming. Or in girl's gymnastics, there's not much integration. On the drill team there isn't much, either. I don't understand it, but there's never been a Mexican girl on the drill team.

QUESTION: What about some of the other activities?

JOSEPHINE: Well, in Pep Club there's usually integration, because everybody's in Pep Club, and Spanish Club is kinda integrated. Also, the Senior Girls' Council and Boys' Council.

QUESTION: In which activities do you find the least integration?

JOSEPHINE: A lot of the clubs aren't really integrated, or things like the Model U.N. For example, I was the only Mexican out of about 300 kids, and there was only about 5 Negroes in the Model U.N.

QUESTION: How about in social activities?

ANNA: Well, we never did try to join activities until about a year ago. More Mexican kids started trying out for things and trying to get into activities. At Catholic High School some of the Mexicans started trying out for drill team and things like that, or for cheerleader. But a Mexican girl's never been elected cheerleader.

JOSEPHINE: I know some Negro girls who'd make better cheerleaders than the white kids. I have this friend from South Center City, for example. In junior high school, she was really great. She really knew how to cheer, and she's beautiful. She could jump real high. She's a Negro. She got to Plains High School, and she didn't make it. I know the Negroes are very disappointed at Plains High School because they can't get a cheerleader. This year again they didn't get one. The Negro kids were very disappointed over this. I always used to say, "Why can't they have a Negro cheerleader? I don't understand it. Some of the Negro kids are better than the white kids." Now I think I know why. They just don't want a Negro girl to represent Plains High School. But the basketball team is almost all Negro. It's very hard to explain. I just don't understand it. I think that the school doesn't want a Negro to represent them that way.]

It is as though, very reluctantly and very slowly, Josephine has decided that there really is such a thing as prejudice at Plains High. The three Mexican-American students interviewed in this section have been reluctant to think of prejudice existing among the "grown ups" who set the school's policy. Actually, the fact that there is no Negro cheerleader seems to be the result of a combination of factors, several of which are not related to prejudice. Nevertheless, the cheerleader situation is one on which prejudice can easily be focused.

It is interesting that the Mexican-American students in this section eagerly deny the existance of prejudice. Probably if they deny that prejudice really exists, then they can deny that it exists with reference to them and that they are victimized by it. It is apparently easier for them to maintain that whatever segregation is directed toward them is actually nothing more than the result of their own lack of motivation to be included in the variety of general activities.

Josephine and Theresa describe attending a graduation party which was sponsored by black students of Plains High. This party sounds as though it had been successfully "integrated," although, as we learned in an earlier chapter, the integration was not total, in that whites and blacks sat at separate tables. Josephine and Theresa speak of how much they enjoyed themselves at this party, and their enjoyment sounds genuine. This sort of get-together is fine witness to the fact that the meeting of Negro, white, and Mexican-American can be natural and does not have to be strained or artificial.

[QUESTION: How do the kids mingle at school activities?

THERESA: Well, at the varsity dances all the white kids are at one end of the gym, all the Negro kids are at the other end of the gym and the Mexican kids are kinda in between. Nobody really mixes. I don't like these kinds of activities. When I go to something, I want to do as I please. I want to go around and see everybody. I don't care if the Mexicans look at me or what they think. But I like to go over and see the Negroes and the whites, and I like to mix.

ANNA: It's always that way. The whites are in their group, and the Mexicans are in their group at all the functions. If there's only one Mexican couple, they'll mix with the others. But when there's another couple there, then the Mexicans stay together, and the whites stay together.

JOSEPHINE: When we had our graduation activities, it was too much. We had this Queen of Courts dance, and you saw all the white kids together, and all the Mexican kids together, and all the Negro kids together. But I told my boy friend that I wanted to go around because, for one thing, I wanted to see who was there. I wanted to talk to a bunch of kids. I didn't care whether they were white, Negro, or Mexican. So we went around and mingled. Let me tell you about graduation. The greatest thing that ever happened, happened at graduation. There was this party at the Highway Motel. It was sponsored by the Negroes, and it was going to be held from 9:30 until 5:00 in the morning. The Negroes wanted to make sure that there wasn't any prejudice, so they invited everybody; whites, Negroes, and Mexicans. I told Jack, my boy friend—he goes to Catholic High—and he said, "Well, if you want to go, okay, we'll go." There was this Mexican party first in Winton. That party was closed. The Mexicans wanted to keep it just for the Mexicans. I felt kinda bad for the white kids because they didn't have any parties like that. I thought they should've been invited to our Mexican party, but the Mexican kids wanted to stay by themselves. We went to the party at Winton first, and then we went to the Highway Motel. It was really nice. I had a great time. Nobody thought about prejudice. We just all danced together. I danced with Negroes, and I danced with whites, and I danced with Mexican kids. It was a great feeling. Everybody was there to have a good time. We were all in there "jamming." That's what we call dancing now. Nobody really thought about prejudice. I thought it was the best party I'd been to in a long time.

THERESA: I went to that party, too. I didn't have a date, so I went alone. But it was great. I danced with Negroes, and I danced with whites. I had a great time. It was really fun. Everybody talked to you. A lot of my friends didn't think I'd go to a Negro-sponsored party.

JOSEPHINE: It was the same way with me. Even the Negro kids didn't think I'd go to a Negro-sponsored party. When I showed up, they were really surprised that I came. But they were happy. It made them feel good that I wasn't afraid to go to a Negro-sponsored party, and it was really great. There were some white kids there, too, and it was a marvelous feeling. Everybody was together, and nobody felt any prejudice. I wish we'd have more of those parties.]

Although the Mexican-American young women severly indict the older generations, and say that the younger generation is more liberal, they follow up this accusation by telling how their friends (of the same age) discourage Mexican-Negro dating. Actually, there seems to be little doubt that the majority of Mexicans (both young and old) discourage Mexican-American students from dating outside their cultural sub-group. Perhaps this is one way the Mexican-Americans are able to maintain cultural integrity.

[QUESTION: Who puts pressure on you not to mingle?
JOSEPHINE: It's the parents and it's your friends, too. Our parents don't like the idea too much. My parents didn't like the idea that I was going to a Negro-sponsored party. I told them about this party that was being held at the Highway Motel, that the Negroes were sponsoring. My parents said, "Well, why do you want to go to a party sponsored by Negroes?" I said I wanted to go, and I went. So, right after we had that party in Winton, I went to the other party at Highway Motel. It was great. It was a dress-up party because the Negroes wanted to show everybody in the community that the Negroes, the Mexicans and the whites could all behave and dress nicely. So everybody was dressed up.
ANNA: I think the kids want to mingle together, but the parents don't want them to mix. This is true of all the parents and the Mexican parents, too, just don't like us to mix.
JOSEPHINE: Mom always says, "Have your fun as long as you're young. Go out with who you want to go out with, as long as you marry a Mexican." I don't feel that way. If I fall in love with a Negro, I'll marry a Negro. If I fall in love with a white, I'll marry a white. I've learned not to pay attention to parents. I know this is kinda bad to say, but I know that if I don't go after what I want, my parents won't go after it for me. So I don't listen to them any more. My mother's half-sister feels the same way as I do. She's very liberal. When they were having that memorial service at the church by us for King, she called me up and asked me if I wanted to go. I said, "Sure." We went. There were some white people there, and you know, we were the only two Mexicans. But the way I look at it, if people don't like what you like, that's too bad. If they can't accept you the way you are, then that's too bad for them.
THERESA: My mother always tells me to marry a Mexican, or a white, but not a colored person. She said a colored person is okay as a friend but not to

marry. I never really consider it, anyway, because I just don't plan that far ahead. I don't like to plan ahead. It's hard for me to explain, though. I don't think I'd ever date a colored person. My parents would never approve of it. I think they'd lock me up if I said I was going out with a colored person. Just before school ended this white guy asked me out. I said I had to check with my mother first. Mother said she'd have to know him first before I could go out with him. She'd have to know what his parents were like and what he was like, so I didn't go out with him. I think, if I married a colored person, my relatives would have a fit. I don't like this prejudice, though, I think it's silly.

QUESTION: Do you think there's been an improvement over the generations: Do your parents feel more liberal than your grandparents?

JOSEPHINE: No, the parents and my grandparents are the same. It's us who's changing. It's happening to us, all of these things, while we're growing up. So we're the ones who're changing. Our feelings are changing. We'll teach them to our children. I don't believe our parents or grandparents will ever change. The older people won't change. They're prejudiced.

ANNA: I don't think my folks would mind me dating a white person. But as far as dating a Negro, they wouldn't approve. The other part of my family, I have a very large family here in town, would have a fit.

JOSEPHINE: They'd frown on us dating a Negro, even if he has higher standards than the Mexicans we date now. Even if the Negro's father was a lawyer or a doctor, and he was a better person than many of the lower class Mexicans that we date now, our parents still wouldn't approve. I just don't understand it. They'd rather see us go out with people who aren't as good as other people, just because of the difference in skin color. They say that they want the best for us, and if the best meant going out with a Negro, they'd deny us the right to go out with that Negro. I just don't understand it.

THERESA: If you went out with a Negro, as soon as you came home from a date, they'd say to you, "Never do it again." My relatives are always talking about white and Negro marriages. They don't like it. It'd be even worse if a Mexican and a Negro married.

QUESTION: How would it be with your friends?

THERESA: Your Mexican friends would put you out of their friendship completely if you dated a Negro.

JOSEPHINE: I'm not ashamed of it. This past year I got crushes on several Negro boys. My friends would say, "Don't ruin yourself by dating him." They'd shut us out. I can't understand this, but they would.

ANNA: I know two Mexican girls who married Negro guys. They get along very well. They love each other. Their parents and a lot of the other Mexicans can't see it, but I don't see anything wrong with it as long as they love each other.]

[QUESTION: Is there much interracial dating at Plains High School?

THERESA: Well, this year there was more interracial dating than ever before. A lot of the white girls dated Negro boys this year. We were surprised. But I think it's up to them. If they like each other, then it's their business whether they date each other or not, and no one else's. A lot of the kids told me that the teachers didn't like it. But I don't think the teachers said anything because, again, it's not their business. I think a lot of the white kids frown on this, though. And they also exclude the white kids who date Negro kids.

QUESTION: How do you think the Negro girls react to it when Negro boys date white girls?

JOSEPHINE: The Negro girls don't understand it. They're always saying, "What's so great about a white girl? Why's she better than me?" They think that these girls are butting in on them. They think that the white girls only like Negro boys if they're basketball players or big football stars, that they don't really like them. They just go out with them because they're stars. At Plains High, usually the Negroes who date white girls are up there. They're the boys who've become stars on the teams.

QUESTION: Do you know of any instances where a white boy's dating a Negro girl?

ANNA: No, I don't think so.

JOSEPHINE: A lot of Mexican boys date white girls, and most of the Mexican girls resent this, too. A lot of the Mexican girls think, "What's wrong with me that he has to date a white girl?" I don't think there's anything wrong with it. My brother married a white girl. They're very happy together. I don't see anything wrong with it.

THERESA: I've a brother who only dates white girls. He said the Mexican girls have hurt him, and he didn't like them any more, so he wasn't going to date them any more. I have another brother who was engaged to a white girl. They broke up because her parents didn't want her to marry a Mexican.

ANNA: I heard that when Mexican boys first started going with white girls, that the Mexican girls even threatened them. They said they'd go out with Negroes unless the Mexican boys paid more attention to them. But it didn't make any difference. The Mexican boys kept going out with white girls anyway.

JOSEPHINE: I have a cousin and he was telling me the other day that a lot of the Mexican men don't like it when Mexican girls date white guys. Lots of Mexican girls date white guys from the air base. He said the guys resent this. They don't know why Mexican girls will date white guys and won't date Mexicans. They will date white guys and give in to them and everything, but they won't date Mexicans. He said, "What's wrong with us? They should give us a chance to go out with them, too. We'd behave and we'd be gentlemen, just like some of the white guys. But they won't give us a chance."

QUESTION: You mean this feeling exists then among Mexican guys as well as Mexican girls, that each one is being excluded by the other if they date interracially?

JOSEPHINE: Yes. The Mexican girls feel left out when the Mexican guys date white girls, and they say, "Why does he date them and not me?" It seems that the Mexican guys feel the same way: they feel like the girls don't like them and are excluding them.]

With reference to dating, one hears many similar themes from the Mexican-Americans as from the Negroes. One difference, however, is that Mexican-American women find it easier to go with white men than do Negro women. Generally, however, they are dated by whites who are not in school. For these young women, dating whites is considered interracial dating, since Mexicans distinguish themselves from "whites." The well-hidden prejudice toward blacks surfaces in Anna's statement that the Mexican girls threatened the Mexican boys by saying they would date Negroes.

[JOSEPHINE: I'm going to tell you something else I don't like at school. In this World Civilizations class there are two Negro girls, and then there was myself. I was the only Mexican. There were a lot of upper class white kids. We were discussing racial discrimination and problems. All we ever talked about was discrimination against Negroes, but they didn't say anything about the Mexicans. This made me mad, because the Mexicans are discriminated against, too. So one day I went in and I said a mouthful. I told 'em about the Mexican's problems. I told them how the Mexican-Americans feel, and how they feel left out, too. There're a lot of other stupid things going on in school. Like white guys will try to say something in Spanish in the hall. Sometimes what they say is real dumb. One time at the Corner Spot, a little restaurant, it was horrible. This couple was made fun of because there was this white guy with a Mexican girl, and everybody was making fun of 'em.]

This is the first time that one of these young women justifiably complains that prejudicial behavior toward Mexican-Americans is generally ignored in Center City. It is ironic that her complaint should be that when people talk about discrimination, the Mexican-Americans tend to be left out. This charge is true since present-day discussions of discrimination, whether in Center City or elsewhere, have almost exclusively been focused on the Negro, often at the expense of other minority groups who are equally discriminated against, such as certain cultural minorities and the American Indian. The tendency to leave other minority groups out of a discussion on prejudice is reinforced by the fact that these other groups have generally not waged an effective protest themselves.

The reluctance to recognize that prejudice might indeed exist against Mexican-Americans at Plains High is broken through briefly as these students describe situations in which they seemed qualified for certain extracurricular positions but could not obtain them. However, this brief admission of possible prejudice is quickly forgotten as another variation of the preceeding own-guilt, inferiority theme is voiced: even if Mexican young men were on the various athletic teams, they would choose a white person rather than a Mexican-American for Queen. Josephine and Theresa also speak about the importance of helping Mexican-American children overcome their expectation that they will not be "chosen," so that they will later try out for the various school activities. While it is true that the lack of Mexican-American effort to join various school activities seems to be an important factor contributing to their uninvolvement in school, at times these young women speak as though it were the only reason.

[QUESTION: Do you feel as much discrimination in school as you feel in the community?

THERESA: I don't feel much discrimination in the community, or in my neighborhood anyway. They're mostly whites and Mexicans there, and one Negro family. We all get along together as neighbors.

JOSEPHINE: You do feel excluded at school. You feel left out, and you wonder, is it because you're Mexican or because you weren't qualified? The first time I felt this was when I was a sophomore. I tried out for usher. My record was excellent, and I thought I had all of the qualifications, but I didn't make it. I didn't know why I didn't make it. I didn't know whether I wasn't good enough and wasn't qualified, or whether I didn't make it because I was Mexican.

THERESA: I had a similar experience, myself. I can't even remember what it was I was trying out for now, but I was a sophomore, and I was turned down. I thought, "Well, is it because I'm Mexican or because I'm not really qualified?"

ANNA: I never tried out for anything, because I didn't think I'd make it. I thought, "I'm a Mexican and there aren't many Mexicans in these things, so I don't have a chance."

JOSEPHINE: I think all Mexicans have felt this in school. They don't try out for things because they don't feel they'll make 'em. I'm trying to help the younger Mexican kids. I'm trying to tell them to go out and try for things. In the Catholic Youth Organization I made a speech and told them to stick together and support each other, and to try out for things. I think kids don't try, because they think they won't make it because they're Mexican. They need to stick together and support each other, because if you know one is behind you, you'll try these things. And I think you'll make 'em, if you keep trying.

THERESA: Another thing is that there're kids who've been in school before you, and they tell you that Mexicans are never in anything in school. So you hear this from the older kids. When you go to school, you don't expect that it can happen—that you could get into things—because you've been told by the other kids, who've been in school before you, that the Mexicans were left out. You've been told that there's never been a Mexican girl for a cheerleader, so you just feel that you'll never make it, that you don't have a chance. I really wanted to be a cheerleader, real bad. I always wanted to be one, but I never tried out because I was afraid. I felt I'd never make it because I'm Mexican.

JOSEPHINE: A lot of cheerleaders who are selected aren't as pretty as some of the girls who don't try out, but still you feel inferior, so you don't try.

THERESA: I think most of the kids feel this way, but I want my brothers and my sisters to try out for these things. I tell them now to try out, and I try to encourage them and support them so that they can do better and help later on in this world.

JOSEPHINE: There's never been a Mexican girl named as Queen of anything at Plains High School. I've talked to some Negro boys about this, and the Negro boys told me, "Well, there's never been a Mexican Queen because the boys don't select them. There aren't any Mexican boys on the teams, and things like that, and the queens are selected by the teams. You don't have any boys to stay behind you." If we did have Mexican boys on the team, though, I think they'd still rather have a white girl as their Queen. I don't believe they'd support each other the way the Negroes and whites do. I don't think a Mexican girl would have a chance anyway.

THERESA: If I had become a cheerleader, I wouldn't act the way some of those girls act. I know a lot of white cheerleaders who, once they became cheerleaders, thought they were better than everyone. They'd even snub their white girl friends. I don't see why they should change because all of a sudden they're cheerleaders. If I had become one, I would've remained the same. Sometimes these kids don't realize that they're snubbing other kids. When we were in junior high school, there was this one Mexican girl. She was really up there. She was in everything and she was in many activities, and she started snubbing us. We wrote a letter to her and told her she was a snob and all the Mexican girls in the school signed it. She came back down and said, "Gee, I'm glad you told me that, because I didn't realize what I was doing." She was a lot friendlier with the Mexican kids after that. I think some of the white girls might also do the same thing if the white girls got together and told her they didn't like the way she was acting.]

[QUESTION: Do Mexican boys and girls go on to college after high school?

JOSEPHINE: Not to a four-year college. Some kids might go to a business college, or something, for a year or so. But most of the kids can't go to a four-year college. They want to get right out now and do things. I only know of one Mexican boy who's gone to a four-year college. He graduated last year from Plains High School. I, myself, I can't see going to a four-year college. I don't want to wait. I want something I can do now. I can't see taking something that takes so long to prepare yourself for.

THERESA: It's hard even to get through high school. The finals gave me a headache. I can't see going to school for three or four years, with homework and everything.

JOSEPHINE: A lot of the boys don't want to bother with it. They want to go out and get things now. A lot of them don't feel they have what it takes to get through college. They just want jobs now, or they go into the service and then come back and get jobs.

QUESTION: Do you get much encouragement from your parents to go on to school?

THERESA: Well my mother encourages me. She wants me to go to a vocational school. I might have a chance for a scholarship to go there. Mother wants me to try for it. Some of my other relatives also want me to go on. I got this graduation card from my aunt who said, "Go on to school because you'll need it." You know, I was really surprised that they felt that way, but I don't think I'll go. I want to go out now and get a job.

ANNA: You know, my folks saved their money so my older brother could go to college. He said he wanted to wait a year and work. My folks have given up on him. I, myself, I don't want to go to college. I want to find a job. I have a nine-year-old brother, though, and he keeps talking about going to the State University already so my parents are saving, and hoping he'll go.]

Apparently, the American value of "going to college" has not captured the young Mexican-Americans. Throughout the discussion on college, one cannot avoid the impression that Josephine, Theresa, and Anna feel less adequate than their white peers. They say that they do not think of themselves as "college material" and that they are eager to leave the learning situation so that they can go out and earn some money and start life. Interestingly, it is the parents who want the children to continue their education, while the children who, partly because they are sick of school, partly because they want to earn a living, and partly because they apparently do not consider themselves college material, leave school and "begin life."

[QUESTION: What has your experience in a desegregated school taught you about the races?

JOSEPHINE: You learn that the Negroes are the same as you. They're just like us. They're the same people. The only thing different is their skin color. Some people think that they are so horrible, but they aren't horrible—they're just darker. They've the same feelings as everyone else.

THERESA: I'd rather go to an integrated school than any other kind of school. If you go to a school with just Mexicans, you have a problem, and all you have to turn to is other Mexicans, while, if you're in an integrated school, you go out and make friends with whites and Negroes and Mexicans. Then you have other people to turn to. I think it's good to know other people from different races.

JOSEPHINE: I'd like to add something else. I think you also learn what life is really like. If I went to a Mexican school, I wouldn't have had the experience, or I wouldn't know what life is really like. You know you're going to have to meet Negroes in real life because they're there. It's better to meet them now than to learn about them later.

ANNA: I'm sorry I didn't mingle more with Negroes and other kids when I was in school. I think it's a good experience to go to an integrated school, but we hardly mingled, so I hardly got to know them.

QUESTION: Would you send your children to an integrated school?

THERESA: Yes, I'd send them to integrated schools, and only integrated schools.

JOSEPHINE: I hope I can send my children to Plains High School. I want them to find out what life is really like. The opportunity will be there for them to find out, if they're in integrated schools.

THERESA: I never want my children not to know what other people are like. For example, there's this boy I dated, and his mother was telling me she has this other son who was three years old, and he came across a Negro boy one time. He asked his mother, "What's that?" He didn't know what a colored boy was. I never want that to happen to my children. I want them to know.]

Although these young women say the "right things," one cannot avoid the feeling that they thought that it was fine to go to an integrated school, not so much because integration was right, but because it was "good for" them. Going to an integrated school, these young women seem to say, rounds out one's life very much as it would to go to a museum. Their tendency to say what is socially desirable cannot be dismissed. For example, Theresa, who has had limited contact with whites and blacks at Plains High, thinks it is a good idea to go to an integrated high school because, "You can discuss your problems with other kids and not just Mexicans." There is little in this interview to suggest that this is what Theresa did.

The Mexican-Americans

Part 2

This interview is with Francis and Manuel, both Mexican-American high school juniors, and Ted, an "Anglo," also a junior. Winton, which is mentioned several times during the interview, is the main Mexican-American community in Center City.

As with the Mexican-American female students, Francis and Manuel vacillate between saying that the social-racial situation at Plains High is problematical and that it is not. The Mexican-Americans seem to feel somewhat in the middle between the whites and Negroes. Being in the middle is a problem, since whites resent it if Mexican-Americans form friendships with Negroes, while Negroes resent most Mexican friendships with whites.

[QUESTION: What pressures do you feel from attending a desegregated school?

TED: Well, they do emphasize academic achievement quite a bit. I feel that as a pressure. Socially, I also found that it was kinda rough because I came from a school where half of my friends went to Adams High, so it took me a while to make friends at Plains High School. But I don't really find it too hard to make friends there.

MANUEL: Well I do. Socially, it's hard for me at Plains High School. I know a lot of Negro kids, and it's hard if you're seen with them, to be friends with the white people. They kinda look down on you if you're friendly with the Negroes.

FRANCIS: Well, I hang around with all races. When you're with Negroes, some white kids will look down on you, and when you're with whites, some Negroes will look down on you. It's very difficult at Plains High School.

TED: You also have to watch your tongue. You can't go to extremes. You can joke and you can kid around about race—there's a lot of that—but you have to be careful about what you say. We get along fine, I think, with the Negroes and the Mexican kids.

FRANCIS: Nobody really feels like it's a big problem at Plains High School.

MANUEL: When one kid starts joking, everybody has fun. It's not really a problem.]

Much of what these three young men talk about is what some Negro students have also mentioned. Of particular interest is the theme of "thinking they are

217

better than we are," which occurs whenever someone tries to leave the old, closed Mexican community and adapt himself to the values of the dominant "Anglo" culture. In this connection, Francis and Manuel speak of the apparent self-satisfaction which characterizes the members of the Winton community and the distrust of, and anger toward, those who have left Winton (i.e. "deserted"). The situation, thus, proves to be similar for the present group of interviewees as for the elite Negroes—the Mexican-American student who tries to achieve success as measured by the dominant culture is not fully accepted by whites, Negroes, or by his fellow Mexican-Americans.

[QUESTION: Are the Mexican kids as involved in school as the other kids?

FRANCIS: No, the Mexican kids aren't nearly as involved as the other kids. In a lot of classes, I'm the only Mexican. I feel kinda strange sometimes 'cause I'm the only Mexican. And also, there's some pressure on me from some of the other Mexican kids, because they think that I think I'm better than most of the other Mexican kids.

MANUEL: In Social Problems Class, I was the only Mexican kid. The rest were white. It wasn't tougher academically, but it really bothered me not seeing any other Mexicans in that class. I'd have felt more comfortable if there was more Mexican kids.

TED: There's something about that, and I think it's kinda hard to explain just what's going on. But you don't see many Mexican kids in the classes with the white kids.

MANUEL: Also, there're some qualified Mexican kids that could run for office, but they just don't take the step forward and run. They just don't run. I think that they're afraid of what the other Mexican kids'll say if they try to run for offices or do a lot of things in school. Most of the other Mexican kids would say they're trying to be better than them.

FRANCIS: Yes, most of the Mexicans are in a rut. They think if you get out, you're trying to be better than they are.

MANUEL: Mexican kids don't associate much with the other kids. Most of the time you'll see the Mexican kids in the chemistry wing, there on the second floor. They usually stay there by themselves. These are the kids from Winton. The rest of the Mexican kids just stick together, too. They don't try to get out and meet the other kids, or do things in school with the other kids.

TED: I notice at school that especially the boys from Winton don't try to associate with the other kids. You can always tell that some kid is from Winton because he doesn't want to associate or mingle with the whites or Negroes or anybody else—he just wants to stay with the kids from Winton.]

Segregation, in its most literal sense, of Mexicans, whites, and blacks, seems at least partially determined by the school subjects each group most commonly takes. But the wish to remain together as a group in all probability also means that each Mexican and each Negro wishes to relax among his friends and to avoid situations in which he will be ignored, treated condescendingly, or verbally attacked. The "segregation" of the white is, of course, based on different reasons: status considerations, disdain for minorities, and the like. However, with a growing militancy in the black community, some whites perhaps self-segregate to protect themselves from verbal attack and guilt.

[QUESTION: What about the other groups? How about the Anglos and the Negroes; do they also keep to themselves in certain parts of the building?

FRANCIS: Well, the Negroes stay in the front and side of the building, but mainly in the front part of the main hall. In fact, if you go to that part of the school you'd think there're a lot of Negroes in school. But actually, in the other areas, you hardly see any Negroes. As far as the whites are concerned, they're all over the place. They don't really stay in one area although a lot of them are on the fourth floor because they have classes on the fourth floor.

MANUEL: Well, the Negroes also hang out on the third floor during class and between classes. But that's because there're a lot of these shop courses and what have you up there, and that's where they have their classes.

FRANCIS: You hear a lot of stories, you know, about kids in the back hall, but there's nobody hanging around in the back halls. They're always empty. The only people who go back there are the people going to their shop classes because the shop classes are in the back hall, and sometimes there're lots of boys going back there, going to class, but nobody hangs around back there. I always heard that there was a lot of violence back there, but I don't see it. I've never seen any violence back there.]

[QUESTION: When you knew you were going to Plains High School, were you afraid to go there?

FRANCIS: A lot of people are afraid because you hear a lot of stories about Plains High School. There was even this teacher I know who transferred from Adams to Plains High School, and when he was going there a lot of people told him that Plains High School was really bad, that the kids carried knives and that they'd knife you in the back halls. Well, he was telling that, for the first couple of weeks, he was really nervous, but he noticed that there wasn't anything going on, so he became more relaxed. It's this way also with the kids. You'll hear a lot of stories, and some of the kids are afraid.

MANUEL: Well, I wasn't afraid to go to Plains High School because I had brothers and sisters who'd went there before. They told me all about it. Now that I'm there, I don't see that it's bad, so my brothers and sisters were right. I wasn't really afraid.

TED: I had a sister who went there before me, too, and she told me it was nice and that she enjoyed Plains High School, so I really wasn't afraid, either.

FRANCIS: Well, I had brothers and sisters, too, who went there before, but they never told me nothing. I was a little bit afraid, and when I found out on the first day that I had a locker in the back halls, I was really afraid. I was looking for my locker, and finally I asked someone, "Well, where's this locker?" and they said, "Oh, that's in the back halls." When I heard "back halls," I was afraid to go back there, but I went, and it's never bothered me, and I've never seen any trouble.

QUESTION: Are there any fights at Plains High School?

MANUEL: Well, there're a lot of fights, but most of the time the fights are between Negroes and Negroes, or between a white guy and a white guy. There really aren't too many Negro-white fights or Mexican-white fights.

QUESTION: What about the girls? Do the girls fight?

MANUEL: Yes, a lot of girls fight.

FRANCIS: I think most of the time, it's Negro girls who do the fighting.

MANUEL: A lot of times, I think they fight over a guy.

FRANCIS: Well, I don't know. I think the girls who get into fights are the ones who don't have dates usually. Nobody wants to date those girls. They're very tough, and all they do is fight.

TED: I think what they're trying to do is attract attention. They don't get any attention any other way, so they start fighting. All the girl fights that I've seen have always been with people from the same race.]

The Mexican-American students are reluctant to tell of any discrimination which is directed against them. Manuel says there is no discrimination; Francis toys at the periphery of a discussion of discrimination in journalism, but when he brings up an example of discrimination, the object of it turns out to be a Negro. Although there seems little doubt that Mexican-Americans are discriminated against in Center City, the Mexican-Americans we interviewed prefer to deny whatever discrimination exists, and themselves assume the blame for differential treatment.

[QUESTION: Do the teachers treat the kids differently, that is, kids from different races?

MANUEL: I haven't found that the teachers treat the kids different. In fact, I think everybody is treated the same.

FRANCIS: Well, I don't know. I like journalism, for example, and there's never been a Negro or Mexican on the newspaper. Next year, I'm going to be on the newspaper. I'm the first Mexican to ever be on the paper. I don't know what to think or what to expect, but I'm glad that I'm going to be on it. I know of this case where there was this one Negro boy; he's tall and skinny, and he's really a nice boy, and everybody likes him. This white girl was molested in the back halls; she said by a Negro. They think she was raped. The girl described a boy who was tall and skinny who did it, so they brought in three boys, and this tall boy was one of them. She said, "Yes, he's the one who did it!" The counselor didn't even listen to the boy's story. He just threw him out of school right away. I think that was discrimination. When our journalism teacher heard about this, she went down and talked to the counselor, because nobody who really knows this boy believed that he could've done that. He didn't do it, and then the counselor had to apologize. But I think he jumped to conclusions. I think that was discrimination.

MANUEL: I think the counselors have all tried to be equal to the students most of the time. I think when people cause trouble, they get kicked out a lot. But they always try to give the guy a chance.]

[QUESTION: Where do you find the most integration?

TED: In sports mostly. The sports are mixed, particularly the basketball team and in physical education. There's a lot of Negroes on the basketball team, and in football.

FRANCIS: Academically, I'd say that the machine shop or the shops in general are where you find most of the Negroes and whites mixing. That's because the Negroes will work with their hands, so they take these courses.

MANUEL: But in a lot of other things you don't see too much integration. Boys' Pep doesn't have any Mexicans, for example. There're only a few Negroes. Hardly any of the Mexican boys go to the basketball games. Some girls go, but the Mexican boys don't. I don't know, it's hard to explain why they don't. But that's probably why they're not in Boys' Pep, too, because they don't go to the games and support the teams.

QUESTION: How about social activities, such as dances?

MANUEL: Well, the kids don't mix at the dances. The colored kids dance on one part of the floor, and the white kids dance on the other part of the floor. But they never mix with each other.

FRANCIS: Well, you know, the Negroes have one way of dancing, and the white have another way. I don't think they like the way each other dances, so they stay apart at the dances.

TED: You don't ever hear of too much mixing at parties, either. There was this one party, though, I know, which was held after the school play. There was this Negro girl there, and there was a lot of dancing at that time. A lot of the white guys danced with this Negro girl. But you have to know her. She's a lot of fun. She's heavy-set and very happy and jolly, so everybody likes her.

FRANCIS: Yeah, she's big and round. Everybody likes her. She's like a boy, anyway.

QUESTION: What about interracial dating?

MANUEL: I only know of one case of mixed dating.

TED: Yeah, that's Jackson and Mary Sears. They date. But this isn't too popular a thing. I don't think either race likes it too much. Both sides think both the boy and the girl are slightly looked down on.

MANUEL: Well, Jackson's a real popular boy, so I don't know if they look down on him that much.

FRANCIS: Well, the girl is also popular, and I think she still has a lot of white friends. But the white boys said they wouldn't date her again.

MANUEL: Yeah, I know this one boy who knows her. He knew her from three years ago. One time he asked me about her, so I told him she was dating a Negro. He kinda looked down on her when he heard that.]

The general integration picture the Mexican-Americans describe is similar to the one described by the other students. It is important to see, however, that the Mexican young men do not attend basketball games. They have no reason, therefore, to join the male Pep Club. This situation would seem to represent another example of voluntary, possibly defensive, segregation.

These young students, the two Mexican-Americans and the "Anglo," further describe their life. It seems that Francis and Manuel are resented as disloyal by the young men of Winton, who maintain a pride in membership in their own community and have little to do with anything or anyone outside of it. As Francis and Manuel attempt to change their values in the direction of the dominant (mostly white) points of view, the Mexican-American young men of Winton attack them and consider them turn-coats. Thus, while the Negro resents being excluded from the white subculture, one has the impression that the Mexican-American does not care so much. He wants little to do with "Anglo" ways of life, and he resents the members of his own ethnic group who seem to desert the Mexican-American way for the "Anglo" one. Perhaps this is one reason why the Mexican-Americans do not find themselves as far in the evolution of their integration as is the Negro. While the Negro is fighting for integration, the majority of Mexican-Americans seem more satisfied to maintain their separateness.

[FRANCIS: The kids from my area don't get along too good with the kids from Winton. The kids from Winton look down on the Mexican kids from my area. Everybody is kinda scared of these Winton kids. They're really tough. These are Mexican kids, too, but they're a little different from the Mexican kids in my area.

MANUEL: If some of the Mexican kids try to get ahead and try to do things, the kids from Winton don't understand it. It doesn't dawn on them that this is important. If the Winton kids don't do it, you shouldn't do it. They'll think you're trying to be better than they are.

FRANCIS: For example, I go to an all-white church. There's only one other

Mexican family there. My mother took me there when I was in the first grade. It's a Baptist Church, and that's kinda odd, too. There aren't many Mexicans who're Baptist. Most Mexicans are Catholic. The kids from Winton look down on me, because I go to a white church, and because I'm a Baptist. They also look down on me because I'm better academically. They don't do it, so they don't want me to do it.

QUESTION: How about with the Anglos—are you supposed to achieve in school, Ted?

TED: I think it's better. The Anglo kids want you to try hard. You're supposed to be good academically, and you're supposed to try to get into activities. The more you can do this, the more status you have with the kids. The more you participate, the better off you are. The counselors and the teachers will help you, and people look up to you. Sometimes the counselors will single out the smart kids and help them more. I've seen counselors do this. I know this one Negro boy who went to the counselor and told him he wanted to go to Boys' State. The counselor told him that he didn't have much of a chance to go to Boys' State, that another Negro boy, like Jack Baldwin, stood a better chance, and it was more in line with something he'd do, instead of the boy who was asking. The Negroes are like the Mexicans. I think the whites are a little bit different. For example, this Negro boy was the vice-president of his senior class last year, and I know that the Negro boys held it against him. The whites are looked up to if they achieve more, but this isn't so with the Mexicans or the Negroes.

QUESTION: Well, what about if a white student achieves? Do the Mexicans and Negroes look up to him?

FRANCIS: Yes, I think they admire a white kid who does well in school and who gets involved in the politics of the school, or other activities. But they don't like it when kids from their own race try to do these things. I know some bullies who'll really embarrass you. They'll say things out loud against you and make you feel real bad. They'll just turn around and say things like, "Here's one who thinks he's better than we are," and this doesn't make you feel very good.

MANUEL: Yeah, the Mexican kids say, "Let the white kids do it. They'll take care of things. They'll run for the offices, and they'll take care of the student government." Things like this. They say, "Why should we worry about it? We shouldn't worry about it. Let the white kids take care of it." They don't want any of the Mexican kids to get involved. If I got an office in student government, I think my friends would look up to me, but not the Winton kids. They wouldn't like it. They'd embarrass me, and they'd laugh at me. I really don't care for the Winton kids. They try to show off, and they whistle at girls in the hallways and make foolish remarks. They like to kid and joke all the time. I just don't like them at all.

FRANCIS: I don't like them, either. We played them in football a couple of times. If they lose, or they see that they're losing, they always start a fight. I don't hang around with the kids from Winton. I don't like them.

TED: Yeah, I find that the Winton boys try to be tough all the time. It's very strange with them, because the opportunities are there. I think they could do things at school, but they just don't want to take advantage of them.

MANUEL: They don't care too much about the school. In Winton, there was this restaurant which they closed up now, but you'd find all the boys in there, playing the pinball machines and things like that, instead of going to the school activities. They just don't care much about school. It's not because they're poorer, because they're not poorer than a lot of the other kids. They just don't care.

TED: I wouldn't say that they're poorer, because their dads work in the same places as our dads. Their dads have some good jobs, just like mine. Mine's a foreman, and I know some Mexicans who're foremen; so they've as much money, and they can dress as well.

QUESTION: What about the Winton girls?

MANUEL: Well, the Winton girls mix a little bit more than the boys do. But they stick together, too. I think the reason why the boys in Winton won't participate in some of the school activities when they'd like to, is because they're scared that the other boys will call them sissies and will get on them real bad. I think this is why more of 'em don't participate.

QUESTION: Well, what are you supposed to do, as far as the Winton kids are concerned, to get respect from them?

FRANCIS: To get respect from the Winton group, you'd have to get drunk, smoke, cause trouble, and have a police record. As a matter of fact, if you have a police record, then you have a lot of respect. These are the kids who'll pull out a switch-blade if there's a fight, particularly if they're losing. If they're losing, they'll cut you up. Not too long ago, at an all-city dance downtown, there was a big fight started by the kids from Winton. This boy was losing, so he pulled out a knife and swung it back. Then he saw this blood, so he started to run. He ran away.

MANUEL: If you fight one of the kids from Winton you have to fight them all.

FRANCIS: Yeah, my cousin and his friend were going to fight a Winton kid. They brought ten guys to fight my cousin and his friend. They always do this.

MANUEL: If you whip the one guy, you have to fight them all. If you lose, it's okay. They leave you alone.

TED: I'll tell ya one thing. If you're gonna get in a fight with a Winton kid, it's better to fight right then and there. They don't like to do this. A lot of times they'll say, "Well, let's meet at such-and-such." But if you meet later, you know damn right well that when they come back they're gonna have a whole army, so you're gonna have to fight them all.

QUESTION: Is this true about Negroes too?

MANUEL: No.

TED: Usually Negroes would rather fight right then and there and get it over with.

MANUEL: I don't know, I think it depends on the individual. If the Negro boy is popular, he may have some friends there.

TED: Yeah, but his friends might only be there to see that nobody else jumps in. I don't think the Negroes jump in like the Mexicans do.]

Ted's opinion of Negroes is quite different from that of the racist and conservative students in an earlier chapter, who said, "If you fight one Negro, you have to fight them all."

Francis and Manuel think of their parents as more broadminded than Ted's as far as interracial dating is concerned. These broadminded attitudes partly support the statement made by one black student to the effect that minority groups are more tolerant of integration than whites. But Mexican-American students nevertheless believe that their parents are more tolerant of Mexican-American and "Anglo" dating than of Mexican-American and black dating.

[QUESTION: Do you find a difference between the generations in terms of how liberal they feel about mixing with other races?

FRANCIS: Well, I think my father wants me to mix. He's a civic worker and tries to get equal opportunity for everybody. If anything, I'd say that I feel pressure to mix from my parents.

MANUEL: My parents don't say nothing to me, but I know that they want me to mix. I've got this basketball court in my backyard, or I used to have it until the wind blew it down. There're a lot of Negroes in the area where I live. These kids always used to come over to play, and my parents never said anything about it.

TED: Well, if I tried to date someone from another race, my parents wouldn't like it. This wouldn't go good with my parents. It's okay to be good friends. They don't mind that. But dating would be a different story. They'd blow up. I think we'd have a good time in the house if I tried to do that.

FRANCIS: Well, I went with this white girl for ten months. My father's philosophy is, if you stay out of my hair or my business, I'll stay out of yours. I never got any pressure because of that.

MANUEL: Yeah, I'm going with a white girl, too. In fact, I never date Mexican girls. One of my brothers married a Mexican, and one of my brothers married a white girl. My parents don't seem to care.

FRANCIS: There aren't as many Mexican girls, it doesn't seem, as there are Mexican boys. Maybe that's why we date white girls.

MANUEL: I don't know about that, but I'd say that there aren't that many Mexican girls you like to date. Most of 'em aren't that pretty. Then when they're nice, they know it, and that's what I don't like. Because when they're pretty, they know they can get dates from anybody, and they show off.

QUESTION: Do the Mexican girls get mad when you date Anglos?

MANUEL: Well, some Mexican girls try to put pressure on you not to date white girls. They talk about you. These girls in CYO—you know I belong to this Catholic Youth Organization—they know that I date white girls. I told my cousin, who's a Mexican girl. She's always asking me these things, and then she goes back and reports to these other girls. In fact, I've decided that I'm not going to tell her anything else. There're a lot of Mexican dances, too. Usually I don't go to them. I don't like to go, and I wouldn't bring a white girl there. When I'm not there, they'll come up and say, "Why weren't you at the dance?" I'll say, "Well, I was out with the guys." And they'll say, "Yeah, I bet. I bet you were out with a white girl."]

Francis now brings up the matter of dating a Negro. While he thinks his *father* would not object to such dating, Manuel thinks his *mother* would not care (although maybe his father would). In any case, one has the impression that at least this particular set of Mexican-American parents reverse the generational pattern that is discussed by the young people in the previous chapters. Insofar as their children perceive them, the Mexican parents seem not to be as conservative as "Anglo" parents.

[FRANCIS: I don't think that my father would object, even if I dated a Negro girl. But it's never come up. My father likes Negroes. I think. He has Negro friends. I don't think he'd object, but I've never dated a Negro girl.

MANUEL: I don't know about that myself, I couldn't say how my parents would feel. I don't think my mother would care, but maybe my father would.

QUESTION: Do you find your generation more liberal?

FRANCIS: Yes, I think we're more liberal than our parents and grandparents. I think one of the reasons, though, is because the older people are worried about their positions. You take a white businessman. If he's seen with a Negro, he might lose some business. So he might stay away from Negroes because it looks bad. I think it's the same way for a lot of Negroes. If they're seen with white people, it doesn't look good as far as some of the Negroes are concerned.

TED: Yes. What's the word they use for people who hang around with whites? Uncle Toms—he might be called an Uncle Tom. They associate with white people. I, myself feel free of mixing with everybody. But I think some of the older people don't.]

[QUESTION: Who do you think mixes better—boys or girls?

TED: I think the boys mix a lot better, because of athletics. There's a lot of progress between the races because of athletics. When you play on the field, you have something in common, so you tend to mix more.

QUESTION: How come Plains High School has never had a Mexican, or a Negro, cheerleader?

MANUEL: Well, there was this one Negro girl who's really good. She was in our junior high school, and she was really a good cheerleader. I thought she was going to get it this year. But they had the election on King's funeral day. They had it before school in the gym. I heard that this girl missed by two votes. I think she should've gotten it.

FRANCIS: Well, I don't know. I missed the cheerleader election, too. I was talking to this kid in the hallway and asked him when they were gonna have the elections. He said, "Today." I looked at my watch and had already missed it. He'd missed it, too.

MANUEL: I think she should've made it.

FRANCIS: As far as Mexicans, none of the Mexicans ever run for it. They're scared. I think they feel, if they fail, people'll laugh at them, so they don't try out.

MANUEL: I think maybe next year they'll have some trouble over the cheerleader.]

Only relatively mild anger is expressed by these students over the "cheerleader issue." Of the three young men, Manuel feels that the Negro cheerleader should have won the election, while Francis admits that he did not vote because he was too late for the election. Thus, in this group, a middle path is achieved, between the anger of those who feel the cheerleader to have been discriminated against, and the placating attitude of those who feel that everything was as it should have been.

[QUESTION: Are there certain kids at school who might cause some trouble? Are there kids who are more militant?

FRANCIS: Well, as far as militants go, there's this one kid, Tim Howard. He's kinda militant. I don't understand him 'cause he has a lot of white friends.

TED: Well, I think he does this to get attention.

FRANCIS: Yeah, you know he's the one who spoke out downtown that time when King died.

MANUEL: I don't understand him, either. You know, he plays on an all-white basketball team. He seems like he's having a good time. Then the next day I saw him, and he was out preaching Black Power.]

[QUESTION: What do you kids think of the principal and the administration at school?

FRANCIS: I kinda like Mr. Ewing. You know, when we had that school-boundary incident, when they were screaming and didn't want their kids to go to Plains High School? I was one of the kids chosen to speak about Plains High School's good points at the Board of Education. You know, the Board of Education didn't want us to speak, but Mr. Ewing told us that when we got there to just go right up and speak. He could've gotten into trouble for saying that. I think he's a real good guy. I think he tries to help everybody.

MANUEL: I really like him, too. I don't know him personally, but I think he's real friendly with everybody. When I see him in the hall, he always says, "Hi." He talks to everybody. I think he's well liked by the students. For example, he always gets a very good ovation at the assemblies. I don't think the kids'd do this if they didn't like him.

TED: I'm sure they wouldn't. Because, remember, not too long ago when we had the assembly, they booed the drama teacher in the assembly. They were supposed to have this assembly on athletics, and this drama teacher got up to talk about the plays and musicals and things like this, and everybody booed. It was really awful.

FRANCIS: Yeah, and then there was this teacher that nobody likes, and it was announced that he was leaving. They said, "Mr. Page is leaving." Well, I'll tell ya, it sounded like people were really happy to see him go, because there was a tremendous ovation.]

Francis, Manuel, and Ted speak very positively of Mr. Ewing, their principal. Other students who have spoken in this book have not always spoken favorably of Mr. Ewing. In discussing their principal, they often selected aspects of his behavior, perceived by them as prejudicial. Why do these students see their principal so positively, while others see him so negatively? In part, the answer may lie in the fact that these three students are not actively involved in the struggle to change the status quo at Plains High School.

[QUESTION: Do Mexicans go to college as often as the white kids?

MANUEL: No. There aren't too many Mexican kids who go to college. I think a lot of it is lack of money, and a lot of them don't try that hard for a scholarship. They just want to get out of school and settle down, and maybe get married.

FRANCIS: A lot of them are real good with their hands, so they go to vocational school. They want to work as machinists, or something like that, but not many of 'em go to college.

TED: Well, I think a lot of it is because their parents didn't go to school themselves, and they pass this on to their kids. They don't really encourage their kids to go to college, either.

MANUEL: I wouldn't say that. I know a lot of Mexicans that are fathers now, who don't even have a junior high school education. I'm not ashamed of it. I don't believe my father went beyond junior high school, but he wants me to go to college. He pushes me to try real hard. He makes a good living, and he supports us well, but he wants me to do a little bit better for myself. I don't think that it's the parents who don't want them to go to college. I think it's the kids who don't want to go.

FRANCIS: Well, some of these homes that these Mexican kids live in, I wouldn't really call them homes. It's just a place to eat and sleep, so the kids are real anxious to get out of there. They go off, and they get married early, and then they find out that married life is not so good either. So then they leave married life, too. I think a lot of 'em want to get out of the homes as quickly as they can. Some of these homes are really lousy. You always see one of the parents walking around in the home with a bottle in their hands. They don't show any love or anything for their kids

TED: Well, I wanta go to college. I wanta have a better chance of advancing in a job. I'll probably try to get my military out of the way as soon as possible, so I might go into the military first. I think most Anglos want to go to college.

The two Mexican-American young men present a fairly similar picture regarding the young Mexican-American's wish not to continue his education by going to college. This was also true of the Mexican-American girls in Part 1 of this chapter. Rather than more school, they emphasize getting out of school and getting a job. This pattern has also been observed in such other cultural minorities as the Italian-Americans, where the younger generation is unwilling to delay immediate gratifications for further education. Although Ted is from a similar socioeconomic level as Manuel and Francis, he has accepted "Anglo" values with reference to a college education.

At first these three young men deny any difference in their relationship to Negroes and whites as they went from elementary to junior high and high school. Gradually, however, they become more vehement in their conviction that things have not really remained the same—that awareness of skin color seems to have increased with age. It is interesting, too, to see a greater identification, both with the Negro as friend and with the Negro as fellow victim of segregation. After their initial denial, the Mexican-American students tell how they, too, can *feel* the prejudice of the white fellow students.

[QUESTION: What have you learned at Plains High School about race relations?

FRANCIS: Well, ya know, we grew up in mixed situations, so we've always been mixed. But I don't think it's really taught me anything, because I don't see it as any different from the way it's been. You know, when we were in junior high school, that was mixed, and grade school was mixed, too. So it seems pretty much the same to me.

TED: I feel the same way, too. When I went all through school, I've been in a mixed situation, so it doesn't seem to be any different at Plains High School.

MANUEL: I've been the same, too. I haven't noticed any difference from elementary to where I'm now.

QUESTION: Do you all agree that there really isn't any difference in how you mix with the other kids in elementary, junior high school and high school?

FRANCIS: Well, when you're a little kid, you don't recognize that this guy is black and this guy is white. He's just fun to play with, and things like that; that's all you think about. You don't think about skin color. I think in high school, we think a little more about skin color. You hear a lot about it on TV, and you hear about it from your parents. In fact, everywhere you turn you hear about it.

MANUEL: Well, yeah, I think there might be a little bit of difference. I knew this girl all the time, almost all of my life. I knew her when I went to kindergarten. We were in school together. We'd play together an awful lot. Now that we're at Plains High School—she's white—we remember each other, but it's different. She has her white friends, and I've my Mexican friends. I think, as you grow older, you start thinking about color. You think about the color of a man's skin.

TED: You can't escape it, somebody's always bringing it out. I liked elementary school. Nobody thought about race. In junior high school, a lot of the kids didn't think about it, either. At Plains High School, most of the kids I knew when I first went there were either Mexicans or Negroes. But then, I had to learn to get to know some of the white kids, too, and I think the kids at Plains High School think about color a little bit more than they do in elementary school.

MANUEL: You know, it's harder for me to meet a white kid than it is for me to try to meet a new Mexican kid or a Negro kid. It's hard for me to know what to say to the white kids, or what they think of you. The white kids'll look down on another white kid if he's seen with a Mexican or a Negro. I feel kinda bad, and I really don't feel comfortable with other white kids. I find it very hard to meet them.

FRANCIS: If you're seen with a white kid in a place where most of the kids are Mexican, you feel that the people are looking down on you. If they're friends, it doesn't matter what he's like. He's just a friend. Most of your friends won't look down on you, but the other kids do.

QUESTION: Have you enjoyed going to an integrated school?

TED: I think going to an integrated school is the best experience you could have.

FRANCIS: If you have the experience with people of a different skin color you learn to get along better in life because in life you're gonna have to get along with kids and people with different skin color. I think it's a good experience.

MANUEL: I really like it at Plains High School. I know all of the Mexicans and most of the Negroes. It's just meeting the white kids that was the hardest. There's lots to do when you have plenty of friends. I really like it. I think it's a good experience.

FRANCIS: I went out for football and met a lot of white kids there. When you share an experience, it makes it easier to get along with them. I think it's easier when you share an experience than when you just try to meet friends in the hall.

MANUEL: Most of the white kids I got to know I met through physical education. I try to be friendly with all of them, but I think the kids from the different junior high schools are different. Some are harder to get along with.

QUESTION: Will you send your children to an integrated school?

TED: [The only one who answers] Well, if I live in an area where there's an integrated school, I certainly would send them there. It's the best place to learn how to get along with other people.

CHAPTER 9

Interracial Dating

Few topics produced feelings as intense as when we discussed interracial dating in our interviews with these young people. All the students expressed their opinions on this topic—opinions which often did not agree, and which ran the gamut from complete acceptance to complete rejection. Interracial dating demonstrates one of the many sources of pressure which the students desiring to integrate have to face—pressures which originate in the community, in the school, from parents and from friends and associates.

There seems to be no case of mixed dating in which the young man is white and the young woman black. In fact, most of the students have difficulty even considering such a pattern. At Plains High School, when interracial dating does occur, it most often involves a Negro athlete who occupies a high status.

The school does not *always* interfere with this type of dating. Instead, both black and white students accuse the school of interfering with mixed dating on a selective basis. They say that pressure from the school and its personnel increases in direct proportion to the white young woman's social status. As one Negro says, "If you're a low white person, the administration could care less, but if you're a higher white person, they're worried you might be dragged down by a Negro."

Gordie and Jean are the most frequently talked about interracial couple at Plains High. Both occupy a high status—Gordie, who is black, occupies his in athletics; Jean, who is white, occupies hers in student government. We could not interview Gordie, for he was out of town and later left Center City for college. Jean, however, agreed to talk with us, and in this chapter, we will meet her and two white girl friends—Marjorie and Carol.

In one of our interviews, a student suggested that "the tuition is high" for interracial dating. Just how high it is, is indicated by Jean's story.

[QUESTION: What pressure do you feel from attending a desegregated school?

MARJORIE: I think you have to learn to watch what you say more closely. I believe that most of the colored people think that white people don't like them very much and are kind of touchy about it, so I'm always careful about what I say around Negroes.

232

JEAN: Well, Marjorie, why don't you tell them about your classroom? [Marjorie is reluctant to tell.]

CAROL: Well, why don't you tell them, Jean?

JEAN: Okay. Marjorie was in a classroom where there were a lot of colored people who were talking and making a lot of noise. She wasn't able to study or anything, so one time Marjorie told them to shut up, and they got real mad. I'd get real mad, too, if Marjorie told me to shut up, but she's my friend, and I can take it, where a lot of these kids can't. If you say something like that to them, they get real mad, and then they'll get after you.

CAROL: This is not so much the color but it's the person. All people react that way, but I think that a colored person might be offended more easily because they may think that what you say was said about their race and not them. This is what I find difficult with the colored people at school. A lot of times you'll make an innocent remark to a person, but it's not taken as a personal remark; it's taken as something said against their race. I've gone to school with colored people as long as I can remember. I never really noticed the difference, until they noticed the difference themselves. This was around junior high school. They began to act as if whites and Negroes are different. It's getting harder to talk to them as people because of the race thing. I think this started pretty much around the eighth grade. There're some individuals to be handled as a race, and they see you always handling them this way, rather than as people, although you're trying to handle them as people and not as a race.

QUESTION: Which sex is more touchy about discussing race?

MARJORIE: I think it's the girls more than the boys. I noticed this particularly in home economics. There're a lot of Negroes in that class. It seemed like they were different there. I like the boys better than the girls. I think the Negro boys have broader minds than the girls.

JEAN: Well, I think that's because the boys go places together, and the girls don't. I think it's because of sports, which is where they get a chance to get together, and they're quite friendly.

MARJORIE: That's right, the girls don't have many sports in which they get a chance to get together like that.]

With few exceptions, the students assume that Negro and white young men get along better with each other because of the "integration" that takes place in sports. Yet sports at Plains High are integrated only in the sense that whites and blacks play on the same team. They tend not to go with each other once the athletic situation is over. The presence of blacks and whites together in the same organized activity is understood as "integration," probably because when the parents of the present generation of students attended Plains High

School, a "Jim Crow" system prevailed. There was an all-white and an all-black basketball team, an all-white and an all-black football team, an all-white and an all-black school party and so on.

[JEAN: I find it different at Plains High School. I came from McKinley Junior High. There're only about five colored kids there. We didn't even think about this thing in junior high school. In fact, I can only remember one Negro in junior high, and that was Jack Baldwin. It's funny that I can't think of the other Negroes' names.

CAROL: Well, I went to a junior high school where fifty percent of the kids were Negro. Some people, in fact, think that it's all Negro. The Negro girls there were a lot more athletic than the white girls, but I think that the girls got along better than we do at Plains High School. One of the reasons, I think, is because it's a small school and you got to know everybody. I made friends there with some Negro girls that are still my friends. I think another reason why kids are more friendly in junior high is that there aren't as many cliques. I remember this daisy chain practice that we had before graduation. Do you know what daisy chain is?

INTERVIEWER: Doesn't it refer to when the junior class girls act as ushers at graduation ceremonies?

CAROL: Right! Anyway, this white girl said something to this Negro girl. The white girl shouldn't have said what she said, because it wasn't very nice. I can't really remember what it was exactly, but it wasn't nice. The Negro girl was going to beat her up. A lot of times, the Negroes say things that make you mad; in fact, if they were white people and said the things that they say, I'd get real mad, but I don't so much when they are Negroes. I let it go.

MARJORIE: That's because there're a lot of fights, and you're kind of afraid.

QUESTION: Are the fights interracial?

MARJORIE: No, most of the fights are between colored girls; even a lot of fights in junior high school were between colored girls, I don't believe I've ever seen a white girl and a Negro girl fight.

JEAN: Well, in junior high we were told terrible things about Plains High school, and we didn't know what to expect. We were told that the back halls weren't safe and that girls had babies in the bathroom and put them in the garbage. We were told that little men that they couldn't find run around down in the back halls; but this isn't true at all. When I was a sophomore, I was a proctor during the sixth hour in the shop, and I had to walk down through the back halls, where a lot of the colored boys were waiting for school to be out. This scared me at first, but then I got used to it.

MARJORIE: I'd be afraid if there was a gang of boys I didn't know, especially lower class boys with long hair, who were kind of dirty—people like that. I'd really be afraid.

JEAN: Whenever there're fights, they usually don't last long anyway. I only know of one racial fight, but it never really got started because this colored guy stopped it. It was going to be a fight between this tough colored kid and a white kid. They were playing around with each other, punching each other and what have you, and then they got mad. They were going to fight, but this colored boy stopped it.

CAROL: I don't think there're fights because of race at Plains High School. I think when fights occur they're fights just between guys or just between girls, but not because of race.]

Most students report that they do not discuss racial problems, either formally, or informally, at Plains High. While there is some joking about racial matters, serious racial discussions are almost nonexistent. Jean, Marjorie, and Carol agree with the other students that the teachers, too, tend to discourage discussions on race. At the same time, these young women are able to tell of more examples in which race is discussed, in and out of class, than were previously reported to us.

[QUESTION: Do you discuss racial problems at school?

CAROL: There's this Negro guy I know. He used to live behind me. We used to talk about race a great deal. He always told me the truth. When guys were talking about trouble, he'd tell me the truth. He seemed to think that it wasn't right for these guys to go looking for trouble.

MARJORIE: When Dr. King was shot, we'd talk about race. One day, we had this whole class period on it. There were some colored kids in that class, and the colored kids thought that the riots were silly. But even though they thought they were silly, they supported the Negroes that rioted. Also, in our history class and in current events, we've talked about race.

CAROL: We've talked about race in our American History class. In fact, the history teacher was upset because there wasn't any mention of Negro history in our textbook, so we spent one whole week on Negro history from some other books. There were five Negroes in that class; one girl was from Tennessee. The girl from Tennessee had been a migratory worker. She was the only one who'd talk in class. I know one thing that she brought up in class which kind of shocked some people. A lot of people never really thought about it, but she said that she noticed that in the cafeteria not only were the boys and girls segregated, but the Negroes were segregated from the whites. They sat at different places. Nobody ever really gave it too much thought until she brought that up.

MARJORIE: Well, people tend to eat with their friends.

CAROL: That's true and Negro boys and girls do eat together, but it's awfully funny that whites don't eat with Negroes.

MARJORIE: I think that most of the teachers keep us away from racial issues in class. I think they're afraid to bring them up.

JEAN: The only other class I know of in which they talk about race was in Social Problems. In that class I was proctor this year, and they had a whole year of giving oral reports. This one colored fellow did a report on "What it would be like in the Summer of 1968." It was the longest report in class and everybody wanted to talk about it, because they never get a chance. In fact, the guy giving the report hardly had a chance to say anything because everybody wanted to put their two bits in—or, how do you say it?—two cents, I guess. In singing I sit with colored girls, and I got to talking to them. It's funny, I thought they'd think differently than me, because they're colored. I thought that their reasons for doing things would be different from our reasons. I was surprised when I found out they had the same reasons, and they thought the same as we did.]

While some teachers may discourage discussions on race relations during class time, they are not directly responsible for the segregation which exists in the school cafeteria, nor do they control the topics the students discuss there. None of the students, however, seem to recognize that the cafeteria could be desegregated if they, themselves, took the initiative. Frequently, the cafeteria situation is dismissed with the comment, "People tend to eat with their friends." Even the liberal students are prone to locate the cause of segregation at Plains High outside of themselves.

Without being asked, Jean relates her parents' reaction to her dating a Negro. We decided beforehand not to ask explicitly about her interracial dating, because we thought she might have omitted parts of her story if she believed that we were already familiar with it.

[JEAN: I had a lot of trouble, too, because around Christmas time I got to know this colored boy real well, and I wanted to date him. There was a big mixup, and my parents didn't like it. I did date him, and we started going together. There was a lot of trouble.

QUESTION: Who gave you trouble?

JEAN: My parents, mostly.

CAROL: When I was in the eighth grade, I went with a Mexican boy. He was in the clique that was "cool," so he was accepted by most of the kids. I didn't have as much trouble with my parents when I started dating him, but that's because my parents are a little more liberal than Jean's parents. [Later we learn that Carol's parents are not so liberal, after all.]

JEAN: My parents put quite a bit of pressure on me not to go out with this boy. They told me not to see him again. I did, and this is the first time any of us in my family have ever been punished. I have some brothers. They're too good to ever get punished. They grounded me for two weeks. It was the longest two weeks I ever spent in my life. My parents are really funny people. They're the type of people, like dad, who says he's not prejudiced at all. He even has them working in his office, but he wants them to stay in their place, and the whites to stay in their place, and then everything is okay.

CAROL: Sometimes the kids talk awfully big about what they're going to do. They say, "If I met a colored person, and I loved him, I'd marry him," or, "If I met a Mexican, and I loved him, I'd marry him." But it really takes guts, when it comes down to it. There're a lot of pressures from parents, from kids and everywhere else. All the pressures from society—there aren't many kids who have the guts, when it comes right down to it.

MARJORIE: The kids, I think, still do react strongly against interracial dating. In fact, I do, myself, and at first I didn't like Jean dating this boy. The boy had to kind of prove himself to me. I got to accept it, because Jean is my friend. I don't think I'd accept it if the person weren't my friend. But once this boy Jean was dating proved himself to me, I got to like him.]

None of the young women being interviewed (including Jean) indicate it is presumptuous of Marjorie to say that Gordie had to "prove himself" before she would accept him. Although Jean might have considered Marjorie's comment to be patronizing, she said nothing—perhaps for fear of losing another "friend."

[JEAN: There was a lot of talking behind my back; snickering when I left the room and when I walked down the hallway. I tried to tell myself that it didn't matter what people thought. I thought I could overcome what they thought, the snickering and everything, but it still hurt. It hurt an awful lot. When I first told my mother that I wanted to date this Negro boy, she said, "Well, you have to make up your own mind on this." Then my brother told her that he didn't like him. My brother played basketball with Gordie, and he didn't like him, so he told my mother this, and this changed her whole mind. She didn't want me to go with him then. I really can't tell you everything that I felt. They made me feel so guilty. They made me feel so cheap. They were worried about what people would say. They made me feel like two pieces of dirt. They kept saying that they were worried about me, but I think they were worried about themselves and what people would say about them because their daughter was going out with a Negro. It was really awful. You know, I never thought interracial dating was a good idea, either. I always thought that my parents and I were on the same side on that issue. But I never really thought of this boy I was going out with as a Negro. I never talked to my parents much about it. We don't really get along. They're always telling me that I should form my own opinions and views. That's fine only as long as my views are the same as theirs, but if I try to form my own views, then it's another story.

MARJORIE: You know it's funny, until this year I liked nearly everyone, but this year I've started disliking people because of some of the things they do. I've found colored people that I don't like, but I've also found white people that I don't like. After a colored person proves himself, and he's worthy of my friendship, then I accept him. But it's funny, I still feel that Negroes, even my Negro friends, are inferior to me. Except maybe for the boy that Jean was dating. I liked him. But on the other hand, there're some white people I think I'm better than, too.

QUESTION: Are you afraid to accept Negroes as equals?

MARJORIE: I've thought about that, too. We've talked about it in church. Mostly, I guess, I can't stand to be around people who're physically dirty, who don't take care of themselves. It's not clothes. I don't have many clothes, myself, but I try to look nice. I think it's people who have torn clothes. I think if they're careless about their clothes, they're probably careless about other things, too. Also, I don't like people who try to act big, who are loudmouthed or dirtymouthed. I don't like people who swear a lot.

JEAN: Well, when you walk down the hall and get propositioned from people, you don't think much of them. There're a lot of people like that at Plains High School.]

Marjorie assumes her attitudes toward blacks to be liberal, particularly since she has not rejected Jean for dating a black student. At Plains High School, such an attitude is sufficient for believing oneself to be liberal, since many students, who once had been friendly with Jean, rejected her once she began to date a black athlete. Marjorie believes that her father's liberal leanings have influenced her, although, at times, she considers him to be inconsistent. But she sees no inconsistency in presenting herself as a liberal, at the same time as she says, "I still feel that Negroes, even my Negro friends, are inferior to me . . . ."

[MARJORIE: My father is from Wyoming. He never saw a colored person until he got here. He was about 20 years old. It was during the war, and he was in the army. I think he has a lot to do with my attitude. He told me in Wyoming there wasn't segregation because there weren't any colored people where he lived, but they had the same kinds of problems between Catholics and Protestants. He said they still had prejudices, but it wasn't between races. He knows that there're good and bad in both races, but sometimes he's not consistent. Dad owns a filling station on the South side. Negroes have given him a bad time.

JEAN: Well, your father has a reason for disliking Negroes, because of what happens to him on the South side.

MARJORIE: That's right. The Negroes have a newspaper, I don't know what it's called. They come around and try to get you to buy it. Every time he refused to buy the newspaper, there'd be a break-in in his gas station, so he's learned it's a lot cheaper to buy a newspaper. He still seems to like them, though, because he likes sports, and he always goes to the Plains High School games, although most of the players are Negro.

JEAN: This year I'm a little bit different. I started meeting people I liked, and I just gave up trying to be nice to people I didn't like. When I found people I liked, I was real nice. It worked out a lot better, because I didn't have to spread it out thin, like I was trying before. When I met this colored guy it changed me, because I've never gone with anybody that I really liked before. I think this changes your outlook and gives you hope, when you find someone you really like.

QUESTION: Do the students accept interracial dating?

MARJORIE: The people that didn't know Jean or Gordie didn't understand at all. They were kind of vicious.

CAROL: I got kind of sick of the kids throwing her to the dogs all the time. There were times when you had to take a stand. You either turned the other cheek, or you fought back for Jean. They thought she was cheap, and they were saying all kinds of nasty things about her. It was very difficult.

MARJORIE: A lot of the kids were saying . . . . You don't mind, Jean, do you, because you've heard all these before?

JEAN: No, I don't mind; I know what they said.

MARJORIE: Well, they were saying she's hard up for dates. They said that she really stooped low to go down to a colored boy.

CAROL: Even a guy I'm dating, he's that way, too. If one of his friends needs a date—just last week I suggested Jean. But he said, "No! I won't let my friend go out with her." He's very prejudiced, but his parents are very prejudiced, and that's why he's that way.]

There seems little question that interracial dating is associated with sex, so that black, white, and Mexican-American young women who wish to date young men from a different race or cultural background are accused of being sexually immoral. Yet there is not even a whisper of sex when students date fellow students from the same race. White young women who date black students are subjected to a white "boycott."

[QUESTION: Do all white boys refuse to have anything to do with a white girl who's dated a Negro?

MARJORIE: Not my boy friend. I think he's in love with her. Well, he kind of likes her because I told him she's my friend, and he had to be nice to her. Also, he has lots of Negro friends. They call each other names. They call each other "nigger," and things like that, so he gets along pretty well with the Negroes.

CAROL: Yeah, the Negroes call the white boys they like "honkies." One time coming out of a basketball game (my boy friend plays basketball), a bunch of the Negro boys came out, and they were kidding with me. My boy friend would say things like, "No colored guy's going to touch my girl." Everybody laughed, and it was kidding, but they all knew it was real. They knew that I wasn't serious about them, and they knew they couldn't be serious about me. I don't know whether they thought that was so because they were Negro, or because I was going steady. I've had a couple of offers to go out with colored boys who didn't know I was going steady, but I didn't go out with them.

JEAN: Nobody from Plains High would ask me out. The Negro guys didn't and won't ask me out; they know better. And the white guys'll have nothing to do with me. I used to date a lot of white guys at school, because I went out a lot before I started going out with Gordie, but I haven't had a date with a white guy since. Last night I dated a white guy for the first time. He's from Mississippi. He's not in school, and he's 20 years old. It's really quite a change. He wants Wallace for President. I'm going out with him again Wednesday night, and I'm going to tell him I used to date a Negro. That ought to be something.

QUESTION: Did you receive pressure from anyone else when you were dating Gordie?

JEAN: At first the counselors called me in and told me no white guy would ever ask me out again.

MARJORIE: The counselors were awful. When Jean and Gordie would try to see each other between classes, the counselors would even come to their class. They stood and watched them so they couldn't meet. They threatened to call her mother.

JEAN: There were other people, though, who made me feel good. There were some friends, once they realized that I liked him and nothing was going to come between us, who'd offer to pick me up and take me to meet him. They were white boys. My counselor, she's a woman, said that this other counselor who's a family friend was going to call my parents when she first called me in. She said that, whenever something like this happens at school, they always call up the parents to let them know, which isn't true. She really upset me. Everybody talked about it. Even the teachers talked about it during their coffee breaks. My first hour teacher talked about it. They didn't say anything about it directly, but they'd say things like, "Remember whatever you do in high school will stay with you a long, long time.]

There is little support from what follows for the view that side-by-side contact between the races by itself improves relations. The quality of the contact rather than contact alone seems to be a much more important factor. For instance, Carol tells of a family friend, a teacher, who dislikes Negroes because they make things difficult for him in class. Jean's mother, after having come in contact with a classroom of rowdy Negroes, thinks all Negroes are rowdy. In both these cases, the quality of their contact seems to have reinforced the ready-made preconceptions of these two adults.

[QUESTION: Do the teachers treat all students alike?

MARJORIE: They say they do, but I think that some teachers discriminate.

CAROL: We have a family friend who's a teacher at Plains High School, and he said the colored kids gave him more trouble. He didn't like them because of this.

JEAN: My mom practice taught one year of English. One of the classes she had was a higher class group, where there weren't any Negroes, and one was a real dumb class in which they were all lower class Negroes who were really quite bad. She's just down on all Negroes. I can't convince her that they aren't all like that. She just won't listen.

QUESTION: While we're on the subject, how many different classes of Negroes are there at Plains High School?

MARJORIE: Well, there're Negro people, and there're colored people.

JEAN: The Negro people are the ones who're really gross. The colored people are nice. They get good grades. They're good persons. The Negroes would burn down the school if they had a chance.

QUESTION: Amongst yourselves, do you call one group Negroes and the other colored?

JEAN: No, we call the Negroes, "niggers."

MARJORIE: I call the Negroes, "niggers," too.

CAROL: I never used to. I never used to call anyone, "nigger," but now I call the lower class ones, the ones who're filthy in looks and mouth, "niggers."

QUESTION: How many classes of white kids are there?

JEAN: There're lower class white kids that we call, "white trash" or "hoods." The hoody guys don't care about their appearances. They have dirty hair and dirty clothes. They steal cars or they light fires in the restrooms. They have filthy mouths, and they're as bad as the niggers. Then there're the sophisticates. They think they're too good for anybody. These are the richer kids—you can always tell them. The ones that I really dislike are the ones who're rich and let everybody know it. There's this one girl that I know—she's kind of like her parents—her parents are that way. I think so much of it is environment. The way you're brought up is the way you stay, unless something happens to you to change you, like it happened to me.]

Few words are minced in describing the various classes of Negro and white students. Presumably, money, or the lack of it does not qualify a person for admission, or omission, from these classes. Membership is based on behavior.

Jean returns to telling about her relationship with Gordie. This time she focuses on the pressures she experienced from her "friends."

[QUESTION: Can you explain what you mean by, something happened which changed you?

JEAN: Before I started dating Gordie, I thought I had a lot of friends. We used to go places together and have a lot of fun. I thought they were friends, but then I found out that they weren't. They talked behind my back. They were as vicious as the other kids.

MARJORIE: I have to admit, if I weren't Jean's friend, I wouldn't approve of it, either. There was another girl in my class who used to date a colored boy. She wasn't my friend, and I didn't approve of it. I still don't like it with Jean, but Jean's my friend.

JEAN: You know I even felt that way. I thought it was terrible that this white girl and this colored boy walked down the hall together, but I'm more sympathetic now.

MARJORIE: I really think it all depends on who they are.

JEAN: You know, when I was dating Gordie, I was surprised at how many white girls wanted to date colored guys. They'd come up to me and ask me things. They really wanted to date colored guys, but they were afraid.

CAROL: That's for sure. I've even seen colored guys that I'd like to date, but you're afraid to date colored guys because you know it's not approved. You know you're going to lose your friends. You know your parents are going to give you pressure. You know that the school's going to put pressure on you. It's very hard. I don't know how Jean's stood it.

JEAN: Most of the kids are afraid of what people would say. The parents always tell you, "Don't let that happen to you." My parents told me that. They told me what was going to happen. They were right, but I still don't like them.

CAROL: I don't know how to explain it. Even though you don't always want to marry the guy you're going with, like, for example, the guy I'm going with now, I don't really think of marriage. Still, in the back of your mind you're always thinking of the future. You always think about this when you're dating. You become afraid, maybe, that you couldn't get a good date if you started dating a Negro. You'd have to end up with someone from the lower class, or another Negro, because kids from the higher class won't date you anymore. I think these are some of the things you think about.

MARJORIE: When I think of Negroes, I think basically that Negroes are lower class, incomewise, anyway. The better percent of them are. I know there're some Negro doctors, but they're kind of the exception, like the movie, "Guess Who's Coming to Dinner."

JEAN: That movie was really idealistic.

MARJORIE: The boy that Jean dates is real light complected. I think that the dark Negroes seem more Negro to me than the light ones. I don't know. It's very difficult to talk about.

QUESTION: What was idealistic about the movie, "Guess Who's Coming to Dinner"?

JEAN: Well, for one thing, there aren't a lot of parents who'd react the way her parents did. That's the first thing. The only thing that impressed me in that movie was that his parents didn't like it—that was realistic. Also, her attitude was idealistic. She was just kind of carefree and didn't even think about the fact that he was Negro, and that's not true. You think about it, because people make you think about it.

MARJORIE: By the way, Jean, I never did ask you, but how did Gordie's mother accept you?

JEAN: Gordie's mom liked me. She said it was his life and he could do what he liked. But I know from my own experience that that movie was idealistic, because it'd take more than one day to get used to the idea.]

The pressure interracial couples face is summarized in Jean's statement that you think about the fact that he's a Negro, "Because people make you think about it." It is this reaction from others, plus the thought of being accepted only by other Negroes or by lower class white young men, which frightens Carol and prevents her from dating a black student. Other factors probably also play a part in this decision, such as parental disapproval.

Carol tells about the disappointment she experienced with her parents who, although they profess liberalism, expressed their dislike when she dated a dark-complexioned Mexican-American.

[MARJORIE: You know, I really don't know what my parents would do if I dated a Negro or a Mexican. I don't know how they'd react to it, because they're prejudiced, far more prejudiced than I am. Maybe they'd send me away, or they'd lock me up. I just don't know what they'd do.

CAROL: I can give you an example of what happened to me because I dated this Mexican-American boy in junior high school. We'd talk on the telephone, and it was all right. My parents knew that he was Mexican. He came to get me one night, that was the first time they saw him. We were going to a party. He was kind of afraid to meet my parents because he said he'd dated white girls before, and he was embarrassed. But I told him that my parents would never embarrass anybody, that he could come over to my house and relax. Anyway, that night when we got back, we had a little party at my house. A bunch of the kids came over around ten o'clock. I was kind of surprised because both of my parents weren't around. My parents usually stay up late until about midnight. I found out later that they were upset because this boy was so dark. In fact, he's darker than Gordie—the guy that Jean was dating. I found out something about my parents that night. They talked big, but they didn't accept it when it actually happened.

QUESTION: Where do the Mexicans fit in at school?

MARJORIE: I don't even notice Mexicans.

JEAN: They're just sort of there. I don't know.

CAROL: Aren't they kind of ostracized from everything? I just don't know where they are. I personally, think that the Mexican people are beautiful because of their coloring—their dark hair and their dark eyes.

MARJORIE: I really think they're beautiful, too. I always wanted dark hair and dark eyes like they have. I think the girls are really beautiful, but you never notice Mexicans. They're always off by themselves.

JEAN: I'll give you an example of what happened once. Mr. Ewing called me into the office. I hold this all-school office in which whenever there's some case of discrimination I'm called in. Mr. Ewing got this anonymous note, saying, "Why don't we have a Mexican fiesta and a Mexican queen?" He was telling me he was surprised. He never really thought much about it, because Mexicans are always off to themselves, and the Negroes to themselves, and the whites to themselves. He didn't know that they ever felt this way. He was really disturbed by it.

QUESTION: In general, how do the students get along with the administration?

JEAN: Well, I have to get along with Mr. Ewing because of my school office. I have to see him about three times a week. He thinks I like him. He tries, but I don't think he gets along too well with the kids.

CAROL: We want to try so many things that the other schools do. He's afraid to try new things. He's very old fashioned in his ideas.

JEAN: A lot of times he gets blamed for things which he's really not responsible for, but I still don't like him that much. He gets a lot of pressure from the NAACP. He gets blamed for everything that happens in school—if a colored girl isn't chosen queen, if a colored girl isn't chosen a cheerleader and things like this. I think he tries, but not enough.]

As is true with each of the other student groups, these students, too, consider sports to be the most integrated activity—although they are also aware that the "integration" does not extend off the field. The fact that Jean seriously explains that the white students support an all black team "even though" their opponents are white, is an indication of the degree to which Plains High is not aware of the extent to which it harbors prejudicial attitudes.

[QUESTION: In which activities do you find the most integration?

JEAN: Sports. Five colored guys played basketball this year. And the kids are right behind the team, even though they are colored. This year there were a number of times when our five guys played against five white guys, but everybody rooted for our colored team.

QUESTION: Is there much mixing off the playing field?

JEAN: Sometimes, but not often.

CAROL: Well, occasionally they'll go out for a drink after a game, but they don't get personal invitations to go to parties, or things like that.

JEAN: When the colored kids have a party, they invite white kids. They try to have integrated parties, but there aren't many kids who participate. I like the colored kids' parties, because they go all out at a party. They hire a band, catering service, the whole works, and they have a lot of fun. There're some white kids who like to go, but some of them are afraid. They feel kind of funny when they go to an all-Negro party. There're other kids who do go and still feel kind of funny, but they go, anyway.

QUESTION: Are the clubs integrated?

MARJORIE: The colored kids don't seem to want to be included in clubs. Honor Pep, for example—there aren't any colored girls in Honor Pep.

JEAN: There are this year. There're seven of them.

MARJORIE: Well, that's right, but in the past there weren't any.

JEAN: Well, the president of the senior class this year is a colored guy, and there'll be four other colored kids in school offices. Before, there were always none.

MARJORIE: But the colored kids in these offices, a lot of them don't really get along with the other kids. This kid, Jeff, who's the president of the class next year, he's not really liked by the Negroes. They voted for him because they wanted a Negro to get in, but they don't really like him.

QUESTION: Where do you find the least integration?

CAROL: In personal relationships. We don't go anyplace with the colored kids. The boys mix more than the girls do. They're more sure of themselves because of their experience in athletics. They even kid with the girls. For example, this Negro this year kidded around with me a great deal. Last year he was very quiet. He knows the guy I'm going with and he flirts—not meaningfully—but just to be nice.

JEAN: Yeah, that guy is really a kidder, he always used to say, "When can I come over to your house?" when he'd be walking behind me. I'd always say, "Later." One time I said, "Okay, why don't you come over tonight with Marjorie's boy friend?" He did come over. You should've seen him. He was really nervous. He couldn't sit down. He kept pacing back and forth. Then he'd sit down and then pace. After ten minutes, he left. He couldn't stand it, and he's never been back.]

Most students had never given much thought to interracial dating involving a white young man and a Negro fellow student. While some students had seen such couples at the state university, or in larger communities, most of them had never even thought of such a combination. Carol's obvious surprise when asked to think about such a pattern of interracial dating is typical of many students.

[QUESTION: Have you ever seen a white boy date a Negro girl?
CAROL: You know . . . wait a minute, that really seems kind of funny. The white boys hang around more with the Negro guys than the Negro girls with white girls. The Negro boys date the white girls, but white boys don't mix with the Negro girls.
JEAN: Now you have it.
CAROL: I never thought about that before.
JEAN: Well, that's the same all over.
CAROL: What do you mean "all over"?
JEAN: Well, everywhere in the whole country, that's the way it goes.
MARJORIE: I have a friend who dated a colored girl once. He wasn't serious, but he took her out. It happens, but not frequently. I think he took her out on a bet.
QUESTION: Do the students mix at dances?
MARJORIE: No one dances with anyone except the person you came with.
JEAN: We used to have lines, and the colored kids don't dance in lines, but the white kids do. The colored guys teach us to dance, but they just show us. They don't dance with us. You can go up to a colored guy and ask him to show you some steps, and he'll show them to you. Then you can go back and show your friends and your date, but the colored boys never dance with the white girls. They may dance beside them but never with them.
QUESTION: What about the students who don't have dates?
MARJORIE: Usually you're not allowed to go to a dance unless you have an escort. Nobody ever goes to dances without an escort.
CAROL: When they have functions, a lot of outside kids come, and they're rough. The stag guys go. Usually the stag guys are drinking, and they think you're just a pick-up. This is considered cheap.

MARJORIE: That's right, if you went alone you'd look like a pick-up.
JEAN: I think the girls get the short end of the stick all around.
CAROL: If I went to a dance all alone, and my boy friend knew about it, that'd be it. He'd think I was just a cheap pick-up.]

As with previous groups of students, there is little of a favorable nature that these young women say about the counselors—not only because they hear that the counselors discriminate against students from minority groups, but also because they consider many counselors to be incompetent.

[QUESTION: Do the counselors treat all the students alike?
JEAN: Well, we hear a lot about this, because I'm on the judicial council, and the Negroes and Mexican kids seem to think that the counselors do discriminate.
CAROL: I don't think the counselors are very good in general. There's this counselor, who's there because he's been there forever.
JEAN: If you really have a problem you want to talk about, you go to a teacher you like, or you might go to Mr. Snow. He's the only counselor you can go to. But the counselors can only go so far, anyway, because they can't oppose school policy.]
[QUESTION: What was school like when Martin Luther King was killed?
MARJORIE: The school was empty.
CAROL: It was mainly kids who didn't care about him. The day after he died, we had a short prayer and some quotes from his speeches. Everybody stayed for a minute after and then left quietly. The first boy that walked out—he made me mad—he was a Negro boy who slept through most of his classes and didn't pay attention to anything. He's the type of kid who'd always say that people were discriminating. He never did anything.
CAROL: This girl and I were crying because it was so quiet and strange.
JEAN: I didn't go to school that day. I was away at a festival, so I really don't know, but I heard a lot about it. I heard it was quiet and very strange.]

Attending a desegregated school has meant various things to different students. The three young women in this chapter think of this school experience as having contributed differently to their lives. Attending Plains High had taught Marjorie she has to be different from her parents; it has given Jean a chance to be herself; and it has taught Carol the "do's and don't's" of interacting with whites and nonwhites.

[QUESTION: What has your experience at Plains High taught you?
MARJORIE: I think you learn to change from what your parents are.
JEAN: I think you learn that you have to find out what you really are and think, and then you must do it.

CAROL: Well, there're so many people at school who're out to make anything you say to them as individuals apply to them as a race. In junior high there wasn't this much difference. In high school it's bigger. Also, most white people would be down on you if most of the people you knew were Negroes and not white. I think you learn these kinds of things. You learn what to say, and you learn little subtleties, like you hang around with more white people than Negro people if you're white.

MARJORIE: I think if Carol went back to junior high school she'd see that it was the same. She just thinks it's different because she's in high school.

QUESTION: Carol, since you're the only one here who attended a desegregated junior high school, has your relationship with Negroes changed in high school?

CAROL: I was closer to more Negro kids in junior high than I am in high school. You don't get to know them as individuals in high school. My best friend in junior high was a Negro girl. We're still close but not as close as we were then.

QUESTION: Has your experience in a desegregated school been good?

MARJORIE: I think anything is good as long as you learn from it, especially if it makes you more broad minded. I think this is good.

JEAN: I wouldn't want to go to any other high school than Plains High School.

CAROL: But I think it's more than school. I think it has to take place at home. I think you have to have parents who're also liberal. My mother's parents are very prejudiced. I think because of this my mother has tried to be more lenient. She tried to bring us up so that we wouldn't be prejudiced. She thought prejudice was being ridiculous. But my mother still is a little bit prejudiced. She says she can accept integration up to the point to where one of her daughters would intermarry. I believe, myself, that I can accept integration, including the marriage of my child. That's the difference.

MARJORIE: My parents would never accept intermarriage. They say you have to think of your child. The child will have to choose between colored people and white people. It'd be very difficult.

JEAN: Well, I thought that way until I knew Jimmy Ford. He's half Negro and half white. He dates Negroes and white girls. He has a lot of Indian on the colored side, and he looks a lot like an Indian. He has a beautiful body.

MARJORIE: He came here from Ireland when he was in the sixth grade. He often talks about the changes he's had to make in his ways, because in Ireland, I guess, there wasn't any discrimination. He'll often say something about Negroes, and then he gets confused and says, "But what am I? I'm a colored person!" But he's really neither. I'd say that every generation thinks it's improving. Yes, my parents think there's been improvement, too. It might be improvement in their eyes but not in our eyes. But I think that we'll really improve race relations because we've lived an experience that they haven't, and I think that what we do will help our children, and our children will be freer.

MARJORIE: Well, I don't think I'd want my kids to marry a Negro. You just wouldn't know the person. It's different, but I really don't know what I'd do as far as intermarriage is concerned.

QUESTION: Would you send your children to an integrated school?

JEAN: I definitely want my children to go to an integrated school.

MARJORIE: Well, probably by the time we have children all schools will be integrated.

QUESTION: Unless the neighborhoods are integrated, the schools won't be. Suppose you live in an area which is all white, will you go out of your way to send your kids to an integrated school?

MARJORIE: No, I'll send my kids to school where I live.

CAROL: If I marry the guy I'm dating now, he's so prejudiced that I'd send the kids to an integrated school. I'd want the kids to get to know Negroes, particularly if their father was so prejudiced. He really comes from a lower class background. They've been laborers all their lives. Many of his parents' friends are actually shocked that I live in a mixed area. They're shocked to know there's a Negro living right behind me; in fact, he's shocked, too. That's how prejudiced they are.

CHAPTER 10

Comments and Observations

It is appropriate, at this point, to think about the significance for race relations of the preceding chapters. Unfortunately, we are not in a position to know if the views of the students in our sample are peculiar to Plains High School, or if these views are held generally among most high school students. Instead, the reader will have to decide if his high school and his community bear any resemblance to Plains High School and Center City.

We have heard a fairly adequate cross section of young people speak about the way they feel and think about blacks, whites, and Mexican-Americans. In our interviews, we were struck, not only by the similar ways in which these young people perceive certain events, but at least as much by the different manner in which they interpret their social world, particularly as these differences appear *within* members of the same race. We hope, therefore, that this book will help explode at least one major myth: the myth that a classification of people into black, white, and Mexican-American is sufficient, so that greater refinements are unnecessary for a true understanding of the ways the various members of a racial group see themselves and others and act according to their perceptions.

As is true in the larger society, some of the students we interviewed accept this myth. Their acceptance is indicated by their answers, which are laden with the familiar sterotypes about "all" blacks, whites, and Mexican-Americans. However, we feel quite certain that few Negroes, when confronted with the alternatives of, say, white "racists" and white "conservatives," would suggest that the two brands of prejudice represent a similarity which can be responded to in the same way. On the contrary, prejudice as open as that which is expressed by the white "racists" is rare. Such open racial hatred is so contrary to what is socially approved nowadays, that responding to it with (counter) violence may even receive the community's tacit approval. On the other hand, responding to the "conservatives'" views with violence might well help crystallize the stereotype of the Negro as a violent person, and so increase racial antagonisms. Similarly, white students who find themselves in classrooms with "elite" Negroes can hardly accept that portion of the myth that holds that Negroes are intellectually inferior to whites. For these white students, the "elite" Negro is often a formidable intellectual competitor.

In general, the students believe good relationships between the races to be an important and desirable goal. By "good relationships," they almost always mean "integration." Many of these young people convey their wish that an end be put to arbitrary and superficial social distinctions between people. Nevertheless, most students, no matter what their race, think of *others* as responsible for maintaining malicious distinctions between races, only a few acknowledge that any of their own ideas about fellow students of another race, or of a different cultural background, are prejudicial. As is often true among adults, these adolescents, too, usually locate the source of racial prejudice outside themselves. Among the "prejudiced" they list their parents, grandparents, teachers, counselors, principals and fellow students; only rarely do they include themselves. One should say, however, in fairness to the students, that they are no different from these same parents, teachers, counselors and principals who, if asked, also would locate the problem of race relations in "others."

Some readers may have found themselves questioning the genuineness of the liberal convictions voiced by some students. To what extent, such readers may ask, do these students honestly believe that social distinctions between races should be eliminated, and that black, white, brown, and yellow should be as one instead of as four? Are these liberal convictions in response to group pressures, or are they in response to personal beliefs in what is right? Such questions are particularly pertinent in connection, for example, with the archconservative students, who, while they openly degrade blacks, still want their children to attend an integrated school so that the children may be more "tolerant" than their fathers.

Individuals who are subtle in expressing their prejudice probably have even greater difficulty recognizing the superficiality of their professed liberalism. When blacks label fellow blacks "Uncle Toms," for example, or when Mexican-Americans label their fellows "un-Mexican" because they accept "white ways" (or because they compete with white students academically, or for school offices, or in extracurricular activities), such disparagement reflects not only an intolerance of each other, but a disdain for whites as well. These same students, however, firmly maintain that all racial distinctions should be eliminated. Do the arguments for such elimination simply represent another example of wanting to be "in" with popular points of view which go counter to attitudes the person might express on other occasions? We are not saying, of course, that a superficiality concerning liberal attitudes is always characteristic of adolescents—only that at times adolescent liberalism may be somewhat suspect.

Some adults may also ask, why is so much emphasis given to a project of such secondary importance as the election of a black cheerleader? While few adults consider the election of black cheerleaders, or black class officers, or the desire for an open lunch hour to be main Civil Rights issues, we nevertheless feel that the issue of a black cheerleader, for example, *is* relevant for the situation in which these black students find themselves. Few individuals, after all, select as relevant racial issures which transend their own immediate situation. When the black students at Plains High School attend a basketball game, the contrast they experience as they watch five black athletes on the court, while seven white girls lead the cheering on the sidelines, is a constant reminder of white prejudice and white exploitation. Focus on the cheerleader issue became even more acute when the regular basketball season was extended at the time the Plains High team entered the state tournament. In the light of such situations, one can certainly consider the cheerleader issue relevant. It is essential that we evaluate the motives of individuals within the situations in which they find themselves.

Aside from the issue of the election of a black cheerleader, the students (regardless of their race) are preoccupied with matters related to interracial dating. Few topics demonstrate the pressures related to the intermixing of races so well as does this issue. These pressures originate from parents, friends, teachers, counselors, school administrators, as well as from anonymous members of the community. We found interracial dating to be relatively rare; when it did occur, it was characteristically between a black male and a white female. Some of the animosity between white and black young women grows out of the fact that occasionally Negro young women feel that white female students take away their black (and only) boyfriends. At Plains High School when a black athlete dates a white girl, he is replaced by neither a high- nor low-status white. Generally, the black young man in question is an athlete with considerable status among his Mexican-American, black, and white peers.

Not all interracial dating at Plains High School is between students who occupy prestige positions. There are examples of interracial dating involving an "average" black and a lower-class white girl. Although the school administration takes a dim view of mixed dating whenever a high-status white girl is involved, they do little to interfere when the young woman seems not to be from a "good family." Both whites and blacks feel that the school interferes selectively with interracial dating, and this tendency increases the student's objections regarding the school's legitimacy in interfering with their social lives. Black students perceive the school's policy of selective interference as still another example of white racism and as still another white attempt to lower the black man's self-esteem. To black students, the school's action seems tantamount to saying, "You can go out with the trash, but we don't want you to drag down the important ones." Whether or not this observation is valid is a moot question—there is little doubt, however, that it seems real to the young people involved.

In discussing interracial dating with the students, it also appears that a number of their parents are inconsistent in their attitudes. While some parents may profess liberalism, they often express prejudicial attitudes regarding racial integration when matters really count. It is generally a young woman who reports that, while one or both parents speak liberally, they act in a prejudiced manner. Young men either do not acknowledge this tendency in their parents, or they test their parents less often, or they test them differently (since there seems to be no interracial dating when the young man is white, so that his parents are allowed the luxury of keeping their prejudicial feelings latent).

Actually, black, white, and Mexican-American parents are all guilty of such inconsistencies, although these inconsistencies are most frequently reported by white young women. Mexican-American, Negro, and white parents are certainly more apt to encourage mixing when there is no threat of actual dating. If dating looks imminent, many parents of the three groups do their utmost to introduce new rules and, in this way, to change the game.

The reader may have noticed that the Mexican-American students in our sample see themselves as belonging to neither the white nor to the black race. Although no Mexican-American students say so directly, their constant reference to whites, on the one hand, and Negroes, on the other, is as though they see Mexicans as belonging to some third race. Officially, of course, Mexicans are classified as white, and if any distinctions are assumed between whites and Mexicans, they are usually attributed to cultural factors. Because many of the Mexican-Americans we interviewed live in a Mexican subcommunity where Spanish is spoken and where thousands of daily references identify the community with Mexico, their thinking of themselves as "Mexican" instead of "white" is understandable. Reference to "white" is undoubtedly not meant in the spirit of a biological classification. When Mexican-Americans refer to "white," it is quite clear that they mean "Anglo." Nevertheless, it is worth noting that Mexican-Americans seem to mix cultural and racial categories in their relations with others outside their own particular group.

The shallow conception of "integration" which these young people have is rather striking. For most of the students, integration is apparently brought about once whites and blacks are juxtaposed in the same area, or when they participate jointly (if momentarily) in pursuit of a common goal such as attending a class or playing on the same basketball team. There are few reports of truly significant integration. In fact, there is no real evidence that Plains High School is significantly more integrated today than it was twenty years ago. At that time, Plains High was integrated insofar as whites and blacks attended the same school, although the washrooms, athletic events, teams and social functions were kept separate for black and white. While the formal barriers of a "Jim Crow" system have been removed, Negroes and whites still maintain their separation. Many of the students are proud that the "Jim Crow" system of segregation no longer prevails at Plains High—they interpret this change as progress and as "integration." They do not recognize that the *formal* system of segregation has been replaced by an *informal* pattern which is almost as divisive as the one that existed two decades ago. Yet, because of the limited number of blacks in Center City's other high schools, a favorite cheer when Plains High plays its intracity rivals is: "Two, Four, Six, Eight, When You Gonna Integrate!" Were Plains High to be taken as the model, however, the integration to which this cheer refers seems to mean little more than "When are blacks and whites going to go to the same school?".

One of the more interesting, and yet perturbing, findings which emerges from our talks with the students is that blacks and Mexican-Americans who actively seek a place in their school are discriminated against by fellow blacks and fellow Mexican-Americans. Such derogatory attitudes are particularly noticeable toward blacks, who, more than Mexican-Americans, may try to compete with white students for academic honors, school offices, and roles in extracurricular activities. Black students bring up the Negro's exclusion from these activities as examples of white prejudice. Yet successful entry into these very activities is also not acceptable to many black students. The black student who enters these activities is called a "white nigger" or an "Uncle Tom" by other blacks. The motives of the few Mexican-Americans who try to enter these activities also are questioned by other Mexican-Americans, who ask, "Do you think you're better than we are?"

In other words, while much lip-service is given to the rights of minorities, once these rights become a reality, members of the minority group themselves accuse their fellows who achieve success within the school setting of acting like whites. For blacks, part of this inconsistency lies in the black students' failure to substitute their *own* goals for white goals (which the black reject as unacceptable). The black students want to be their own architects for accomplishment and change, but they have so far constructed little that begins to satisfy this wish.

In a sense, it is especially tragic that the schism between the races is so great that preparing for college, for example, is labeled "white" behavior. Education, and the right to it, should certainly transcend both the color of a man's skin and his cultural background. That the process of education becomes tainted with a pejorative label of "white" is particularly tragic since, unwittingly, such a position among blacks can only serve to revitalize white half-truths about the Negro's intellectual inferiority. A reality of modern day occupations is certainly that an ever-increasing amount of education is necessary to qualify individuals for decent employment. While the repudiation of things white may help to build positive black identities, such a repudiation may, at the same time, keep blacks socially inferior.

What we refer to as the "they" phenomenon also tells us a good deal about the state of race relations. By the "they" phenomenon, we mean the tendency to refer to members of another race simply as "they," as if all were identical—not really worth being differentiated—equal to each other and fit only to be placed in one great individuality-negating caldron. While such a tendency to oversimplify and negate personality is most marked among the racist archconservatives, who claim that all Negroes belong to the same ("nigger") class, the more liberal respondents also tend to differentiate blacks into fewer classes than they do whites. Such a tendency to underplay individual differences is a prime characteristic of "theyness."

That white students are not alone in their tendency to see an entire race in a poorly differentiated fashion can be seen when blacks tend to speak of the "black community" as though it were a homogeneous mass. In this way, blacks tend to wipe out the individual differences in their own race. "Whitey," of course, is a symbol with no three-dimensional personality at all. And both whites and blacks speak of Mexican-Americans as though they were made of cardboard.

It is understandable how, in the kind of interviewing that has been done in these pages, there is a tendency to aid the process of "theying"—of objectifying groups—because groups, after all, are easier to manipulate verbally that way. Still, the denying of individuality involves perhaps one of the most basic problems in race relations—people tend to neglect the truism that groups are made up of individuals, with individual attitudes, wishes, feelings, behavior patterns and so on. When adolescents and others speak of "they," the people to whom they make reference are made into a thing; they are demeaningly objectified and lose their character as persons. Referring to individuals of another race as "they" is a symptom, rather than a cause—a symptom of the need to degrade.

Ironically, these and even subtler prejudicial attitudes, as has already been indicated, are more dangerous and also more difficult to deal with than more blatantly racist ones. The very subtlety of mildly prejudicial comments sometimes makes it difficult to recognize their antagonistic implications or to remonstrate against them without appearing foolish. Most often, condescensions or stereotypes embedded in "well-meaning" comments (such as, "They're wonderful musicians" or "They're always happy") are not recognized as prejudicial over-simplifications by the person who makes them. In fact, it usually surprises him whenever an objection is raised to such comments. He is not fully aware that when he praises Negro students (for example, for being "such good basketball players"), he delivers, at the same time, his subtly expressed (and silent) opinion about the Negro's abilities in areas other than certain types of sports. Persons who "praise" minorities this way usually consider their own attitudes to be positive, benevolent, not at all derogatory and generally far from destructive. They feel virtuous because they believe that they totally accept other races. They feel hurt, puzzled, and angry when it is suggested that their racism is insidious and therefore particularly dangerous. Condescension is a difficult attitude with which to deal effectively because the person who condescends tends to feel somewhat righteous about being well disposed toward the minority group involved. While one can thoroughly and explicitly take exception to frankly derogatory statements, one has much more difficulty doing so with "pleasantly" belittling ones.

As we said in Chapter I, any prejudice has a narrowing and "shallowing" effect on the attainment of knowledge about the surrounding world. Prejudice is like an inflexible filter which, rather than refining, distorts incoming information. Instead of being "open," the prejudiced person, with his distorting filter, is relatively "closed" to incoming information. Rather than perceiving things that surround him clearly and truly, he tends to make emotional judgments about them; instead of finding out and discovering, he makes a statement and gives an opinion before he knows the factors which are involved. The tendency to prejudge and judge faultily and immaturely is particularly the case with those areas in which the individual is prejudiced. A prejudicial person cannot afford to wait and "get all the facts"; he delivers himself of unvalidated opinions and acts impulsively rather than in a more considered fashion. To the degree that such a person's view of people and situations around him is distorted by his prejudice filter, to that degree is his broad and valid understanding limited.

The adolescent, understandably, is concerned primarily with himself as he actively tries to find out more about what and who he is and where he is going in life; as he is more or less actively creating an identity for himself. As we reread the preceding chapters, we are struck by the degree to which these adolescents seem so intensely preoccupied with themselves. Even the "hippies," who express so much concern with the plight of the blacks, actually seem more concerned with *their particular role* in improving the Negro's situation than with the Negro's situation itself.

As these adolescents express their sensibility to problems associated with race relations, another adolescent characteristic comes into view: the "all or none" quality of adolescent reactions, a characteristic frequently found in this age. It is not uncommon for the adolescent to pursue one extreme position or another and almost never choose a position of compromise; compromise cannot separate the conglomeration of feelings which are so troublesome.

Among the adolescents found in these pages who say they wish to solve the tangled racial situation in some way, the reader may find that a particular adolescent lacks genuine involvement, or displays involvement for mistaken reasons (e.g., "Negroes are such good athletes"). Others show a fiery involvement in maintaining the status quo (as with the archconservatives). And still other adolescents may demonstrate an equally fiery involvement, the singleminded purpose of which is to bring about desirable changes in the racial situation *right now*. Compromise is held in contempt, particularly by adolescents who are genuinely striving toward a solution of the acutely disturbed racial situation, even when compromise is intended as an entering wedge to accomplish what is felt to be necessary and desirable. Compromise is slow; it is often bumbling; it usually does not contain the strong feelings which the adolescent wishes to express. But the adolescent probably finds compromise unsatisfactory mainly because it does not cleanly dichotomize into issues of either-or.

The situation concerning the relationship between races is constantly changing—attitudes and behaviors are forever shifting. Even while this book was being written, the black students at Plains High School exerted influence to have the school change its voting rules to enable Negroes to elect two additional cheerleaders who would be black. This symbolic change was a small one, however, and did not begin to touch the problem of black impoverishment and other examples of black secondary citizenship. The blacks also organized a Black Student Union, and some white students organized a Student for Democratic Society (SDS) chapter. The Mexican-American students have formed a group to foster involvement in school activities, so that they, too, can be visible and counted on in the school setting. All groups continue to strive for greater involvement in administrative decisions. While in this academic year, then, there appears to be improved communication between the school administration and the students, there is another addition at Plains High: three security guards, ostensibly there to prevent "outside agitators" from entering the school.

A major question concerns the direction in which change in the racial situation will continue to take place, both nationally and locally. If change continues, will it be in the direction of increased racial *integration*, or in the direction of increased voluntary racial *separation*? The recent changes at Plains High School, after the initial movement in the direction of racial integration, have suggested a movement toward increased cohesiveness among the black students (with an increased drawing away from the whites), together with increased white cohesiveness (with a resultant separation from the blacks). The black students, for example, requested that they be given the opportunity to choose their two black cheerleaders purely among themselves, so that their cheerleaders would be exclusively a black choice. The black young woman, who was said to have lost her election as cheerleader by only two votes, was rejected by her black fellow students because of her (relative) popularity among the whites. The blacks wanted to choose their own cheerleaders, without nodding in the direction of white preference and condescension. It is certainly possible that integration can take place only after an initial separation of the blacks, by virtue of which Negroes can achieve an increased cohesion and feeling of unity and worth. Perhaps only after such an experience of separation can blacks allow true integration to take place— permitting themselves to mix freely, while maintaining their selfhood.

EU Authorised Representative:
Easy Access System Europe
Mustamäe tee 50, 10621 Tallinn, Estonia

www.ingramcontent.com/pod-product-compliance
Lightning Source LLC
Chambersburg PA
CBHW032124020426
42334CB00016B/1057